THE DIEPPE RAID

THE DIEPPE RAID

THE STORY OF THE DISASTROUS 1942 EXPEDITION

ROBIN NEILLANDS

First published 2005 by
Aurum Press Limited
25 Bedford Avenue
London WC1B 3AT
www.aurumpress.co.uk

A catalogue record for this book is available from the British Library.

ISBN 1 84513 116 9

10 9 8 7 6 5 4 3 2 1
2009 2008 2007 2006 2005

Text design by Roger Hammond

Maps by Reginald Piggott

Typeset by SX Composing DTP, Rayleigh, Essex

Printed and bound in Great Britain by
MPG Books, Bodmin

CONTENTS

MAPS

ACKNOWLEDGEMENTS

As with all my previous books, a great many people and institutions helped me with this one. My thanks go first to my Canadian friend and supporter, Paul McNicholls from British Columbia, a colleague at the Oxford University Summer School, especially for his help in finding Canadian veterans, papers and books. Thanks then go to Eric Garner, my British researcher, for his help in tracking down information on the Internet and in discarding a great deal of dross.

As always with these military works, my thanks to Major-General Julian Thompson, CB OBE, an expert in amphibious operations, for reading the text and making many helpful comments. Also to Lieutenant-Commander Tristan Lovering, RN, Royal Marines Corps tutor of Fleet Command, and my friend and student Bruce Chinery for reading and commenting on the text. Critical comments from those in the know are always worth having.

Much of what I know about the Dieppe Raid I have learned from the participants, so thanks go to Major-General Robert ('Titch') Houghton, once of the Royal Marines 'A' Commando, and former Sergeant-Major James Dunning of 'C' Troop, No. 4 Commando. Also to a great number of Canadian veterans and to those of the Commando Association who responded to my plea for recollections – they are acknowledged in the text.

Thanks must also go to a number of institutions: to the Department of Documents at the Imperial War Museum, London, to the Musée du Débarquement at Arromanches in Normandy, to the Canadian Legion in Ottawa, Canada, to the Royal British Legion, the Liddell Hart Archive at King's College London and the National Archives at Kew. Thanks also to my American friend, author and historian Carlo d'Este, for pointing me towards the JUBILEE correspondence in the Liddell Hart Archive.

Others, too numerous to mention – not least for fear of leaving someone out – were also helpful in providing information or driving me on. Chief of these last has been my dear wife Judy, for her amazing tolerance of those interested in military history.

Robin Neillands
Beckhampton, England, and Barrou, Touraine, France, 2005

ABOUT THIS BOOK

> To throw good money after bad is foolish. But to throw away men's lives where there is no reasonable chance of advantage is criminal. In the heat of battle mistakes in command are inevitable and amply excusable. But the real indictment of leadership arises when attacks that are inherently vain are ordered merely because if they could succeed they would be useful. For such manslaughter, whether it springs from ignorance, a false conception of war, or a want of moral courage, commanders should be held accountable to the nation.
>
> B.H. LIDDELL HART, *History of the First World War*

This is the second time I have used these words of Liddell Hart as the opening quote in a book – the first occasion was in my book on the Great War generals, which recounted many larger disasters. I have used them again here because they encapsulate almost every negative point that will appear in the pages that follow.

Ignorance, incompetence, a false concept of war, a want of moral courage – not least the courage to call the operation off – permeate the story of the Dieppe Raid. These errors contributed to the losses suffered by the troops that went ashore in an assault that was indeed 'inherently vain'.

The Dieppe Raid of August 1942 was one of the great tragedies of the Second World War; in percentage terms, the losses equalled or exceeded those in any First World War battle. The Raid has also been a potent cause of controversy ever since, not least because no one has ever come up with a satisfactory, controversy-killing explanation of what it was actually *for.*

This alone is curious. Military plans usually begin with a clear statement of the aim, but while the Dieppe Raid has plenty of objectives, the prime aim of Operation RUTTER/JUBILEE remains obscure. Most of the reasons advanced to justify the Raid, that it was 'a reconnaissance in force', or a necessary preamble to D-Day, or an attempt to see if it was possible to capture an undamaged, working port, were voiced after the Raid when reasons – or excuses – were needed to justify the losses.

This being so, it seemed a worthwhile project to take Operation JUBILEE apart, clear away some of the more common myths and account for the tragic loss of so many men. On a personal note, may I add that I am sick and tired of reading accounts in which the courage of brave men is used to distract attention from the glaring incompetence of the commanders.

The first requirement of any military commander is that he should know his job, but the job can vary; it is apparent that many of the commanders on JUBILEE had only a slight grasp of the problems and difficulties involved in amphibious operations. They failed to understand the most basic principles of amphibious warfare and the skills needed when putting a force ashore and extracting it afterwards. All this has to be demonstrated and will be covered in detail in the pages that follow.

The origins of my interest in Operation JUBILEE go back to my first visit to Dieppe in the summer of 1949, just seven years after the Raid. First impressions are often powerful, and I can still recall that overriding smell of postwar France – public lavatories and strong cigarettes – that seemed to hang like a miasma over French towns at that time.

Dieppe was still somewhat battered and the Imperial War Graves Cemetery, just outside the town, was still new and raw. So, aged fourteen, I first became aware of the Raid, if not why this event cost the lives of so many men. To move forward from that position took much longer.

By the time I returned to Dieppe several years later I had served in the 3rd Commando Brigade and was more closely acquainted with the practicalities of amphibious warfare. The officers and senior NCOs in the Corps had all served in the Second World War, usually in Commando units, and the Commandant of the Commando School when I passed through was Colonel – later Major-General – R.D. Houghton. Known to me as 'Sir', but to his closer acquaintances as 'Titch', he was a very splendid and much-loved Marine officer who had landed at Dieppe in August 1942 with the Royal Marine 'A' Commando – later 40 (Royal Marine) Commando – and been captured on the beach before the town.

Having served as a Commando soldier, my main impression after studying the landing beaches, and especially the one in front of the town, was one of amazement that anyone with the slightest knowledge of amphibious warfare could contemplate such a place for an amphibious assault. Someone, it appeared, had blundered.

And so, over the years, I began to take a closer interest in the Dieppe Raid, urged on later by Brigadier Peter Young, once of No. 3 Commando, who took part in it. Even so, it was not until sometime in the 1990s that I began to consider the possibility of examining the Dieppe Raid more closely and seeing how many of the stories and popular myths about that operation stood up to historical analysis . . . and the more I learned, the more I wondered.

There is usually a purpose to military actions. In the majority of cases they are not *discrete* operations; they arise from what has gone before and contribute, for good or ill, to what follows. They are, in other words, part of a train of events heading towards victory or defeat. They may even be the decisive action in a war or campaign, but if they are to make any worthwhile contribution to that train of events, they must serve some purpose of their own . . . and at that point a certain measure of disquiet set in as far as the Dieppe Raid was concerned.

Many books have been written about the Dieppe Raid disaster and most of them concentrate on where to pin the blame. Churchill, Montgomery, Lord Louis Mountbatten, the Americans, the entire British

Chiefs of Staff Committee and Major-General Hamilton 'Ham' Roberts, commander of the 2nd Canadian Division, have all come in for a hammering in this process; if finding blame is the sole object of the exercise there is probably enough of it to go around.

This book is not a hunt for some particular scapegoat. I am not wildly interested in conspiracy theories and, having trawled the records and applied a little common sense, I have found it impossible to single out any one man for particular condemnation. The focus of this book is on why the planners and many of the participants got it so terribly wrong and what factors contributed most directly to the chaos and slaughter on the beaches. As an example of 'how not to do it' a study of the Dieppe Raid is very useful. It should be a text in every military academy and a topic on every War Studies course.

The story of Dieppe – of what it was for and why it went so spectacularly awry – remains an enigma. The end result of some fifty years of quiet brooding over Operation JUBILEE and two years' intensive research on the ground and in the archives is this book. It will, I hope, explain not only what happened but why. In addition, since my corner in the military history world is devoted to myth-busting, I hope to show which of the stories surrounding this tragedy stand up to close inspection. It will also be a small tribute to the gallant Canadian soldiers who landed on that fatal shore – and were doomed before they even left their ships.

THE ROAD TO JUBILEE

1939–42

Too big for a raid, too small for an invasion . . . what were you trying to do?

German interrogator to Canadian prisoner, Dieppe, 19 August 1942

THIS IS THE STORY OF A CATASTROPHE. On 19 August 1942, in the space of just six hours, a force of Canadian and British troops some 6000 strong, engaged in assaulting the seaport of Dieppe on the Channel coast of France, lost 4131 men, killed, wounded or captured, the vast majority from the 2nd Canadian Division. No other Allied operation of the Second World War saw such a loss in such a time.

Nor were the Allied losses confined to manpower. One hundred and six RAF aircraft were destroyed, half the pilots being killed – compared to just forty-eight Luftwaffe fighters. All the brand-new Churchill tanks that went ashore that day were destroyed or fell into enemy hands. British naval losses included the destroyer HMS *Berkeley*, a large number of landing ships and assault craft and their trained and experienced crews. By any standard and for every Service that took part, Operation JUBILEE was a disaster.

These figures grow worse on closer inspection; the losses among the Canadian assault battalions storming these beaches reached First World War proportions. The Essex Scottish, landing in front of Dieppe town, lost 90 per cent of its ration strength, only 52 of the 553 men who went ashore that morning returning to England. The French-Canadian Fusiliers Mont-Royal, sent ashore in support, lost 459 men out of 584 and 27 out of their 31 officers. The Royal Hamilton Light Infantry lost 372 out of 582 – and half the men who returned to England were wounded, including the only officer to survive the landing.

Other units recall similar losses. The Cameron Highlanders of Canada and the South Saskatchewan Regiment took a combined total of 1065 men ashore at Pourville, west of Dieppe, and lost 685 of them. On the eastern flank, the Royal Regiment of Canada lost 94 per cent of its men and very few of those who went ashore even got off the beach. Nor was there any compensation in the form of losses inflicted on the enemy: total German losses on 19 August 1942 did not exceed 600 men.

Terrible images arise from this stark litany: of beaches littered with dead and dying Canadian infantry, burning tanks on the steep shingle and wrecked landing craft bobbing offshore or in flames, vast quantities of abandoned kit strewn about on the beach – Churchill tanks, Bren guns, mortars, rifles, piles of ammunition and grenades – the decks of the destroyers offshore piled with wounded and dying men while, for hour after hour, the sound of gunfire never ceases until, finally, in the early afternoon, the last resistance on the beaches is snuffed out. The long, hard years of the Second World War record no tragedy greater than Dieppe.

After tragedy comes recrimination, and so it was here. The causes of this disaster have been endlessly debated for more than six decades, with all manner of reasons and not a little pure speculation advanced to account for the debacle. In the circumstances, such debate is inevitable and indeed desirable, but the argument has often done no more than muddy waters already clouded by controversy.

An objective analysis of this event suggests that the basic cause of these appalling losses at Dieppe is actually quite simple: mistakes were made that should have been avoided had the people involved in this operation known more about amphibious warfare. At every level, from planning to execution, those responsible simply did not know what they were doing – and we have evidence of that from one of the survivors. Major-General Robert Houghton was a Major and second-in-command of the Royal Marines 'A' Commando when he landed on White Beach at Dieppe on 19 August:

> It would be hard to overestimate the appalling ignorance and inexperience of many people at the beginning of the war – especially what utter ignorance there was about amphibious operations. No one had really thought about opposed landings, there was no study of the problems involved and our training was not very good. A hard thing to say, but that is what I firmly believe.[1]

Mistakes in war come from various causes – the most common of which are underestimating the difficulty of the task and underestimating the strength and aggression of the enemy. The task of putting a force ashore at Dieppe was gravely underestimated – for which accusation we have the harsh fact that most of the troops never even got off the beach. As for the enemy, every military historian and every soldier, and especially every general, should remember the heartfelt cry of that sagacious Polish officer, Major-General Sosabowski, at the end of the briefing for Arnhem – 'What about the Germans?' There was a conviction among the planners that the German forces at Dieppe were 'second-grade troops', whatever that means. When push came to shove on 19 August these 'second-grade troops' stood their ground and stopped the Canadian assault in its tracks. Underestimating them was only one of several, quite fundamental, reasons why the Dieppe operation was doomed from the start.

The prime aim of this book is to set the Dieppe Raid in the context of its time and to illustrate how a series of events and pressures, political as well as military, personal as well as official, led to this unprecedented and unnecessary disaster. It will also examine the Raid as part of the history of amphibious warfare, that long and painful 'learning curve' that took the Allies from Dunkirk to D-Day. It has been claimed and can be cautiously admitted that lessons were learned at Dieppe, and it is certainly arguable that some of these lessons might not have been learned in any other way. We shall see how those claims stand up to close inspection in the course of this book, but it is fair to add that the arguments supporting the benefits of JUBILEE are not always convincing. Moreover, it is very clear that a great number of mistakes could have been avoided on JUBILEE, either because the planners had ample prior evidence of where their proposals might lead, or because a little thought might have led them to some more sensible conclusions, or because some basic principles of warfare, and especially of amphibious warfare, were either ignored or not understood.

It also seems important to examine a few of the popular myths surrounding this tragedy, of which more anon. Many military operations are surrounded by myths and the Dieppe Raid is no exception, many of them arising from the numerous attempts made by politicians and historians over the last decades to fix the blame for the horrendous losses on some particular individual. Unfortunately, for all their endeavours, the documentation to support some positive accusation is either scanty or completely lacking – a fact which, in itself, has led to a considerable amount of speculation and not a few accusations of duplicity and lies. Only by taking the entire venture apart can we see how and why the Dieppe operation went so disastrously awry. We cannot change what happened; we can, perhaps, discover why it happened and in so doing prevent such a catastrophe happening again.

The problem facing the British military in the first years of the Second World War was that many of the difficulties confronting them were essentially new. This is not to say that the failure to tackle these problems is excusable, but it largely arose from the First World War experience and a failure to appreciate that the military world had changed. For example, though the British had invented the tank and first employed it on the Somme in 1916, by 1939 they had still failed to grasp the true nature of tank warfare or decide what kind of weapon the tank actually *was*. Was it an infantry-support weapon, which could therefore be slow and lightly armed, or was it armoured cavalry, heavily armed and capable of great mobility? The British opted for the former role and the Germans for the latter – and the Germans were right. Sound tank and anti-tank tactics were developed by the Germans in the interwar years, while the British handling of tanks in the Western Desert in 1940–41 was lamentable, allowing the enemy to run rings round them – usually with inferior forces.

Moreover, there was an element of hubris in the British high command, much of it probably arising from the Great War experience. The British and their Allies had won the First World War, and their officers and generals returned from that conflict convinced that they had 'found the formula' for victory in the all-arms battle and could repeat that success when called upon to do so. As a result of this conviction, the changes in kit and military philosophy and methods of warfare forced on the Germans by their defeat completely passed the British by.

In spite of the fact that Britain was a maritime rather than a military power, her skills in amphibious warfare, in the projection of power ashore, were little short of pathetic, to the point of being non-existent. The First World War had seen a series of amphibious catastrophes, notably at Gallipoli and Tanga in East Africa, with only the small Zeebrugge Raid of 1918 to lighten the gloom. Basically, when it came to handling a major amphibious assault in 1942, the British did not know how to do it, a fact that this story will reveal in stark clarity. Fortunately for the British, the need to develop an amphibious capability also passed the Germans by. Germany was a land-based military power and the blitzkrieg strategy that enabled the Wehrmacht to shatter the Polish, Dutch, Belgian, French and British armies in 1939–40 ground to a halt on the Channel coast of France. But for that twenty-mile-wide Channel ditch, the German panzers would have kept on coming and rolled triumphantly into London.

Given that the expulsion of the British Army from France must sooner or later require an invasion of the Continent, this ignorance of amphibious warfare – 'amphibiosity' as it is now called – was bad enough, but the rot went much further. The Dieppe Raid illustrates that ignorance of amphibious warfare two years after Dunkirk was still widespread, even to the point of abandoning the most basic and normal requirements of operational planning.

The need 'to learn how to do it' has been put forward to justify the Dieppe operation, but that reason will not wash. While amphibious operations have their own particular and peculiar problems they still fall within the military remit, and some basic requirements apply as much to assault landings as to a land-based attack: good intelligence on the enemy and the ground, a realistic appreciation of the possibilities of success, a sound plan, well-trained troops, adequate support and so on. These elements have to be present or any attack, across a beach or anywhere else, tends to go seriously awry – as it did at Dieppe.

Operation RUTTER/JUBILEE was a great leap forward from all preceding amphibious raids. The Commando raids mounted between 1940 and 1942 had involved small groups of highly trained infantry soldiers, a few hundred at the most, even for the major attacks on Vaagsø and St Nazaire in 1941–2. Both of these were raids on coastal targets. Now came Dieppe where some six thousand troops were sent into the attack with armoured support from a regiment of tanks – and orders to head inland, sometimes for miles. This may well have been a 'beach too far' – a landing well beyond the current experience of Combined Operations Headquarters and the three Force Commanders charged with planning and executing the Raid. In the words of that great Danish Commando soldier Anders Lassen MC** VC, himself killed in the last days of the war, 'You can do this raiding business now and again for quite a while but you cannot do it all the time for very long.'

Dieppe is a fishing port on the northern coast of France, set midway in the high chalk cliffs that run between Boulogne in the Pas de Calais and the large port of Le Havre at the mouth of the River Seine. With a population in 1942 of some 25,000 people, Dieppe also served as a seaside resort and a market centre for the farmers of the *pays de Caux*, that chalky hinterland behind the coast that rolls south and east towards the Seine.

Dieppe, town and port, lies behind a one-mile stretch of steep shingle beach at the mouth of the River Arques. In more peaceful times the town was best known to British visitors as the Continental end of the cross-Channel service from the English port of Newhaven in Sussex. This pacific reputation tends to conceal the fact that, in its time, Dieppe has seen a great deal of history . . . and not a little war.

From the time of the Norman Conquest privateers from Dieppe preyed on English shipping in the Channel. In 1415, Henry V, King of England, passed by the port on his way from the siege of 'girded Harfleur' to his victory at Agincourt; his bedraggled column was fired on by the guns of the great castle at Arques, which stands a few miles inland from the sea, guarding the landward exit from the Arques Valley.

The hot breath of war continued to blow on Dieppe at regular intervals from the early Middle Ages until the end of the Napoleonic Wars. After that Dieppe became a mecca for painters, French and English, all attracted by that clear, sharp Channel light that picks out the colours in the surrounding countryside and seascapes. After the artists had made their mark came the summer visitors and the tourists, each accretion adding to the town's prosperity while not distracting from its prime roles as a port for inshore fishermen and a market for the farmers of the *pays de Caux*. Dieppe, in short, is a small, pleasant French coastal town with narrow streets and alleyways, an attractive harbour but, even in 1942, of no particular military significance.

However, the most significant question about Dieppe *as a military objective* – a target for a raid – is how to get at it in the face of some considerable natural obstacles. Even without any military defences, Dieppe is not an easy place to attack, especially from the sea. The town is completely overlooked, east and west, by two headlands, the western headland crowned by a medieval castle. These two headlands dominate the Arques river mouth, the harbour and the beach before the town. The beach is backed by a sea wall which bars access to a large and open promenade or esplanade, about 100 metres wide, leading across the open to a series of tall hotels. This was the situation in 1942 and remains the case today; in 1942 the western side of this promenade was occupied by a large casino, a three-storey building that ran from the edge of the beach back to the hotels and houses on the landward side.

From this promenade streets lead off into the town, but in 1942 the street exits off the promenade had been blocked by concrete obstacles and, at one point, by a French tank turret, concreted into position and armed with a quick-firing cannon. The sum total of all this, plus those numerous German gun positions overlooking the beach, was to turn both beach and promenade into the perfect 'killing ground' for any troops foolish enough to come ashore here. Anyone with the slightest knowledge of amphibious operations will shudder at the thought of making a landing on the steep shingle beach, below the beetling cliffs that overhang the landing area. When the Canadians and the Marines of the Royal Marine 'A' Commando went ashore on that central beach they were going to their deaths – and most of them probably realised that fact as their landing craft took them into the assault.

What was the operation for? The raiders were not without a series of objectives – far from it. These ranged from destroying coastal batteries to blowing up harbour installations and seizing German invasion barges in the harbour and sailing them back to Britain; the troops committed to raiding Dieppe were given plenty of tasks to perform. The problem that confronts historians is what this motley collection of *objectives* adds up to in the way of an *aim*. Even after six decades no one is sure why the Dieppe Raid was launched – and the popular explanations do not stand up to even cursory inspection.

It is alleged, for example, that the failure of the Raid revealed the impossibility of the Allies seizing a major port in an undamaged condition and so led to the development of the prefabricated Mulberry harbours for D-Day. This argument falls down in the face of Winston Churchill's famous memorandum to Lord Louis Mountbatten of May 1942 – three months before the Dieppe Raid took place – enquiring about the development of artificial harbours and concluding, in typically Churchillian fashion, that 'the piers must float up and down with the tide. Do not argue the difficulties, the difficulties will argue for themselves.' The actual design and construction of the Mulberry harbours did not begin until 1943, but the idea was certainly around before the Dieppe Raid. That fact is recorded in the Musée du Débarquement at Arromanches on the Calvados coast, a museum entirely devoted to the creation of the Mulberry harbours, one of which was built just offshore.

It has also been alleged that the Raid was simply an extension of other raids and a small leap forward in scale, Winston Churchill coining the phrase – or offering the hopeful explanation – that it was simply 'a reconnaissance in force'. Unfortunately that remark was made after the Raid had taken place, when the full extent of the disaster was becoming all too apparent and some justification for the losses had to be found. Perhaps – and, when lacking any evidence to the contrary, one may speculate – the Dieppe Raid *was* simply an attempt to mount a cross-Channel Commando raid in considerable force; one far in excess of anything previously committed, employing the very latest Churchill tanks and a full division of infantry to see what would happen. But if so, why was that intention not made clear before it took place and why has it proved so difficult to extract a reason for the Raid from those responsible for planning it?

The essential difference between a raid and an invasion is in the intention to remain ashore. If the intention is simply to get ashore, do the necessary business and get away again quickly, that is a raid. If the invaders intend to stay ashore for a while, say a few days or a week – or as long as possible while developing a bridgehead – that is an invasion. By those criteria, the Dieppe operation, for which assault and withdrawal all took place within the space of one tide, was clearly no more than a raid, but it was a far bigger raid than anything mounted previously. That fact alone – the sheer scale of the operation – presented the planners with a range of problems they either did not appreciate or chose to ignore. The assault plan was flawed and failed to deliver the first and most fundamental objective of any amphibious operation: getting the troops off the beach, the killing ground of any amphibious operation. It will be stressed again and again – it cannot be stressed too often – that the prime aim of any amphibious assault is to get the troops off the beach.

Getting ashore was only half of it – what about the withdrawal? A raid requires surprise and stealth but the Dieppe Raid was too big for stealth; certainly after the first shots were fired the enemy would be alert and active and anxious to hit back and drive these aggressors into the sea, not least during the withdrawal phase. How were these tanks and infantry to re-embark on their craft – a slow process at the best of times – and get back to the safety of Britain, with the enemy fully aroused and the Luftwaffe active over the Channel? Surely, by the summer of 1942, halfway into this war, the British should have learned how swift and violent any German reaction to this incursion was likely to be? Apparently not; as we shall see, a large proportion of the Canadian losses came during the withdrawal phase.

The notion that JUBILEE was 'just a raid' is also challenged by Vice-Admiral Lord Louis Mountbatten, Chief of Combined Operations in 1942, who claimed later that 'the battle of D-Day was won on the beaches of Dieppe', harking back to Wellington's famous dictum that the Battle of Waterloo was won on the playing fields of Eton. Mountbatten's comment was self-serving: Dieppe and D-Day were wildly different in almost every way. Two essentials for winning the D-Day battle of 1944 were air superiority over the landing area and an adequate amphibious lift for both the initial assault waves and the subsequent battle of supply, of which only the latter was present at Dieppe.

But the British already knew the importance of air superiority and amphibious lift. They had learned it from their own experience with the enemy, two full years before Dieppe. In the summer of 1940, Adolf

Hitler's plan for the invasion of Britain, Operation SEALION, had been abandoned by the Führer because the Luftwaffe had found itself unable to defeat the RAF and so establish the necessary air superiority over the Pas de Calais – and the Wehrmacht did not have anything like the necessary amount of amphibious craft or the knowledge of amphibious operations needed to mount such a venture with any hope of success.

In the next two years nothing much changed on the British side, although some of the difficulties of amphibious warfare were made apparent by Commando raids during that period – and there were some successes, notably the two most recent Commando operations, the Vaagsø Raid of 26 December 1941 and the St Nazaire Raid in March 1942. Employing cruisers and aircraft of RAF Bomber Command, as well as Nos. 3 and 4 Commandos, Vaagsø was a true 'Combined Operation'. The raiders were able to overcome the brief but fierce enemy resistance and do considerable damage ashore before withdrawing, destroying large supplies of a vital commodity – fish oil – and in addition obliging the Germans to maintain garrisons on the coast of Norway, a long way from the real centres of war.

The St Nazaire Raid – Operation CHARIOT – was another success, albeit at a heavy cost in lives. Under cover of darkness a British destroyer, HMS *Campbeltown*, her bows crammed with explosives, sailed up the river Loire, escorted by motor launches crammed with Commandos, and rammed the dock gates of the *Forme Ecluse*, the largest dry dock on the Atlantic coast and the only one capable of containing a capital ship like the German battleship *Tirpitz*, which as a result remained in the safety of the Norwegian fjords for most of the war.

Surprise, adequate air and naval support, a rapid attack and withdrawal were the keynotes of the Vaagsø and St Nazaire operations but, as we shall see, these necessary principles were either lost or abandoned in the planning for Dieppe. Even by the summer of 1942, the British had no clear air superiority over the Channel and the beaches of Dieppe. The

Royal Navy were therefore naturally reluctant to commit capital ships to the risk of air attack when supporting the landing, yet another reason why a major amphibious operation was fraught with risk. In such circumstances – the lack of naval gunfire support – anything more than a minor raid on the French coast was a recipe for disaster, and the British Force Commanders and planners should have known this. In fact, in the planning stage, such support *was* available, or at least promised. The mistake came when this support was withdrawn and the operation went ahead anyway.

The Dieppe Raid, however, has a further dimension. It was, in many ways, a product of its time, of the particular circumstances facing the three major Allies – the United Kingdom, the United States and Soviet Russia – in the summer of 1942. These circumstances produced pressures that, while of no direct bearing on the Raid, may well have created the atmosphere in which it could not be abandoned. These factors will be evaluated, but now we must go back to the event that made it necessary to develop the entire branch of warfare that came to be known as Combined Operations – the expulsion of the British Army from Dunkirk in the summer of 1940.

AFTER DUNKIRK
1940–41

We must be careful not to ascribe to this event [the Dunkirk evacuation] the attributes of victory. Wars are not won by evacuation.

WINSTON S. CHURCHILL,
JUNE 1940

OPERATION DYNAMO, THE nine-day Dunkirk evacuation of the British Expeditionary Force from France in 1940, can be regarded in various ways. For the British Army it was clearly a defeat; although some 338,000 British and French soldiers were evacuated from under the noses of the enemy, the bulk of their equipment had to be left behind.

For the Royal Navy, Operation DYNAMO was a success. Although a number of precious destroyers were lost, the Regular Army, the only trained soldiers Britain possessed, had been extracted from the jaws of captivity and the Royal Navy rightly got the credit. As for the British people, they were euphoric; anticipating that all was lost in May, they had got the bulk of their Army back by the middle of June – and now they had no unreliable Allies to worry about or defer to. Indeed, the national air of jubilation in Britain post-Dunkirk was so extreme that Winston Churchill, the new Prime Minister, found it necessary to issue a public warning in the House of Commons that 'wars are not won by evacuation'.

It is arguable that Hitler allowed the British Army to escape from Dunkirk. Certainly, had he ordered his generals to attack and wipe out that slender, shrinking BEF pocket on the coast, it is hard to see how Operation DYNAMO could have been carried out or the Army saved. Various reasons have been advanced for this failure: some allege that Hitler wished to do a deal with the British that would preserve the British Empire and thought that his present successes would be enough to bring the then British Government to the conference table. Others contend that Hermann Goering, commander of the Luftwaffe, had convinced the Führer that air power alone could shatter the BEF; or that Hitler simply wanted to avoid the mistakes made by the German Commander-in-Chief, General von Moltke, in 1914, when the German armies failed to round up and destroy the retreating French and thereby permitted Joffre to regroup and counterattack on the Marne. This time the German Army would finish the job and destroy the French Army; if that meant letting the

British get away to their island, so be it. This was the course the Germans adopted and it can be argued that Hitler's failure to destroy the BEF at Dunkirk was his first major mistake.

Wandering along the northern coast of France between Dunkirk and Calais, among the piles of abandoned British guns and trucks, herding some 60,000 British soldiers into captivity, the Germans cannot have been unaware that Britain's situation was now desperate. When the British declined to negotiate, let alone surrender, the Führer did indeed prepare an invasion force and draw up plans for a seaborne assault – Operation SEALION – but apart from a basic shortage of amphibious expertise and landing craft, the Germans lacked the first requirement for a landing – air superiority.

When Napoleon Bonaparte was planning to invade England in 1805, Admiral St Vincent, the First Lord of the Admiralty, explained his optimism to the House of Lords. 'I do not say the French cannot come,' he said briefly, 'I only say they cannot come by sea.' In this the Noble Lord was quite correct; the storm-battered ships of the Channel Fleet commanded the Narrow Seas and while they were on station the *Grande Armée* had to wait, frustrated, in its camps at Boulogne and look across at the white cliffs at Dover – so near and yet so far.

Matters were somewhat different in 1940. By then a new and entirely accurate doctrine dominated military affairs: 'he who commands the air commands the battlefield'. The Royal Navy could still block the seas off the Pas de Calais but if they tried to do so their ships would soon come under attack from the Luftwaffe – unless the Luftwaffe could be kept at bay by the pilots of Fighter Command.

During the interwar years a number of Air Force officers, most notably Colonel Billy Mitchell of the US Army, had demonstrated that even large warships were very vulnerable to aerial attack and this lesson had been learned by the Admirals. Day after day, throughout the long summer of 1940, the twelve hundred pilots of RAF Fighter Command rose from their airfields to defeat the Luftwaffe in the skies over the Channel. Marshal Goering had to admit that, while the British had control of the air, launching Operation SEALION was impossible. This being so, the Germans went over to another tactic, the Blitz, an attempt to break the will of the British people by aerial bombing. This put the Führer on a collision course with the British who, inspired by the words of Churchill, were fully determined to defend their island, whatever the cost might be, and did so. By the spring of 1941, Operation SEALION had been long abandoned. The Blitz did not break the will of the British any more than the later bombing of Germany broke the will of the German people – and so the war went on.

It gradually became clear that with the Dunkirk evacuation the nature of the war in the West had changed. Watching old newsreels of the BEF marching off to France in 1939, it sometimes seems as if the cameras have simply been put in reverse and are showing the old BEF marching to the Great War in 1914. The uniforms, the kit, all seem much the same and those generals who now commanded the British Army, having served in the First World War as junior officers, were gloomily anticipating a re-run of that terrible conflict, right down to the wire and trenches and rat-infested dug-outs, artillery bombardments and night raids 'over the top'. It was not to turn out like that.

The German generals had brooded long and hard over the causes of their defeat, not least on the failure of the Kaiser's Battle, their great offensive of March 1918. They had concluded, correctly, that the reason for that defeat was a lack of mobility, and therefore concentrated on equipping their armies with the means to advance quickly, overcome or avoid fixed defences and keep the battle fluid. They called this tactic *Blitzkrieg* (lightning war) and when Hitler's armies drove forward in May 1940, it proved highly effective; the Wehrmacht panzer divisions carried all before them and drove the British into the sea at Dunkirk. In this war there would be no trenches in Flanders, no dug-outs at Ypres, no muddy battles of attrition on the Somme, no Passchendaele blood baths. But if the British were to fight in France again they must first mount an invasion of the Continent – and that required the creation of an entirely new force, equipped and trained for amphibious operations.

The first step towards winning a war is to avoid defeat. Thanks to those assets listed above, the British were able to avoid defeat – albeit narrowly – in 1940. The snag was that these assets were largely defensive. The British also needed to show aggression and demonstrate an *offensive* capability, to prove to the enemy and the world at large – not least in the United States – that Britain still possessed the will to hit back and carry the war to the enemy across the Narrow Seas. If the British did not display such aggression, the enemy would gain confidence for further attacks and Britain's allies would start to back off. The first answer to that problem was the creation of the Commandos.

Operation DYNAMO ended officially at 1423hrs on 4 June 1940. That evening Lieutenant-Colonel Dudley Clark, Military Assistant to the Chief of the Imperial General Staff (CIGS), General Sir John Dill, was struck by a sudden thought when walking home from the War Office. Clearly, something must be done – and done quickly – to strike back at the enemy, but the available assets to do this did not exist . . . or did they? It might not be possible to strike the enemy with overwhelming force – the kit and the competence for a major assault were simply not available – but surely a body of lightly equipped troops could maintain a British presence on the Continent with raids on the French coast? That night Clark put down his thoughts on a single sheet of paper and on the following day passed it up to Dill. Dill duly endorsed this proposal to create a raiding force and sent it to the Prime Minister, Winston Churchill.

Churchill was the last man to refuse such a request; throughout his life he had an interest in and a hankering for raiding operations. He was also blessed with some personal experience of what guerrilla forces could do, for during the South African War of 1899–1902 the young Winston had been captured by a Boer Commando, which derailed an armoured train in which he had been travelling. He approved the scheme on 5 June and on 6 June Clark was summoned to Dill's office and told to get on with it.

Getting on with it turned out to be the hard part. Britain had no trained raiding forces capable of coastal raids, an amazing omission in the armoury of a maritime power. The Royal Navy has always been seen as the national bulwark against the enemy, and time and time again it has indeed 'seen off' the enemy and kept the State secure. This was certainly true in the ninety-nine years of peace that followed the Napoleonic Wars; even though Napoleon was finally defeated at Waterloo rather than Trafalgar, it was the Navy that got the lion's share of the attention – and the money – in the following century.

For just over a hundred years the Royal Navy dominated the oceans and carried the British flag and British trade to the furthest corners of the world. The Army was seen as the poor relation and indeed, at the turn of the twentieth century, the then First Sea Lord, Jacky Fisher, could assure the Government that, in his opinion, 'The Army was simply a missile to be fired by the Navy'; and he produced a number of highly dangerous schemes to do just that on the Baltic coast in the event of war with Germany. One outstanding flaw in Fisher's thinking was in the matter of reinforcements: he could not appreciate that the land-based Germans could bring up reinforcements to oppose a landing far quicker than the Navy could put more troops ashore – a point the Dieppe planners failed to grasp forty years later.

The notion that amphibious warfare, and coastal raiding, were a specialised branch of the military art never entered the naval mind, and in that respect matters had not changed at all by the summer of 1940. Coastal raids were called for by the Prime Minister, but who was going to carry them out? Clearly not the Royal Navy; while overwhelmingly powerful afloat, the Navy lacked the means to project British power ashore. This called for a combination of maritime and land operations – amphibious operations – for which the Admirals had not the kit, the men or the slightest interest.

This is not to say that the Royal Navy completely lacked an amphibious force at the outbreak of the Second World War. This took the form of that stern regiment of sea-soldiers, the Corps of Royal Marines, formed in 1664 as the Duke of York and Albany's Maritime Regiment of Foot, a body of men which has served in every British naval engagement – and most of Britain's land campaigns – from the seventeenth century to the present day. However, at the start of the Second World War the Royal Marines were almost entirely ship-bound. They manned 25 per cent of the main armament of gun-armed capital ships, like cruisers and battleships, and were an integral part of the ship's company. Capital ships and the newly arrived aircraft carriers also carried a detachment of Royal Marines for employment on any coastal operations the Admiral or the ship's captain might fancy, including raiding.

This might sound promising, but the Royal Marines lacked the necessary training and amphibious craft to carry out more than the smallest landing operation. Equipped with rifles and bayonets, they went ashore, when required, in ships' boats rowed by sailors using muffled oars. In terms of amphibious warfare, matters had not moved on much since the days of Nelson.

The Marines had long realised this fact. Their senior officers were well aware that the Admirals might choose at any moment, or in times of financial stringency, to replace the Royal Marine gunners with sailors and then disband the Corps, thereby saving enough money every year to buy a cruiser. What the Corps needed to survive was some specialised role. The most obvious one was expertise in amphibious warfare and an understanding of the requirements for force projection ashore which the Lords of the Admiralty currently lacked.

The Admirals were not entirely blinkered either and this matter had been aired from time to time. In 1913, interest in amphibious operations led to the establishment of a joint Army–Navy Committee which published a manual, *A Handbook of Combined Operations*, setting out the problems involved in amphibious warfare and proposing some solutions. In the event, the First World War saw only three serious amphibious operations: the disastrous Gallipoli campaign of 1915, the equally disastrous Tanga landings in East Africa and the smaller but much more successful Zeebrugge Raid on the Belgian submarine base on St George's Day, 23 April 1918.

Creating a new arm takes commitment as well as men and money and although the Madden Committee of 1924 again pressed for the development of the Royal Marines into a fully equipped amphibious force, Admiralty commitment was lacking and no funds were provided for men, equipment or training until 1930, when a new amphibious venture set sail with the establishment of the Inter-Service Training and Development Centre (I-STDC) at Portsmouth. This unit was commanded by a naval officer, Captain L.E.H. Maund, supported by an RAF officer, a major in the Royal Artillery and a Royal Marine officer, Captain J. Picton-Phillips, whose brother was to command the Royal Marine 'A' Commando in the Dieppe Raid.

The I-STDC did good work, not least in the field of equipment and assault craft. They studied the need for assault troop transports, selecting as their ideal a new type of fast passenger ship operated by the Glen Line; four of these Glen ships, the *Glengyle*, *Glenroy*, *Glenearn* and *Breconshire*, were duly taken up from trade at the start of the war, equipped with davits strong enough to carry assault landing craft (LCAs) and took part in most subsequent amphibious operations.

The I-STDC studied the problems of landing tanks, of clearing underwater obstacles, and the landing of logistical supplies like fuel and water. They also studied the problems of command during an amphibious operation, advocating the need for dedicated command ships equipped with state-of-the-art communications equipment, as well as the problems of co-operation between naval and Army officers with their different systems and priorities. These matters had never received the necessary attention and we shall see how that neglect would affect matters at Dieppe. Most of all, though, the I-STDC concerned itself with the matter of assault craft.

When they opened for business in 1930, the I-STDC possessed exactly three landing craft; the most advanced of these drew four feet of water, had a top speed of five knots and was extremely noisy. Over the next ten years this little fleet expanded to six landing craft, none of improved design. The best landing craft in the world at this time were being designed on a private basis by an American, Andrew Higgins, a millionaire boat fanatic from New Orleans. Myopia reigned even in the USA; lacking any official backing, Higgins funded his research into landing craft with his own money and the discreet help of the United States Marine Corps, who found the 'Higgins boats' far better than anything the US Navy could provide. The I-STDC would have dearly loved a few 'Higgins boats' but funds were not available. Starved of money but full of enthusiasm, the I-STDC became a lobbying unit, pestering the powers that be for more men and money and doing everything possible to point out the undoubted fact that a naval power like Britain clearly needed an amphibious arm.

By 1938, the officers at the I-STDC had gained a considerable expertise in amphibious warfare. In theory they knew how to do it – at least for small-scale operations. Landings should be made at night, from fast, shallow-draft landing craft launched by larger craft or transports out at sea, anchored well beyond the range of coastal batteries. Smoke and naval gun protection should be provided during the assault and while the initial landing parties established themselves ashore. After the landing area had been secured from fire, more troops should come ashore and, finally, supplies and ammunition to maintain the force should be landed. The prime necessities were surprise, good intelligence on the enemy and sound planning.

Much of this was common sense and caused no great alarm at the Admiralty, not least because this doctrine – or rather, these ideas – currently cost no money. In 1938 the I-STDC set out to get the craft, the kit and the men, pestering anyone who would listen or could help flesh out their doctrine with the necessary equipment. The outcome of this pestering came in 1939 when, following the despatch of the BEF to France, the I-STDC was disbanded, its officers and men returned to other duties. After all, or so went the reasoning in Whitehall, with the British Army in France anticipating a re-run of the Western Front fighting of the Great War, there would be no need for amphibious forces. A year later came Dunkirk.

The I-STDC did not remain long in the doldrums and had been re-formed in a somewhat truncated version by the spring of 1940 – even before Dunkirk – in time for the Norwegian expedition, an Anglo-French attempt to forestall the invasion of Norway, and another costly failure. The Combined Operations history refers to the Norway assault as being 'as unhappy as a campaign can be; unplanned, unprepared, divergent instructions, non-tactical loading of ships, inadequate equipment . . . a real hurrah's nest'.[1] There were, however, a few bright spots to lighten the gloom; the I-STDC landing craft did heroic work at Narvik and a new force (the Independent Companies, forerunners of the Commandos) gave a good account of themselves in those snowy mountains.

And so to the aftermath of Dunkirk. Clark's orders to form what became Commando units were followed by some necessary action on the command and administrative front by the Chiefs of Staff, the Committee which handled the day-to-day running of the war under the close direction of the Prime Minister – who had retained the Defence portfolio. This body was understandably alarmed at the notion of Winston Churchill creating private armies, largely consisting of wild spirits who wanted to crawl about at night with blackened faces, cutting throats.

On 14 June, the Chiefs of Staff (composed of the heads of the three fighting Services – the Chief of the Air Staff, the CIGS and the First Lord of the Admiralty, Sir Dudley Pound, who acted as Chairman and reported directly to Churchill) appointed the Adjutant-General of the Royal Marines, Lieutenant-General Sir Alan Bourne, as 'Commander of Raiding Operations on coasts in enemy occupation and Adviser to the Chiefs of Staff on Combined Operations'.

This title is interesting and seems to offer General Bourne two roles: one active, one advisory. Taking the Independent Companies and the Commando units now being formed under command – and possibly paratroopers at a later date – Bourne could mount small raids on his own authority, provided he could get his hand on some ships. In his second advisory role he was to be the Chiefs of Staff consultant on all matters affecting opposed landings while supervising Combined Operations training and overseeing the production of all special craft. None of this meant that Bourne had a free hand; he was a Royal Marines officer, the Royal Marines were paid by the Navy and General Bourne was accommodated in the Admiralty, where the Admirals could keep an eye on him.

One result of this was that nothing much happened. There were a couple of minor operations. On the night of 24 June, one day after the French leaders surrendered to the Germans in the railway carriage at Compiègne, a force of British Commandos from No. II Independent Company, 115 strong and led by Major R.J.F. Tod, later of No. 9 Commando, raided the French coast at four points between Boulogne and Berck Plage. This operation was accompanied by the Commandos' godfather, Lieutenant-Colonel Dudley Clarke, anxious to see how his new venture would work out in practice.

In the event the results of this raid were mixed. One group advanced half a mile inland but met no one and withdrew. A second group came across a seaplane and were about to attack it with grenades when it took off. The third group had better luck, killing two sentries, while the last party was surprised and shot up during the withdrawal, Lieutenant-Colonel Clarke being shot in the head and slightly wounded; his ear was almost removed but sewn back on later.

Three weeks later, on 14 July, the first Commando unit, No. 3 Commando, commanded by an Artillery officer, John Durnford-Slater, put in an attack on the island of Guernsey; like its predecessor the raid did not achieve very much, and Churchill later described it as 'a silly fiasco'.

The Royal Marines were not closely involved in the creation of these new units. To their considerable chagrin, this role was delegated to the Army, who naturally had little knowledge of naval procedure or amphibious warfare. Britain's newly fledged Commando soldiers therefore had a lot to learn, and how they set about learning it will be fully described in the next chapter. The point at issue here is the establishment of Combined Operations as a viable and useful asset, accepted as an integral part of the British military machine.

In June 1940, Winston Churchill was a man in a hurry and not to be argued with or delayed by any foot-dragging among the military establishment over new units and fresh ideas. He soon realised that the current Combined Operations set-up, such as it was, was being held back by the powers that be in Whitehall who, perhaps understandably at this time, were more interested in the training and re-equipping of conventional forces than in creating new and unconventional forces of parachutists and Commandos.

General Sir Alan Bourne, though willing and competent, simply lacked the clout to deal with this resistance and so a new commander had to be found, someone fully capable of fighting the 'Combined Ops' corner and seeing off any opposition. Looking around for an iconoclast, Churchill's eye chanced on Admiral Sir Roger Keyes, who had been the overall commander of the successful Zeebrugge Raid in 1918. By now aged sixty-eight, he was a noted fire-eater and a Westminster MP. On 17 July 1940, Keyes took over Bourne's portfolio of responsibilities as Director of Combined Operations.

In his history of Combined Operations, Bernard Fergusson comments, or at least hints strongly, that this change of title went to Keyes's head.[2] If he was the Director, Keyes intended to direct, and he regarded himself as the fount of all knowledge in matters affecting amphibious operations, capable of initiating operations as well as advising on them; in short, anything to do with Combined Ops was now Keyes's area of responsibility and woe betide anyone who got in his way. It should be pointed out that Fergusson was a stout supporter of Lord Louis Mountbatten, the man who succeeded Keyes at Combined Ops, and a certain amount of prejudice in favour of the latter colours Fergusson's account.

Keyes took on this new command with considerable energy and did not hesitate to lobby Churchill and General Ismay, his contact at the War Ministry, for anything he needed, establishing his new headquarters – COHQ – in Richmond Terrace, well away from the Admiralty. COHQ was a Combined Services operation from the start, with departments headed by officers from the Army, Navy and Air Force. When Keyes finished reviewing his command – the process took less than a day – he discovered that it amounted to COHQ, about 1000 Commandos, with more being recruited, and three specialised shore-based establishments ('stone frigates'): HMS *Northney* on the south coast, where landing craft crews were trained, HMS *Tormentor* at Warsash, which was used for advanced training and as a base for cross-Channel raids, and the old I-STDC, which was still beavering away at the problems of command and supply.

The big problem was landing craft; assault craft of various kinds, for landing men and vehicles and tanks, still had to be designed and constructed or there would be no amphibious lift and therefore no major raids. Some of these could be built in the UK, but one of Keyes's first acts was to order from Mr Higgins's boat yard in New Orleans no fewer than 136 landing craft, each capable of carrying 25 fully armed and equipped Commandos and known as 'Eurekas'. An establishment to train troops in amphibious techniques was also necessary, and the first Combined Training Centre was set up at Inveraray in the Western Highlands of Scotland; the training of Commandos was later moved to Achnacarry, just north of Fort William.

All this was to the good and would pay off later, but it was not what Churchill wanted. He expected Keyes and his merry men to spend most of their time harassing the enemy, not messing about in boats in the Western Highlands. Granted, there were some Combined Operations in hand, but these were big affairs, outside Keyes's remit – and usually disastrous. The most important of these, mounted in August 1940, was Operation MENACE, an attack on Dakar, the capital of Senegal in West Africa, a territory occupied by the hostile forces of Vichy France.

This was an Anglo-Free French operation, which might charitably be described as a shambles. The Anglo-French forces slunk home having learned, one hoped, a useful series of lessons. The most important of these, one with relevance for future operations, including Dieppe, was the need for a dedicated headquarters command ship, equipped to liaise with the rest of the amphibious squadron and the forces ashore. As it was, the Force Commander on MENACE, General Irwin, was embarked on a battleship, and, as he recalls:

> Seldom have I felt so impotent as during this expedition when I was separated from my forces and tied to any naval operation which might become necessary at short notice. On one occasion I was heading northward at twenty-five knots while my forces were proceeding south at twelve knots and on another I was returning to the advanced base at five knots while the transports preceded me at twelve knots.

Commanders in a Combined Operation, Irwin concluded in his report, must *not* be embarked on a bombardment ship even if this meant building a specialised headquarters vessel – as it clearly did. This lesson was taken on board and headquarters ships were duly commissioned but not in time for Dieppe, where General Roberts, the Land Force Commander for JUBILEE, exercised his command from HMS *Calpe*, one of the supporting destroyers, with command back-up on another destroyer, HMS *Fernie*.

The development of Combined Ops under Keyes's direction continued for the next eighteen months. Full credit should be paid to Keyes and his staff for the work done at that time; landing craft, including LCTs (landing craft tanks; shallow-draught vessels capable of landing three tanks on open beaches), were built, crews were trained and more Commando units were raised. The problem was not the creation of a new Commando force but the will to commit it to battle – and the failure to do more in that area was the cause of increasing frustration at COHQ and especially among the battle-thirsty Commando units.

Here again, this was not for want of trying; various raids were proposed or planned, on Pantelleria in the Mediterranean and on the Canaries or the Azores in the Atlantic, but only a few minor raids were actually implemented. Three Commando units under Brigadier Robert Laycock – and therefore referred to as 'Layforce' – were sent to the Middle East but found very little action there, except for an attack on the Vichy French forces in Syria, a number of small raids along the North African coast and the famous raid on Rommel's headquarters in the Western Desert; this last was yet another disappointment, for Rommel was not in residence.

By the early spring of 1941 Keyes was at odds with the Chiefs of Staff, partly over a lack of support for raiding operations, partly over the question of how the Commando units – now nine in number – should be organised. The War Office, nothing if not conventional, wanted the

Commando organisation, which currently consisted of rifle platoons of fifty men, known as 'fighting troops', plus a support and small headquarters troop, re-formed on the same lines as an infantry battalion, albeit a rather small one.

Neither did the powers that be care for the newfangled name, 'Commando', that the unit commanders seemed to have adopted. The War Office preferred to call these units 'Special Service Battalions', which became 'SS Battalions' on official communications and therefore vastly unpopular with the troops. A final blow was the War Office's rejection of Keyes's request for a special headdress – later the green beret – for his Commandos.

Fortunately, the War Office gave in on some of these points. The Commando organisation was retained within the newly formed 1st Special Service Brigade, but the great leap forward came in March 1941 when the Brigade sent 500 Commandos to raid the Lofoten Islands off the coast of Norway, a major raid and a chance to show what such units could do. There was no German garrison to eliminate, but the raid did destroy several factories producing fish-oil, a strategic commodity at the time, and brought back a large number of Norwegian volunteers to join the Norwegian forces in Britain.

Gratifying though this operation was, it did not greatly improve relations between Admiral Keyes and the Chiefs of Staff, who, in March 1941, issued a directive that placed Keyes and COHQ firmly under their control and changed his role to a subsidiary one. From now on, the Director, Combined Operations would be responsible for the training and command of troops specially organised for landing operations and the initiation, planning and execution of raids involving up to five thousand men. He would also advise the Chiefs of Staff on amphibious warfare and retain control of establishments like the I-STDC. This sounds a very clear brief, but there was a hole in it: to mount a truly Combined Operation would require the assistance of the Royal Navy and the RAF – and who was to issue orders to these naval and RAF units and ensure their compliance?

Matters came to a head in August 1941 – a year before the Dieppe Raid – when a COHQ exercise involving naval and RAF units went badly wrong. In his subsequent report, Keyes complained bitterly that this was because the naval and RAF Force Commanders had taken their orders from the Chiefs of Staff rather than from him. The Force Commanders had also put in a report listing their complaints, and so the whole matter of what Combined Ops were to do and whom the Director of Combined Ops reported to had yet another airing.

The end result was one that Keyes could not accept. This shifted the responsibility for the actual execution of raids to the Force Commanders, one from each Service, who would report to the War Cabinet. The Force Commanders should also be responsible for the planning and execution of specific operations. Responsibility for major operations – say the invasion of Europe – should fall in the remit of the Commander-in-Chief, Home Forces.

Keyes was demoted from 'Director' to 'Adviser' and COHQ would henceforth concern itself with giving advice when asked and with the development of craft and amphibious techniques. On 30 September 1941, Churchill wrote to Keyes, expressing the hope that the Admiral would go along with these arrangements. On 2 October Keyes wrote back, saying that he could not accept the terms of this new appointment, and two days later he was relieved of his command.

Keyes was a warrior and he went down fighting. Once dismissed, he donned his full Admiral's uniform and, in spite of a none too subtle warning to desist, in the shape of a hand-delivered copy of the Official Secrets Act, he delivered a devastating speech in the House of Commons on his recent efforts and travails, which concluded:

> After long naval experience which had recently embraced the appointment of Director of Combined Operations, I must fully

> endorse the Prime Minister's comment on the strength of the negative power which controls the war machine in Whitehall. Inter-Service committees and sub-committees have become the dictators of policy instead of the servants of those who bore full responsibility; by concentrating on the difficulties and dangers of every amphibious project the planners have succeeded in thwarting execution until it is too late. Procrastination, the thief of time, is the key word in the War Office. We continue to lose one opportunity after another in a lifetime of opportunities.

Please note the date; we are now in October 1941, less than a year before the Dieppe Raid, and the command and control function governing Combined Operations like Dieppe has *still* not been settled, more than a year after Combined Operations was first established. This is no light matter; having the right organisation in place and functioning properly is vital to any planning and particularly so in the case of wartime operations, not least amphibious operations. Until this matter was sorted out – what Combined Operations HQ was *for*, what it was authorised to do and to whom it was responsible – it would be impossible for any operation to be properly planned.

This abrupt but hardly unexpected dismissal was a considerable blow to Roger Keyes who, a few days later, heard that his son Geoffrey, then serving with Laycock's Commandos in the Middle East, had been killed in the Rommel raid. So, after fifteen months in his post and having achieved a great deal in the teeth of established and entrenched opposition from the powers that be, Keyes departed. His replacement was a very new broom indeed: Captain Lord Louis Mountbatten, the dark angel of the Dieppe Raid.

THE COMMANDER, THE COMMANDOS AND THE CANADIANS

1940–42

Enterprises must be prepared, employing specially trained men of the hunter class, who can develop a reign of terror down the enemy coast.

WINSTON S. CHURCHILL,
INSTRUCTIONS TO THE CHIEFS OF STAFF, JUNE 1940

Lord Louis Mountbatten – or Prince Louis Francis Battenberg to give his original title – a man known to his intimates as 'Dickie', was very well connected, not least among the royal family, the Royal Navy, the aristocracy and Britain's political establishment. A professional naval officer and a fully committed playboy, Mountbatten had devoted his ample leisure time to polo, travel, fast cars, befriending the Prince of Wales – later and briefly King Edward VIII – and marrying a rich and beautiful heiress, Edwina, daughter of the financier Ernest Cassell. In the happy years between the wars – happy at least for those with money and the right connections – Dickie Mountbatten was a leading light in British society.

He was also brave, ambitious, charming and extremely devious; in later life he was told to his face that he was 'so crooked, that if you swallowed a nail, Dickie, you would shit a corkscrew'. One postwar colleague at the Ministry of Defence told of how the Chiefs of Staff Committee were often disenchanted to find that a matter they had assembled to discuss had already been settled in a private chat between Dickie and the Secretary of State for War, adding that 'Dickie Mountbatten would much prefer to come in down the chimney than walk in through the door'.

Mountbatten's war career so far had been marked by fame, danger and folly in roughly equal amounts, with recklessness as its most significant characteristic, a career recently culminating in the loss of his destroyer, HMS *Kelly*, to air attack during the Battle of Crete. Here again, though, in the sinking of the *Kelly*, Mountbatten redeemed himself with a display of his great virtue, outstanding physical courage. He fought the *Kelly* until she sank under him, with every man at his post, all guns firing and Captain Mountbatten still on the bridge, clinging to the compass standard. When Churchill summoned him to take charge of Combined Operations, Mountbatten was in the USA, about to commission his new command, the aircraft carrier HMS *Illustrious*, making many friends in Washington and very eager to get back to the war.

The overall picture is of a man with an engrained capacity for intrigue and cutting corners – and one therefore seen by the Prime Minister as just the man to slap away the dead hands currently obstructing the much-needed development of Combined Operations. To Winston Churchill, Mountbatten's not entirely attractive character was more important than his limited military experience and expertise, which had not yet covered amphibious operations.

Indeed, Mountbatten's initial appointment in October 1941 was as 'Adviser' on Combined Operations, not 'Director' or 'Commander'. This is a point we shall return to but it raises an obvious question: as a former destroyer captain, flotilla commander and naval Signals expert, it is hard to see from where Mountbatten drew the experience required to advise anyone on amphibious operations, let alone the British Chiefs of Staff. When one considers that the Prime Minister was surrounded by generals, admirals and air marshals, the selection of a mere naval captain for one of the most important posts available – and then for membership of the Chiefs of Staff Committee – is more than a little surprising, until one considers the fate of Roger Keyes. That episode suggests that Churchill did not appoint Mountbatten to COHQ because of his expertise in amphibious warfare – Mountbatten had no amphibious expertise – but because he thought he was the man to short-circuit the road blocks in the Whitehall machine.

Whatever his title, an 'advisory' post was not the role Churchill had in mind when he selected Mountbatten for this job. Mountbatten's job was to 'think offensively' and carry the war to the enemy, always bearing in mind the eventual need for a cross-Channel invasion. Even without the warnings from Keyes, the Prime Minister had noted that the Chiefs of Staff and their subordinate rank and file at the War Office were frequently dragging their feet over his raiding concept and where the accumulated experience might lead.

In the circumstances of the time the elevation of someone like Louis

Mountbatten to the higher echelons of the military establishment was therefore both a breath of fresh air and quite understandable. The British military mind is essentially conservative and there was little enthusiasm at the senior Army level for the creation of Commando units, paratroop battalions or much else of an irregular nature. The British have a talent for irregular warfare and during the Second World War no nation produced or supported so many irregular units – SAS, SBS, LRDG, COPP, SOE, the Chindits, the Commandos, Popski's Private Army, Force 136 . . . the list is almost endless.

At the same time, the commanders of these units are united in recording the engrained resistance they endured from the Whitehall warriors, the 'Gaberdine Swine' and assorted 'brass-hats'. Nor was this resistance restricted to the higher echelons of the Army. The battalion commanders in the infantry resented having to part with their best men and did everything they could to keep them back, often sending the sick, lame and lazy in their place. Special forces units had to fight for equipment as well as personnel, and most of all for actions and operations.

Nor was it just the Army that caused problems. The naval commanders had no boats to spare for assault training, or so they said, and, as we shall see, were less than forthcoming with large ships for transport or gunfire support. Furthermore, the admirals were not keen to supply good personnel; when considering the post-training appointments at shore establishments, the answer to the posting problem for 'bottom of the class candidates' was, 'Well, we can always send them to Combined Ops.'

Sir Roger Keyes had flung himself against this dire situation with commendable vigour, but the resistance was well entrenched and he got nowhere and made many enemies in the process. Hence his dismissal and replacement by Mountbatten, an officer of comparatively junior rank perhaps, but Britain's most handsome and charismatic war hero – and a very wily cove indeed.

*

By the time Mountbatten took control, the structure of the Commando units was on the way to becoming established. The initial idea was to form ten raiding battalions – 'SS' or 'Special Service Battalions' as they were first called – each of 500 men divided into ten 'fighting troops' or platoons; this would create units about half the size of a normal infantry battalion. All the men had to be volunteers, trained soldiers, fit, active, skilled in weapon handling and capable of displaying aggression. When the call for such volunteers went out it was accompanied by a letter to Commanding Officers throughout the UK, instructing them to release any man who came forward – an instruction that the battalion COs deeply resented, not least because it required them to give up their best men. And having the best men was the fundamental reason for the success of Commando operations.

In the beginning, however, many of the volunteers who came forward were far from suitable, as Major Milton of No. 7 Commando can confirm:

> With another officer, I went out to interview volunteers from the Eastern Command. I don't think any of us knew how to pick men for an enterprise of this sort. We knew that toughness would be essential but I think that the idea that a rigid, strong discipline must underpin Commando operations and is desperately needed if you are to fight in a co-ordinated manner, somehow escaped us.
>
> We tended to go for men who stood out because they had done something unusual in civilian life, like the one who had gone around the Horn in a Finnish sailing ship or another who had been with the International Brigades in Spain or one who had been the leading light in a Glasgow razor gang. I came to regret every one of those but when the Commando finally formed up it contained men from no fewer than fifty-eight corps and regiments of the British Army.[1]

It soon became apparent that the old military virtues – smartness, sound training, discipline, high standards of drill and cleanliness, sensible handling in camp and field – were as essential for Commando soldiering as for any other kind of soldiering. Peter Young of No. 3 Commando, an outstanding Commando soldier, confirms this:[2]

> The majority of men in No. 3 were recalled reservists; many of them having already served seven years with the Colours, mostly in India. The average age was about twenty-six, they had seen some fighting and wanted more of it. How do you select them? Well, you talk to them, don't you, see if they have something to offer, weed out the bullshitters, select the men with potential, the kind who will always get their shot in first.

The wilder spirits were sent back to their original units, the iron hand of discipline descended on the rest and serious training commenced, concentrating on fitness, field craft, shooting, night movement and – when suitable craft could be found – small boat handling and the landing of raiding parties. Great efforts were made to teach the men self-reliance, and one popular step in that direction was to take them out of barracks and put them in 'civvy billets', as Stan Wetherall of No. 6 Commando recalls:

> The whole Commando was placed in civilian billets in Scarborough. We got civvy ration books and a billeting allowance of 33p a day (6s 8d). We paid our landladies £1 10s a week – £1.50 in modern money – so we were quids in at a time when fags cost 6d for twenty and a pint of beer was sixpence – say two and a half pence today instead of a couple of quid![3]

Commando training became legendary, both for its intensity and for its toughness; wars did not stop on Sundays, so training went on seven days a week. Fighting did not stop in foul weather, so the men went out in blizzards and pouring rain and stayed out until the scheme was completed – and if it was not done well, it was done again. Most of this training employed live ammunition and a certain level of casualties was accepted; more than forty men were killed under training at the Commando Training Centre at Achnacarry.

The Royal Marine 'A' Commando, an all-volunteer force, can also produce some examples of life in a Commando unit prior to Dieppe. This unit, the first Royal Marines Commando, was formed at Deal on 14 February 1942, and largely composed of 'H.O.' (Hostilities Only) Marines from the Royal Marine Division. It had a total strength at Dieppe of 18 officers and 352 other ranks, commanded by Lieutenant-Colonel Picton-Phillips. Bill Hefferson writes:

> I was a Corporal and I took a party of thirty-five Marines to open up a part of the Deal North Barracks. The officer arrived later, led by Lieutenant-Colonel Picton-Phillips, a great officer, who had been my Adjutant back in 1938. Major 'Titch' Houghton was there too and Captain Peter Hellings, and we spent several months at Deal, training and weeding out the unfit or unwilling, men we called RTUs (Return to Units).

The training and discipline soon denuded the Commando of unsuitable candidates and the unit diary records forty RTUs on 17 February, thirty on 21 February and thirty on 27 February. Fortunately more volunteers were coming in.[4]

Kenneth Richardson remembers the early days of the 'A' Commando:

> On the morning parades at Deal, Colonel Picton-Phillips always inspected the unit while on a white horse. Once, when he saw

> someone move, his voice bellowed out, 'Sergeant, that man in the front rank moved, take his name.' The Sergeant replied, 'That man is a Corporal, Sir,' and the Colonel replied, 'Well, damn it all, Sergeant, then take the name of the man standing next to him.' We all respected the Colonel but God help you if you batted an eyelid on parade.[5]

From Deal, the 'A' Commando, now mustering around 250 officers and men, went to Scotland, first to Glen Borrodale, and later to the Commando Training Centre at Achnacarry, the estate of a Highland chieftain, the Cameron of Locheil, at Spean Bridge near Fort William. Charles McNeill remembers their arrival at Achnacarry:

> We got off the train at Spean Bridge, and were met by a big Highland soldier, wearing a kilt, who told us to put our kitbags in the transport, then fall in on the road. We then speed-marched seven miles to Achnacarry Camp, doing a mile every ten minutes, and believe me, that was tough in full kit and with platoon weapons and after sixteen hours on the train. Outside the gates we were halted, tightened slings and marched in at the slope, past a line of graves. I found out later these were fakes, but the remarks on the gravestones still stick in my mind. '*This man ran in front of the Bren.*' '*This man forgot to wet his toggle rope.*' . . . things like that.
>
> Reveille at Achnacarry was at six or thereabouts when a piper marched right through the Nissen huts, leaving all the doors open. That's no joke in March in the Highlands. Most of the training was physical. You ran everywhere at Achnacarry, even when off-duty, even to the sick bay to have the blisters cut off your feet. Officers had to do the same and all exercises used live ammo but it was a very fit, united unit that marched out a few weeks later.

All Commando soldiers who passed through Achnacarry recall how the tough training extended to every level of activity. Ken Richardson writes:

> All washing and shaving was done in cold water and every morning, rain or sleet or shine, began with PT, stripped to the waist. The huts were heated, if at all, by a small stove, and we each had one blanket and a groundsheet. Most of all I remember the series of assault courses: climbing cliffs, crawling through bogs, under barbed wire, while the staff shot over us with Brens or chucked grenades about. It rained all the time so we were never dry, and then there were the speed marches, six or seven miles in an hour, for hour after hour, in full kit with platoon weapons. Many would have fallen out, but were helped on by their mates.[6]

C.E. 'Knocker' White joined the 'A' Commando at Achnacarry directly from a ship's detachment:

> Coming from a ship it proved very hard, and I remember pulling myself up some of those peaks on hands and knees. However, we soon got super-fit. The only thing was, we got so hungry we'd eat anything. We were organized in companies at that time, not in Fighting Troops like the Army lads. I was in 'A' Company when we moved down to civilian billets on the Isle of Wight before Dieppe.[7]

The tactical unit of the Commando was the 'section', divided into three 'sub-sections', which usually consisted of about fourteen men, commanded by a sergeant, with a corporal in charge of the rifle or assault group and a lance-corporal in charge of the light machine-gun or Bren group. The support section would contain a 2in mortar man and later on an anti-tank team armed with a PIAT (Projector Infantry Anti-Tank) was added to this role. The Commandos were soon all divided into Rifle Troops or, as they were then called, 'Fighting Troops', with an HQ Troop and a Support or 'S' Troop armed with 3in mortars and Vickers MMGs; this Troop usually included an Assault Engineer Section to carry out demolitions and clear mines.

Marine Commando units also contained an administrative element of clerks, signallers and drivers. All were equally adept with their weapons and had a place in the line of battle – a useful practice which was adopted by Army Commando units in 1943. As a link with their naval gunnery tradition Marine Commando 'Troops' were later listed as A, B, X, Y and Q Troops, since these are the initials used to distinguish gun turrets on capital ships, but the 'A' Commando was organised on a company basis until after Dieppe, when the unit became No. 40 (Royal Marine) Commando and went to Italy. The strength of these wartime Commando units varied considerably but the establishment in 1942 was for about 460 in all ranks, although this was rarely achieved.

Apart from their platoon weapons, the individual Marines were heavily armed. Ken Richardson recalls:

> I carried a Tommy gun, a .45 automatic pistol, a fighting knife concealed in a sheath sewn into a seam of my trousers, a pair of knuckledusters and a couple of grenades, plus ammunition. Each man carried his personal weapon, a rifle or Sten sub-machine gun. For platoon weapons we had the Bren light machine-gun, the 2in mortar or anti-tank PIAT, and each man carried a toggle rope about 6ft long, with a wooden toggle at one end and a loop at the other. Linked together, these could be used to scale walls or make a bridge. In the beginning we had rope-soled boots, or ammo boots, but these were eventually discarded and we got the rubber-soled type. We never wore steel helmets, even in battle, just the green

> beret which came in about this time or sometimes the traditional woollen cap-comforter.[8]

From Achnacarry, the 'A' Commando moved to the Isle of Wight for more training. Here they were in civilian billets and spread out by Troops among the citizens of Sandown, Shanklin and Ventnor. The idea was to give the men personal responsibility and the chance to practise self-reliance, for they were responsible for getting on parade each day without the usual barracks coercion. This practice also spared the Commando from carrying an administrative 'tail'. The men, more practically, enjoyed all the comforts of home while not on exercise.

'Life on the island was pretty good,' recalls Charles McNeill, 'but the locals weren't very observant. One day the CO got some men to dress up in German uniforms and walk about the town, but nobody even noticed.'

Says Ken Richardson:

> I was billeted at Ventnor and we worked long and hard there to improve our ability, notably in street fighting, with lots of cliff-climbing and speed-marches to keep us fit and build up stamina. I remember we used our toggle rope to span a breach in the pier at Ventnor – it had been gapped to stop the enemy using it, had they invaded in 1940. When my section was crossing, a rope snapped and we fell about thirty feet onto rocks or into the sea, fully loaded. I managed to loosen my kit and swim free, but I was convalescent for four or five days – and then I was put on a charge for losing my kit, regardless of saving myself from drowning.

The final land element in the Dieppe raiding force was a fifty-strong company of US Rangers, a force raised in Northern Ireland soon after the Americans arrived in the UK in 1942. These Rangers also trained at Achnacarry and formed up as the 1st Ranger Battalion. As we shall see they played a useful role at Dieppe when attached to Nos. 3 and 4 Commandos.

The greatest incentive offered to these first Commando soldiers was the possibility of action, and this came quickly – at least at first. The operation on 24 June 1940, described in the previous chapter, marked the start of a long series of Commando raids between 1940 and 1942, notably on the Lofoten Islands, at Vaagsø and at St Nazaire in March 1942. An examination of these raids, especially the larger ones like Vaagsø and St Nazaire, shows that such operations were gradually increasing in size and complication as the techniques of amphibious warfare were rediscovered or developed or expanded by the necessities of the operation in question. The aim was one of gradual progression and both Vaagsø and the St Nazaire Raid provided lessons the planners for the Dieppe Raid should have absorbed.

The Vaagsø Raid, mounted on 27 December 1941, was the first example of a true Combined Operation, employing soldiers from Nos. 2, 3, 4 and 6 Commandos, plus the cruiser HMS *Kenya*, four destroyers, HMSs *Offa*, *Chiddingfold*, *Onslow* and *Oribi*, the submarine HMS/M *Tuna*, two of the newly converted infantry landing ships, HMSs *Prince Charles* and *Prince Leopold*, and ten bombers from No. 50 Squadron, RAF Bomber Command – a Combined Operation indeed and one which ran very much according to plan.

The attack began at 0845hrs on 27 December when *Kenya* illuminated Maaloy Island with starshell and naval guns poured some four hundred shells down on the defenders, who were taken completely by surprise – Maaloy was taken in just eight minutes at the cost of one man killed and one wounded. The attack on the main target, South Vaagsø, was a more drawn-out affair, not least because the existing German garrison was quickly supported by some fifty well-trained soldiers who happened to be in the town on Christmas leave.

When the Commando attack faltered, the Commanding Officer of No.

3 Commando, John Durnford-Slater, sent for the troops on Maaloy and his floating reserve. With their assistance the remaining enemy were quickly overcome, the battle ended at 1345hrs and an hour later the raiders withdrew to their ships after five hours ashore, having lost twenty men killed and fifty-seven wounded. The contrast with the Dieppe operation eight months later could hardly be starker and repays a brief analysis.

The first difference is that the Vaagsø Raid had an adequate amount of support, from bombers and a cruiser, and that support was *employed*, regardless of damage to the town or civilian losses ashore. Secondly, the raiders got ashore quickly and struck the enemy hard; they were not pinned on the beach and when they were held up in the town, more troops were quickly brought in from Maaloy to assist them. Surprise was achieved, the troops ashore enjoyed close support from naval gunfire and RAF bombers, and the Luftwaffe failed to put in an appearance. Finally, the attack was well within the training and competence of the troops; they were in complete control of the situation, blessed with good communications and clear, decisive leadership and working to a sound plan.

Vaagsø was a landmark operation and the lessons learned and employed here might be remembered when we come to consider the actions that took place during the Dieppe Raid. Above all this was a *combined* operation, to which all three Services made a worthwhile and integrated contribution. Vaagsø proved that Combined Operations were perfectly possible, providing a great boost to British morale and a good way of infuriating the Führer. The next operation, Operation CHARIOT, the raid on St Nazaire, was rather more costly.

The great port of St Nazaire lies in Brittany, six miles upstream from the mouth of the Loire. The objective of the raid was to destroy the huge dry dock in the shipyard, the *Forme Ecluse*, then the largest dry dock in Europe and the only one capable of receiving and repairing large capital ships, like German battleships. This last feature was of particular interest to the Royal Navy who were fully behind this operation. Since 1939 the

Admiralty had been obliged to keep capital units of the fleet based at Scapa Flow to check any foray into the North Atlantic by German battleships and in particular by the mighty *Tirpitz.* The menace of the *Tirpitz* was no idle threat; in 1941 the *Bismarck*, sister ship of the *Tirpitz*, had broken out into the Atlantic, ravaged merchant convoys and sunk HMS *Hood*, the pride of the Royal Navy, before she was finally sunk herself while heading for St Nazaire and the *Forme Ecluse.*

Without the security of St Nazaire and the possibility of repairs there, the likelihood that *Tirpitz* could repeat the voyage of *Bismarck* was considerably smaller. Bombing this vast dock into ruin was not considered possible, not least because any attempt to do so would certainly cause heavy casualties among the French population – a forerunner of the later reservations about bombing Dieppe. It was therefore decided to mount a raid and land men to destroy the dock and the harbour installations. This task was entrusted to Lieutenant-Colonel A.C. Newman of No. 2 Commando.

The main force for this task would consist of a hundred men from No. 2 Commando who would attack harbour gun positions and provide cover for demolition parties drawn from the assault engineers of other Commando units, Nos. 1, 3, 4, 5, 9 and 12. The gates of the *Forme Ecluse* would be rammed by a destroyer, the bows of the ship having been packed with high explosives, and these charges would be detonated after the landing parties had withdrawn. The destroyer would also carry part of the landing force, while the rest would be conveyed to the attack in motor launches. Lieutenant-Colonel Newman would command the landing parties while the naval contingent would be led by Commander R.E.D. (Red) Ryder, an officer who would later take part in the Dieppe operation.

St Nazaire is a large town, somewhat bigger than Dieppe and more industrial, with a population in 1942 of some fifty thousand people, many engaged in dock work. To this can be added a large German garrison, who manned coastal and estuary batteries and maintained tight security in and around the port, which since the summer of 1940 had become a major submarine base for operations against the Allied North Atlantic convoys. The reaction of this garrison to the raid will illustrate how the Germans could hit back swiftly against any surprise incursion. Attacking St Nazaire would stir up a hornets' nest and it was conceded that while, with surprise and luck, Newman's force might get in and do the job, their chances of getting out again were slim.

Newman and Ryder's plan called for a bold approach, straight up the river with no firing at least until the destroyer, a former US Navy four-stacker, the USS *Buchanan*, one of the fifty old American destroyers sent to Britain in exchange for bases in Bermuda and now renamed HMS *Campbeltown*, rammed the gates of the *Forme Ecluse.* Then the landing parties would swarm ashore to carry out their tasks and, with luck, withdraw to the Old Mole, which lay slightly downstream from the *Forme Ecluse*, re-embark and head back out to sea. The Chiefs of Staff approved the plan on 3 March and the Raid took place twenty-three days later. Readers may care to note that this raid, one well within the competence of COHQ, was nevertheless approved by the Chiefs of Staff Committee.

While the demolition teams and Newman's protection parties began to train, though without knowing for what, HMS *Campbeltown* was stripped of as much equipment as possible to reduce her draught for the shallows and the sandbars of the Loire, which must be crossed before she could ram the gates. In addition, the four funnels were reduced to two, both of them cut and altered to resemble those of some German Möwe-class frigates based at St Nazaire. This weight loss was balanced by the tons of explosive packed into her forecastle, and by special steel bulwarks welded along the decks to give some protection to the Commandos lying there as HMS *Campbeltown* surged in to ram the dock gate.

Corporal Arthur Woodiwiss from No. 2 Commando was detailed to sail in *Campbeltown*:

> Every man chosen for Operation CHARIOT was given a general briefing and then each man was briefed on his particular task. Each man had to produce his own plan to achieve that objective, and then all the plans, from the Privates' to the Colonels', were discussed and criticised.
>
> We had plans of the dock area, which we had to draw and re-draw, and a wonderful scale model which we could study, to help us identify our targets. As an assault group commander I rehearsed street fighting our way up to the gun positions I had to demolish. By the way, our full-dress rehearsal at Devonport was an absolute disaster. Our 'enemy', the old boys of the local Home Guard, were delighted at running rings round us, but though the rehearsal, Exercise VIVID, went disastrously wrong, for some reason everyone regarded this as most encouraging.[9]

The models used by Corporal Woodiwiss and his comrades were drawn from air photographs and from detailed plans of the *Forme Ecluse* which the British happened to possess; it is hard to believe that similar attention was not paid to the planning for Dieppe.

The first task facing the naval forces and the Commando units was a formidable one. The ships had to sail up six miles of heavily defended shallow estuary before even reaching the dock gates. The tides had to be just right, so the timings were crucial. Then air photographs revealed a new snag. In addition to a flak-ship moored permanently near the dock gates, five German Möwe-class frigates had recently berthed close to the landing area.

Then, as at Dieppe, came a further complication. The RAF bombing programme, designed to distract the enemy's attention while the landing force sailed up the river, was suffering from contradictory orders even at the planning stage. On the one hand, the RAF were asked to rain bombs on St Nazaire and keep defenders looking skywards during the naval approach, while on the other hand they were told to avoid civilian casualties at all costs. Colonel Newman rightly predicted that the bombing plan would not work and would indeed alert the Germans.

Escorted by two Hunt-class 4in-gun destroyers – the same vessels used at Dieppe – the CHARIOT force, totalling 630 soldiers and sailors, sailed on the afternoon of 26 March embarked on HMS *Campbeltown* and sixteen Fairmile 'B' class launches supplied by coastal forces. These were wooden launches with a maximum speed of 16 knots, armed with machine-guns and Oerlikon cannon; in addition to their normal fuel-tanks, they carried a 500-gallon petrol tank strapped on the upper deck. The Fairmiles were, in effect, floating petrol tanks, very vulnerable to enemy fire.

Sailing in three columns, the CHARIOT force first headed west into the Atlantic in the hope that any German aircraft or submarines which saw them would report this activity as an anti-submarine sweep. A German submarine was sighted on the second day and engaged by HMS *Tynedale*, and at 2000hrs that night (Friday 27 March) Lieutenant-Colonel Newman transferred to the motor gunboat (MGB) 314. At 2200hrs the convoy sighted the beacon of the submarine HMS *Sturgeon*, which was marking the entrance to the Loire, and, with *Campbeltown* in the van, the CHARIOT force entered the river.

The RAF bombing raid began about 2330hrs, but the strange behaviour of the aircraft soon alerted the defenders. There was no rain of incendiaries and high explosives as on any normal air raid. Instead the bombers cruised about over the town and estuary, dropping one bomb at a time. After half an hour of this, Captain Mecke, the officer commanding the anti-aircraft defences around St Nazaire, sent a warning order round his area command posts: 'Conduct of enemy aircraft inexplicable . . . suspicion of parachute landing.' The CHARIOT operation began to unravel.

On receipt of this signal, one of his subordinates turned his attention to the estuary and saw a force of small ships forging upstream. This was reported back to the Harbour Commander, who confirmed that no convoys were expected. Therefore, at 0120hrs on Saturday, 28 March, Captain Mecke sent another signal to his outposts: 'Beware landing.'

When that signal reached the defending batteries, HMS *Campbeltown* was within two miles of the dock gates and working up to full speed. The first sign of enemy action came when a big searchlight snapped on to illuminate HMS *Campbeltown* and her supporting craft. Two German signal stations at once challenged this strange flotilla, and one or two gun positions fired warning shots.

On Ryder's instructions *Campbeltown* signalled back in German using codes discovered on the Vaagsø Raid: 'Proceeding up harbour in accordance with orders'. The firing stopped and the searchlight snapped out; the CHARIOT force had gained a precious few minutes.

There was another brief exchange of signals until, at 0127hrs, with the *Forme Ecluse* gates in plain sight, HMS *Campbeltown* hauled down the German colours, hoisted her own battle ensigns to the mastheads and every gun in the CHARIOT force opened up on the defending batteries.

'For about five minutes the sight was staggering,' wrote Ryder in his after-action report, 'both sides loosing off with everything they had. The air was full of tracer, flying horizontally, and at close range.'

HMS *Campbeltown* struck the dock gates four minutes late, at 0134hrs, ramming her bow deep into the caisson. Corporal Woodiwiss remembers the run-in:

> When the German searchlight picked up HMS *Campbeltown*, it first shone on the German flag at the masthead, which confused them. When the Germans finally engaged us, the swastika was pulled down and quickly cut into pieces for souvenirs. When we hit, the *Campbeltown* rode much higher up the caisson than we expected and my assault ladder did not reach the dock so I had to

jump down to attack the nearest gun position which was raking us with enfilade fire.

Pausing to get my bearings, I saw a potato-masher grenade flying towards me. I fly-kicked this, luckily hitting the handle. It went back where it had come from and sorted out the group who had hurled it. After bitter hand-to-hand fighting, I eliminated the sentries, forced my way into the gun position and sprayed the crew with my Tommy-gun. I then wrapped my prepared explosive charge around the breech and destroyed the gun. I returned to my assault group and we attacked all the remaining gun positions then placed our incendiary charges into the oil storage tanks.

Lieutenant Roderick then ordered our withdrawal. I covered this so that our survivors could re-cross to the ship and then climbed the lashed ladder up to the bows and pulled this up to prevent pursuit. A burst of fire indicated a counterattack, pretty quick work. A large group of Germans were forming to cross the open area we had just left. Lying abandoned on deck behind the shrapnel shields were Brens with 100-round magazines, which had been fired as we sailed up the Loire. I set up three of these behind the shields and began firing each in turn to prevent their advance and forced them to withdraw.

The fuses in the six tons of ammonal below had already been activated, the fire below decks still smouldered and I was lying feet above the charge so I thought discretion was the better part of valour and decided to leave. I dropped all the spare weapons I could find into the Loire, collected all the Tommy magazines I could carry, rejoined my section and shared out the ammo. We assaulted across the dock bridge and advanced into the town. Lieutenant Hopwood joined me and we formed a rearguard, breaking down back doors and climbing over garden walls, when things went very quiet.

> When we ran out of ammunition and had gathered a large number of seriously wounded, we were forced to surrender. The German then asked why the English were so very optimistic about winning the war when they had already lost. I told him no one back home was optimistic but all were confident. The interrogation was terminated when a tremendous explosion heralded *Campbeltown*'s completion of our task, taking a lot of Germans with it.

With *Campbeltown* embedded in the dock gates – she did not blow up for several hours – the time was now right for the survivors of the landing force to withdraw. The withdrawal was to prove the tricky part, for, with all surprise gone, another battle was raging on the river between the motor launches and the shore defences, the motor-launch crews using Tommy-guns and Brens as well as their 20mm Oerlikon cannon against German shore batteries, artillery, cannon and heavy machine-guns. The motor launches had swept in to land their troops with every man at his post and every gun firing, while the defenders from rooftop positions in the docks returned their fire at close range, the whole scene lit by tracer, searchlights and blazing craft.

These fragile wooden craft, loaded with petrol and ammunition, made excellent targets. ML192 was hit by shellfire off the Old Mole and caught fire, running in ablaze to put her troops ashore; only five men made it. ML262 forged up the river, pinned by searchlights and under heavy fire, and tied up to *Campbeltown* to put the survivors ashore while Stoker Ball provided covering fire with his Lewis gun. ML268 was set ablaze by tracer and blew up, with only one man surviving. Half an hour into the operation and MLs were drifting across the river in pools of blazing petrol, being steadily shot to pieces.

Those launches which could manoeuvre still came in to land, taking it in turns to pour fire into a German flak-ship which was raking the dock-side with her cannon. Fortunately, the five German Möwe-class frigates were at sea that night, but seven MLs, with many of their Commandos and crews, were lost on the way in; most of the rest were destroyed during the landing phase or the withdrawal.

The losses on the St Nazaire Raid were severe; some 25 per cent of the force committed were killed, and most of the rest were made prisoner. Yet the raid was considered a great success as its prime object, clearly defined in the operational orders, to destroy the *Forme Ecluse*, was achieved; the dock was not repaired until after the war.

It can therefore be argued that the Dieppe Raid, which took place five months after the St Nazaire Raid and eight months after Vaagsø, was simply a continuation of this process, though the steps were not always in a forward direction; the St Nazaire Raid needed bomber support and the 6in-gun cruiser HMS *Kenya*, and RAF bombers supported the Vaagsø Raid – no such support, either air or naval, was made available at Dieppe.

Three points have to be made about these operations. First of all, in line with the original concept, they demonstrated Britain's resolve to hit back as hard and often as possible – and with a growing range of resources. Secondly, most of these raids had a strategic element. Vaagsø destroyed Germany's prime source of fish oil and obliged the Wehrmacht to keep troops in Norway that might have been better employed elsewhere. The attack on the great dock at St Nazaire not only deprived the enemy of a useful ship-repairing asset, it also limited the range of options open to larger German commerce raiders like the battleship *Tirpitz*. Knock out the great dock at St Nazaire and the risks of employing *Tirpitz* – the Führer's pride and joy – increased considerably.

St Nazaire revealed another problem inherent in operations at this time: the need to avoid causing casualties among the French population. The dock at St Nazaire *might* have been destroyed by bombing – though that is doubtful, given the size of bomb and the accuracy of bombing raids at the time – but only at the cost of shattering the town. A Commando raid seemed more certain and less costly in civilian lives, and to further reduce the possibility of civilian casualties a diversionary bombing raid was replaced by a series of single bombers cruising over the port dropping the occasional bomb – and helping to alert the defenders. This factor, the need to save civilian lives, would appear again in the planning for Dieppe.

Nor was this all. Following Dunkirk, it was clear to all that sooner or later the British must return to the Continent and carry the land war to Germany. That called for a cross-Channel invasion on an unprecedented scale, but in 1940–42 the British had neither the ships, the men nor the expertise even to contemplate such a major venture; the shadow of Gallipoli hung over all, and not least in Downing Street; Prime Minister Winston Churchill had been author of the 1915 Gallipoli operation, the disaster which put a crimp in his political career.

When it came to mounting an amphibious attack, everything had to be learned, from the right type of landing craft to the necessity for close support, to an understanding of tides and currents and the difficulties of maintaining a force on a hostile shore. The best way to do this, to learn the lessons, decide what was needed, and develop the necessary kit and craft, was by a series of exercises and operations, each one more complicated than the last – and that constant search for the right way to go about things was another motivation for these raids and the development of Combined Operations. They also helped to display aggression and irritate the Führer, in which they succeeded, to the point that in October 1942 he issued an order, the 'Commando Order', decreeing that all soldiers caught on these raids should be murdered out of hand:

The Führer.
No. 003830142

TOP SECRET

Führer HQ
18.10.42
12 Copies
12th Copy

1. For some time now our enemies are using methods in their prosecution of the war, which are outside the agreements of the Geneva Convention.

Especially brutal and vicious are the members of the so-called Commandos, which have been recruited, as has been ascertained to a certain extent, even from released criminals in enemy countries. Captured orders show that they have not only been instructed to tie up prisoners, but also to kill them should they become a burden to them. At last orders have been found in which the killing of prisoners is demanded.

2. For this reason it was announced in an appendix to the Wehrmacht report from 1.10.42 that Germany will in future use the same methods against these sabotage groups of the British, i.e., they will be ruthlessly exterminated wherever German troops may find them.

3. I therefore order: That from now on all enemy troops which are met by German troops while on so-called Commando raids, even if they are soldiers in uniform, be destroyed to the last man, either in battle or while fleeing. It doesn't matter whether they are landed by ship, plane or parachute. Even if they want to surrender no pardon is to be given on principle. A detailed report of any such surrender is to be made at the OKW for publication in the Wehrmacht report.

4. Should single members of such Commandos either as agents or saboteurs reach the Wehrmacht, e.g., through the police of the occupied countries, they are to be handed over to the SD [Security Service] without delay.

5. They are not to be kept even temporarily in military custody or POW camps.

This order does not affect the treatment of enemy soldiers taken prisoner during normal battle actions (major attack, major seaborne or airborne landings). It also does not affect prisoners taken at sea or flyers who saved themselves by parachute and were taken prisoner.

I shall have all Commanders and officers who do not comply with this order court-martialled.

(Signed): A.Hitler

Nor was this an idle threat; captured Commando soldiers were murdered and tortured for the rest of the war, though a number of German commanders refused to implement the terms of the Order and sent their Commando prisoners to the safety of POW camps. It certainly did not deter the Commandos or halt the growing number of volunteers coming forward for Commando service; if anything they gloried in the fact that their operations were increasingly dangerous.

These early Commando operations had various purposes but the dominant theme was to develop skills and techniques in this new amphibious art, and get three disparate, often competing Services to work together to a common end. In the words of the new Chief of Combined Operations, Lord Louis Mountbatttten, before the Vaagsø Raid: 'We have not tried this [a fully Combined Operation] before and we have to see if it works.'

This may have been especially so in Mountbatten's case. He had had little to do with Vaagsø, which had been planned during the tenure of Sir Roger Keyes – a fact that did not inhibit Mountbatten from claiming the subsequent credit for a successful operation. St Nazaire had also been largely planned under the previous occupant of the Combined Operations chair; now Mountbatten would be responsible for planning an operation on his own.

With the background to amphibious operations and the early history of Combined Operations ventilated and Mountbatten now in post, it would be as well to look at the background and composition of the 2nd Canadian Division, the two Army Commandos and the Royal Marine 'A' Commando. These were the landing forces that would actually carry out the Dieppe Raid; their capabilities and limitations have to be understood before we move on to the planning stage of Operation RUTTER/ JUBILEE.

It should be appreciated that there were two plans for the Dieppe Raid, one code-named RUTTER and the other JUBILEE; only when we have examined these plans, the units involved and some of the political background to this operation of war will the numerous difficulties start to reveal themselves.

The first point to be made is that the Dieppe operation employed crack well-trained troops; the causes for failure will not be found among the men. Both Army Commando units, John Durnford-Slater's No. 3 and 'Shimi' Lovat's No. 4, were outstanding infantry units, battle-hardened and full of aggression, while the Royal Marine 'A' Commando was a fully volunteer unit, imbued with unit pride and very anxious to show what the Royal Marines could do in a raiding role which, many Marines felt, the British Army had usurped.

As for the men of the 2nd Canadian Division, they came from the same background and stock that had filled the ranks of the Canadian Corps in the Great War, when the Canadians had established their enduring reputation in the ranks of the Empire Armies. As in the First World War, every man in the Canadian forces was a volunteer, anxious to get into the fight and carry the war to the enemy.

In both world wars, the first significant forces to join the British in the field came from Canada. The Canadians first made their mark in the Great War when they held the line at St Julian in the Ypres Salient during the gas attack that opened the Second Battle of Ypres in 1915. If the Canadians had broken at St Julian, the vital city of Ypres could not have been held.

From then on no major Great War battle was complete without the Canadians. The Canadian Corps, effectively the field army of the Dominion of Canada, fought on the Somme in 1916 and took Vimy Ridge in 1917. Commanded by a Canadian general, Arthur Currie, one of the finest Allied commanders of that war, the Canadians took the Passchendaele ridge at the final bitter end of the Third Battle of Ypres. In 1918, the Canadian Corps distinguished itself in the final assault on the German armies and returned to Canada covered in glory and well-earned esteem.

The Canadians were to rack up an equally splendid record in the Second World War, although much of this lay in the future in 1942. In 1941 Canadian battalions fought to the last in the defence of Hong Kong against the Japanese. Committed to battle in the Mediterranean in 1943, the Canadians fought in Sicily and mainland Italy, in the advance on Rome up the Liri Valley from Cassino, and distinguished themselves in particular in the street-fighting battle at Ortona on the Adriatic. The 3rd Canadian Division was to land on JUNO beach on D-Day and the Canadians were to take part in all the bloody struggles on the advance into Germany, from Normandy to the Baltic; by May 1945 the First Canadian Army had seen a lot of war and produced at least one outstanding battlefield commander, Lieutenant-General Guy Simonds.

The Canadian commitment to the war was considerable. Canada declared war on Germany on 10 September 1939. At that time Canada was woefully unprepared for any kind of conflict; her Regular Army consisted of 4500 soldiers, her Navy of a few old ships, frigates and destroyers and some 1800 men, and the Royal Canadian Air Force of just 3100 men and women, air and ground crew. By the end of the war, the Dominion of Canada had sent an entire army, the First Canadian Army, to fight in Italy, Normandy and north-west Europe, and a full bomber group, No. 6 Group, RCAF, to serve with RAF Bomber Command, while the Royal Canadian Navy supplied about half of the ships that fought and won the Battle of the Atlantic against the German U-boats.

It is hardly surprising that Canada produced good military units. Canadian soldiers were tough, well educated and independently minded. On the other hand they were not the easiest men to handle and had little time for formal discipline. One story circulating around the British Army in 1915 told of a sentry challenging various units approaching his post:

'Halt, who goes there?'
'The Grenadier Guards.'
'Pass, Grenadier Guards.'

'Halt, who goes there?'
'The Gordon Highlanders.'
'Pass, Gordon Highlanders.'

'Halt, who goes there?'
'Who the bloody hell wants to know?'
'Pass, Canadians.'

In that respect at least, not much had changed since the Great War and on arriving in the UK the Canadians soon found much of the British Army's discipline restrictive, pointless and vastly irritating. The Canadian units arrived in Britain in early 1940, very anxious to get into the fighting as soon as possible, and when the immediate prospect of battle began to dim, these eager Canadian soldiers became discontented, even a touch mutinous.

In the eighteen months prior to the Dieppe operation the 2nd Canadian Division alone racked up the impressive total of twenty-one thousand military offences of various kinds and proved a sore trial to the police and publicans of Sussex and Hampshire. Visits to Canadian units by senior officers or politicians were also fraught with tension; General Montgomery was booed and invited to go away when he came to inspect the Canadian Corps, and on 23 August 1941, when the Canadian Prime Minister Mr Mackenzie King visited the Canadians under training at Aldershot and addressed the troops on parade, he got a very frosty reception.

Mackenzie King told his troops that 'while he realised how difficult it was for men who had come overseas to fight to find the moment of battle constantly postponed, they were in fact performing essential services in Britain'. However true, this statement did not go down too well with the soldiers. They had not crossed the Atlantic for endless exercises and garrison duties; they had come to Europe to fight.

Therefore, according to the official account, there were 'some interruptions which perhaps received disproportionate attention in the Press'.[10] This heckling of their premier, said one Canadian newspaper account, 'merely indicated the men's desire for action'. This statement is surely correct, but if the Canadian Corps soldiers were frustrated and impatient in August 1941 their feeling by August 1942 can only be imagined. These were good troops and they had spent two years on exercises and garrison duties; they *had* to get into the fight. After all, or so their commanders would argue, they had been waiting long enough. This factor must be borne in mind as part of the background to the Dieppe operation; participation in this raid was the Canadians' first real chance of action and they were desperate not to lose it.

Canada's road to Dieppe began in December 1939, when the 1st Canadian Division took ship for the United Kingdom from Halifax, Nova Scotia. The first convoy arrived in Greenock on 17 December and was followed by two others bringing the rest of the Division, which finally assembled at Aldershot – the 'Home of the British Army' – in February 1940, the total number present amounting to twenty-three thousand officers and men, a strong division in 1940.

The 1st Division then endured a number of frustrations. They took no part in the Narvik expedition in the spring of 1940 or in those operations in France and Belgium which culminated at Dunkirk in June 1940, and the detachment of a number of Canadian units to Brittany in the aftermath of Dunkirk ended in fiasco; the Canadians landed, rolled about France for a while and were then shipped back to Britain from St Malo without firing a shot.

This is not what the Canadians had volunteered for. Although it was generally accepted by all ranks that the Canadian Division needed time to train, the necessary equipment to make this training relevant was in desperately short supply, especially after Dunkirk. Nevertheless, training commenced on the thorny heaths of Bagshot and Camberley and the grey, damp weather that passed for an English summer proved challenge enough.

Nor was the Division happy socially. Aldershot may have been the 'Home of the British Army' but this meant that the locals were very used to soldiers, and they proved less than hospitable to the newly arrived Canadians; hard training days were soon interspersed with night-time fights in the local pubs and disputes with the townspeople. The Division moved about, first to Oxford and then to a region south of London, and by early 1941 the Canadians had effectively been gathered into that garrison of troops charged with defending Britain against a German invasion, the threat of which had long faded.

The 2nd Canadian Division had been formed at the same time as the 1st Division, but with weapons and kit being in short supply the 1st Division got priority. It was not until the spring of 1940 that the 2nd Division was despatched overseas and its first destination was Iceland, where it arrived in mid-June. Post-Dunkirk, it was then decided that the best place for the 2nd Division was in Britain where, with the 1st Division, it would form a Canadian Corps. This process also took time; the last units of the 2nd Canadian Division only arrived in the UK on Christmas Day 1940, when the joint strength of these two divisions amounted to 57,000 officers and men.

Although the Royal Canadian Navy and Air Force took an increasing part in the war during 1941 and 1942, the Canadian Corps saw no action at all. Based now on the south coast between Hastings and Portsmouth, the divisions endured an endless round of training and growing frustration with this lack of action, and at one time it was proposed that the Canadian Corps, or one of the divisions, should be sent to join the Eighth Army in North Africa.

Nothing came of this proposal, probably because there had already been mutterings in Empire circles that Commonwealth troops – from Australia, New Zealand, South Africa and India – were doing more than their fair share of fighting in the Desert War. This allegation was not true; the Empire certainly provided the infantry but Great Britain provided the tank crews, the gunners and the engineers – as well as some fifty infantry battalions. Nevertheless, one result of this rumour was to keep the Canadian forces in the UK, mainly engaged in drinking the beer and chasing the girls.

In this latter activity the Canadians were most successful. Wartime marriages between Canadian soldiers and British girls became a weekend feature in south-coast towns; it was said with some truth that 'between 1940 and 1942, the Canadian Corps' birth rate greatly exceeded its death rate'. In August 1942, all that was to change.

The underlying truth in this situation was that the Canadian soldiers were hungry for action. Training can only be taken so far and after two years in the UK the Canadians had been trained to distraction. Denied action against the enemy, they found it by brawling with the police, publicans, British soldiers and civilians – and discipline suffered accordingly. It is hardly surprising therefore that when the prospect of some decisive action was offered in the spring of 1942, the Canadian generals were both relieved and delighted.

By 1942 the command structure of the Canadian Army in Britain was as follows. The overall Commander of the Canadian Forces in the UK was Lieutenant-General Andrew McNaughton. He was responsible to the Canadian Government for the welfare of his troops, and while they were serving under British command he was entitled to consult his home Government and register objections if he felt they were being improperly or recklessly used; the Canadians were willing but they were *not* expendable.

Under McNaughton was another experienced officer, Lieutenant-General Harry Crerar commanding the 1st Canadian Army Corps; this Corps consisted of the 1st and 2nd Divisions. The 2nd Canadian Division was commanded by Major-General John Hamilton Roberts, an officer known to his intimates as 'Ham'. In 1942 the 1st Canadian Corps formed part of the UK's South-Eastern Command, under Lieutenant-General B.L. Montgomery – the soon-to-be-famous 'Monty', victor of Alamein.

All these Canadian officers had battle experience, at least in the Great War, and were certainly as experienced as most of the general officers in the British Army. General McNaughton had served in France and Flanders as an Artillery officer where he won the DSO and was twice wounded. Harry Crerar had started his first war as a second lieutenant and finished it as lieutenant-colonel commanding an infantry battalion.

'Ham' Roberts was fifty years old and another veteran of the Great War, in which he had served with the Artillery and collected both a wound and the Military Cross. When Roberts arrived to take command of the Division, he began by getting rid of the sick, lame and lazy and started a programme of exercises and physical training to get his men ready for front-line action, which, he recognised, was all they really needed.

One answer to the problem of engaging the Canadians in active operations was to employ them in cross-Channel Commando raids from their bases in Sussex and Hampshire, and it is hard to understand why this was not done. The US Army raised a Ranger Force, the Rangers being the US equivalent of the Commandos, within months of arriving in the UK and sent fifty of them on the Dieppe Raid, but the Canadians spent two years in the UK and were not given the opportunity to do likewise. The possibility of using the Canadians in Sussex for cross-Channel raids was discussed in September 1941 but the result was further frustration: various operations were proposed for the winter of 1941–2 but all were cancelled.

These two frustrating years created a situation in which the Canadians were more than ready to take on any operation that promised action, whatever the risk, and none too particular about the nature of the risk involved. As we shall see, accounts vary as to who actually offered the Canadians the leading role in Operation RUTTER/JUBILEE, but one fact is not disputed: when it was offered, the Canadians seized their chance of action with both hands.

POLITICAL PRESSURES 1942

There were many reasons why 'Jubilee' miscarried. But for a start, I suggest our Allied and political background – the plight of Russia and the clamour for a Second Front – be carefully examined.

LORD LOVAT, NO. 4 COMMANDO,
MARCH PAST

THIS STORY HAS now arrived at the start of 1942, by which time most of the actors for the forthcoming drama at Dieppe were in post and Britain was no longer fighting the Axis Powers entirely on her own. It will be clear by now that a number of external factors influenced the operational planning of RUTTER and the eventual execution of the remounted Dieppe Raid – Operation JUBILEE. To these we must now add the effect of events taking place in other theatres of war and the pressures for action in the West that were building up on the British Government, not least from Soviet Russia and the United States.

The Dieppe Raid was not simply another British Commando raid, albeit on a larger scale than heretofore. It was a major operation of war, influenced by a number of strategic factors, and it is necessary to examine these factors in order to put the Raid in context and explain how, perhaps indirectly, they influenced the decision to remount Operation RUTTER as JUBILEE after the initial operation was cancelled. It is also important to put the Raid in the context of its time.

Most books on the Dieppe operation begin by making the point that the summer of 1942 was the blackest time for Britain in the Second World War, and up to a point that is perfectly true. That said, it is also true that matters were either looking up, or about to look up, in many theatres of war, on land, sea and in the air. The British trials in this war so far, which had largely consisted of hanging on desperately and trying not to lose, were already coming to an end. However, that view is inevitably tinged with hindsight, and to put the Dieppe Raid in context it would be as well to review the events of the war, post-Dunkirk, if only to underline the precarious nature of Britain's position at this time and why the various demands made on her by her new-found Allies in 1941–2 were not capable of immediate fulfilment.

Following the fall of France in June 1940, Italy entered the war on the side of the Axis, moved into southern France and attacked the British in North Africa. As a result of these rash adventures the Italians were soon in considerable trouble. Britain's Western Desert Force had no difficulty in thrashing the Italians, inflicting a crushing defeat on the Italian forces at Beda Fomm at the end of 1940, and the Italian venture into Greece was no more successful.

Beda Fomm and the numerous setbacks suffered by the Italians in Greece obliged the Germans to commit forces to North Africa and the Mediterranean, and after General Rommel and the Afrika Korps entered the fray in February 1941 matters went seriously awry for the British. Defeat followed defeat in the Western Desert, the British intervention in Greece proved equally disastrous and in 1941 the island of Crete fell to a German airborne invasion, with great British losses in both men and *matériel*.

Not all of these disasters were entirely the fault of the generals. Apart from the fact that British kit and competence were simply not up to the standard of the Germans', their generals were suffering from strategic overstretch; Wavell and Auchinleck and their subordinates had too much to do, too much territory to cover – from Eritrea to the Western Desert, Vichy-held Syria, Greece and Iraq – and not enough men with which to do it.

Nor was there much comfort elsewhere in 1941. The RAF bomber offensive against Germany was a total failure, and aided by the acquisition of bases in western France, at St Nazaire, La Pallice and Bordeaux, the German submarine fleet was now taking a grievous toll on those trans-Atlantic convoys on which Britain's very existence depended; British shipping losses for the first six months of 1942 exceeded those for the whole of 1941. The U-boats were also sinking vast numbers of American ships off the east coast of the USA. These American losses – the second 'Happy Time' for the submarines – were mainly due to the US Navy's reluctance to introduce convoys, and partly to the blaze of coastal lights which displayed shipping against a floodlit backdrop.

Britain's problems were not eased by the entry into the war on the

Allied side of Hitler's erstwhile ally, Soviet Russia, in June 1941. The fact that the signing of the Ribbentrop–Molotov Treaty in August 1939 had freed German hands for an attack on Poland and the start of the Second World War did not embarrass the Soviet leadership in the least. After Germany invaded Russia in June 1941, a loud scream for British assistance went out from Moscow and Britain's already slender resources were stretched still further by the need to supply tanks and guns and trucks, boots and fighter aircraft, to a country that, until a few weeks previously, had been Britain's devoted enemy.

None of the liberal assistance given by Britain stemmed the Soviets' demands for more, and eventually Churchill summoned M. Maisky, the Soviet Ambassador, to Britain and delivered the following rebuke:

> Until a few weeks ago your country was numbered among our enemies. Until recently, we did not know what you were going to do and now you are insisting that we support you in every way possible, regardless of the situation. Few countries, and certainly not your country, are in any position to criticise us at the present time.

M. Maisky held his tongue after that, at least for a while, but the entry of Russia into the war against Germany was generally seen as a good portent for the future – the fate of Napoleon's *Grande Armée* in 1812 was taken as an example of the fate awaiting anyone invading Russia. This was anyway no time for prolonged recriminations about the recent past. As Churchill also remarked, 'If the Germans invaded Hell, I would find it possible to say a few kind words about the Devil the next time I spoke in the House of Commons.'

However, apart from military hardware, what the Soviets really wanted, as the German onslaught drove their armies back in retreat towards Moscow, was a British attack in the West – a 'Second Front' as it came to be called – and they were not interested in any of the cogent reasons the British advanced for failing to deliver this assistance. The reluctance to open a Second Front in 1941–2 was entirely due to the fact that Britain was already fully stretched and currently at the end of her resources; the Soviets must have known this but their demands continued.

In pressing his demand for a Second Front, Marshal Josef Stalin, the Soviet leader, got considerable support from the British trade unions, the British working class and the nation's leftward-leaning intelligentsia, who were soon actively painting 'Second Front NOW' on their factory walls and organising rallies in Trafalgar Square to repeat the demand. This was a new departure; up until now the mainly left-wing or Communist-led trade unions in Britain had taken a somewhat ambivalent attitude to this war, regarding it as a struggle between rival capitalist and Fascist powers and of no interest to the horny-handed proletariat. Indeed, if the People's Paradise in the Soviet Union was allied to the National Socialist Government of Germany – as they were from August 1939 to June 1941 – then perhaps the Nazis and Communists were waging a war for the workers against the bosses and the capitalists? Putting a gulag or two and a few dozen concentration camps to one side, perhaps the Russo-German alliance was the one to support?

Trade-union bosses of this opinion and in particular the loathsome Harry Pollitt, editor of the main Communist newspaper, the *Daily Worker*, could not push this argument too far. Post-Dunkirk, the bulk of the British working population were patriotic and solidly behind Winston Churchill and the prosecution of the war against Germany, but it is clear that the attack on Russia – Operation BARBAROSSA – greatly eased many Socialist minds. Now they could concentrate all their energies in support of the Soviets and attempt to pressure the British Government to accede to Stalin's ever-greater demands, especially the one for a Second Front. It will therefore be seen that in the latter half of 1941 and the first half of 1942 the advent of Russia as an ally was a distinctly mixed blessing to the British Government, now under pressure at home and abroad.

Popular sentiment and political pressures could not simply be ignored. The maintenance and increase of industrial production was vital, not least in providing weapons of war and producing those export goods that would pay for them. In this effort the support of the trade unions was vital – and that meant paying at least lip service to the notion of a Second Front and demonstrating that Britain too was fighting hard in this war. By early 1942 the British Government was facing pressure for a Second Front from both the Soviets and its own working population, pressure the Government could well have done without.

Six months later, in December 1941, came the Japanese attack on Pearl Harbor and the entry of the United States into this spreading conflict, an otherwise beneficial action that nonetheless added yet another problem to the existing burdens on the sorely stretched British military machine which, already burdened by fighting the Germans and Italians, had now to cope with the Japanese. It should be recalled that the Japanese did not only attack Hawaii and the American-occupied Philippines in December 1941; they also attacked the British possessions in Malaya and Singapore, at Hong Kong and in Burma. The next few months saw a string of disasters in the Far East: the sinking of the battleships *Prince of Wales* and *Repulse* by Japanese air attack off the coast of Malaya, the fall of Singapore, the loss of Tobruk in the Western Desert and the headlong retreat of the Eighth Army to the frontiers of Egypt.

If all this were not enough the British also had to face a new burden on the political front – US and Russian insistence on some positive action by the British in the West in 1942, specifically a landing on the coast of France to aid the Soviets, who were now under great pressure in the East. The US argument was that with the Russians in danger of defeat, the British must launch an offensive in the West as soon as possible. The British belief was quite the opposite; in their current circumstances they would only launch such an offensive if the Germans were in danger of defeat, though in fact Britain lacked the resources to mount a worthwhile attack in either eventuality.

The Soviets and the Americans were not impressed with this argument. There is some irony in the fact that Britain, the smallest of the Allied nations, was now being criticised by Soviet Russia – until recently an ally of Germany – and the United States – until recently a neutral – for failing to prosecute the war as they wished. One might ask what the Soviets and the Americans had been doing for the last three years that left them so woefully unprepared to stand off the Germans or take a rapid part in this conflict. Military help they neither provided nor offered. Until the middle of 1942 there was no direct US participation in the European war – the first US action, a bombing raid on Holland, took place, suitably enough, on 4 July, Independence Day, 1942, using bombers borrowed from the RAF. The US presence in the European Theatre of Operations took time to arrive. What was never in short supply from the USA or the Soviet Union was copious amounts of criticism.

Indeed, in February 1942, Stalin went further, issuing a public declaration that he was willing to treat with Hitler and discuss an armistice since Russia was not getting much help from the Western Allies. Exactly what terms Hitler would have been willing to grant the Soviet leader, or even whether this declaration was genuine, remains a mystery; it is far more likely that this was simply another crude attempt to exert pressure on the British and get some action in the West.

That some such action was a possibility occurred to Adolf Hitler, who in March 1942 issued an order to his commanders in the West, stating that Stalin's demands would probably lead to some form of raiding action on the coast of France. The Commando raids were continuing and mounting in size and frequency but, though annoying, they were essentially pin-pricks. The Wehrmacht had plenty of divisions in the West – between twenty-five and thirty at any time, some of them armoured – more than enough to deal with any possible British incursion without the need to bring formations back from the Russian front. Soviet Russia apart, a more serious form of pressure on the British was now coming from the US Administration and the US Joint Chiefs of Staff, who felt that the British were dragging their feet in the prosecution of the war. This pressure was exerted through the Allied command organisation, the Combined Chiefs of Staff.

In December 1941, shortly after Pearl Harbor, the British and American Chiefs of Staff met in Washington for what became known as the Arcadia Conference. Arcadia reached two decisions that were to have a profound effect on the conduct of the war. The first was to set up the Combined Chiefs of Staff Committee (CCS), composed of the British Chiefs of Staff and the US Joint Chiefs of Staff, to handle the strategic direction of the war under the political direction of President Franklin D. Roosevelt, Prime Minister Churchill and, though at a distance, Marshal Stalin. This decision enabled the Anglo-American Allies to develop a common strategy and so avoid the mistakes and confusions of the First World War, when for some years the British, French, Russian and Italian allies were in effect fighting separate wars and so prolonging the conflict.

That would not be allowed to happen this time. There is no doubt that the setting-up of the CCS played a major role in the ultimate defeat of the Axis Powers – which is not to say that the Allied military and political alliance was always sweetness and light or that the arguments over strategy were conducted without large amounts of chauvinism and not a little animosity. The CCS realised that Allied unity was the key to victory but the policies they united around were subject to debate. Timing is the essence of politics, and so it was in 1942. The Anglo-US arguments centred not so much on what should be done but when it should be done, and the Americans wanted most of it done now.

From the time the United States of America entered the Second World War in December 1941, her high commanders – the US Joint Chiefs of

Staffs (JCS) – began agitating for a return to the Continent, a cross-Channel invasion of German-occupied Europe 'as soon as possible'. If the pressure exerted on the British by the JCS in the early months of 1942 is anything to go by, 'as soon as possible' meant shortly after the smoke cleared from the wreckage of Pearl Harbor. This demand formed part of what the US Government and their senior military commander, General George C. Marshall, saw as their quid pro quo for the second major strategic decision taken at Arcadia – the decision for 'Germany First'.

'Germany First' stated that the first task of the Allies was the defeat of Nazi Germany rather than Germany's Italian or Japanese allies. This decision was in line with the well-known strategic doctrine that when faced with an array of enemies the strongest shall be defeated first, for this will lead to the collapse of the junior members of the enemy alliance. The notion that the first task is to defeat the minor players – 'knocking away the props' as it was commonly called in the First World War – has no strategic validity.

This decision to concentrate on the war in Europe came as a considerable relief to the embattled British and represented a certain sacrifice on the part of the Americans. The United States had been treacherously attacked at Pearl Harbor; the Americans were naturally anxious for revenge and saw the need to carry the war deep into the Pacific theatre and evict the Japanese from the Philippines before the latter could establish themselves too firmly in their recent conquests.

There were also some personal issues: Admiral Ernest King, Commander of the US Navy and a most devoted Anglophobe, knew that the Pacific War would be a naval war in which his branch of the Services would shine, provided the resources the US Navy needed were not squandered, as he saw it, in Europe and on the British. In the aftermath of Pearl Harbor there was a brief time when it appeared possible that the USA would concentrate its energies on Japan. Then, most unwisely, Germany brought the Americans into the war by declaring war on the

United States, barely a week after Pearl Harbor. It is interesting to speculate on what might have happened if the Führer had refrained from such a declaration of war, as the Italians had done vis-à-vis the British when the Second World War broke out in September 1939. Italy, though allied to Germany by the 'Pact of Steel', did not enter the war against the Anglo-French until the June of 1940, and then only in the hope of sharing the spoils of what was seen as an inevitable German victory following the fall of France. The German declaration of war and the Arcadia decision for 'Germany First' prevented any possibility of such an outcome in Anglo-US relations.

However, the point to grasp is that the Arcadia decision came with certain strings attached, in particular that 'Germany First' also meant 'Germany Soon', and the two Allies were soon at odds over exactly how soon that should be. This argument has led to at least one persistent myth, a legend prominent in US history circles since the war, that the British were never keen on the eventual cross-Channel operation, the D-Day landings of 1944, Operation OVERLORD, and dragged their feet over it for the next two years while dissipating Allied resources in the Mediterranean.

This accusation is pure myth and an excellent example of 'cherry-picking' the facts of history. The British were perfectly willing to invade France and had indeed been preparing to do so since the time of Dunkirk. They were not, however, willing to invade France *in 1942*. They felt that other factors took priority, that the time was not propitious, that their forces were not sufficient and that the necessary kit, notably in the form of landing craft, was not available. In all these conclusions the British were absolutely right.

The Americans regarded this reluctance to plunge into cross-Channel adventures in 1942 as an example of British caution or timidity, but since the USA currently lacked the military resources to take over this task themselves, the result was a stalemate, interspersed with argument and some dangerous pressure. Pressure began in a letter from Roosevelt to Churchill on 18 March 1942, just three months after the USA entered the war:

> I am becoming more and more interested in the establishment of a new front this summer on the European Continent, certainly for air and raids. From the point of view of shipping and supplies it is infinitely easier for us to participate in because of a maximum distance of about three thousand miles. And even though losses will doubtless be great, such losses will be compensated by at least equal German losses and by compelling the Germans to divert large forces of all kinds from the Russian front.

Roosevelt neglected to add that this 'new front' he was interested in would have to be established by the British – who already had their hands more than full on other fronts.

Three weeks later, on 8 April, General Marshall, the US Chief of Staff and head of the CCS, and President Roosevelt's confidant, Harry Hopkins, arrived in the UK to press the American plan – or rather plans. The first was for a landing in France by forty-eight Allied divisions, eighteen of them British, supported by 5800 combat aircraft, 2550 of them British. This operation, a full-scale invasion, was codenamed ROUNDUP and would be mounted before April 1943.

The second plan advanced by General Marshall called for an attempt to seize the French ports of Brest or Cherbourg, preferably the latter but possibly both, during the early autumn of 1942. This operation would have to be almost entirely British as the Americans could only field two or three divisions by September 1942. Churchill's response to this proposal was that it was 'more difficult, less attractive, less immediately helpful or ultimately fruitful than ROUNDUP', an operation which later became OVERLORD, the D-Day landings of 1944.

The JCS plan for 1942 was urged on the British by General George C. Marshall. The objective was to seize Cherbourg and some of the Cotentin peninsula and hold it through the winter of 1942–3, filling it with Allied troops, including some from the USA, then mounting a breakout in the spring of 1943. This idea gained rapid currency and a codename – Operation SLEDGEHAMMER – and Mr Hopkins gave some political weight to the proposal by adding that if public opinion in the USA had anything to do with it, unless an invasion of the Continent took place shortly, the weight of the American effort would be directed against Japan.

This was little short of blackmail. Besides, to put it bluntly, Operation SLEDGEHAMMER was lunacy. None of the elements necessary for such an invasion (air superiority, adequate amphibious lift, adequate forces or, most crucially, the logistical back-up for the post-invasion phase) currently existed either in the UK or the USA, but that point carried little weight in Washington. The JCS thought that SLEDGEHAMMER was not only desirable but quite feasible, and in this they were totally wrong. In the circumstances of 1942, a major landing – a full-scale invasion of the Continent of Europe – was simply not a viable proposition. That harsh fact did not concern the Americans; after all, they were not the ones nominated to do it.

What the Germans would be doing during this SLEDGEHAMMER operation was not seriously considered but can be readily imagined. The Germans had twenty-five to thirty divisions in Western Europe, several of them armoured; the British could put ashore just six. Assuming it could even be formed, any Allied bridgehead in the Cotentin would be quickly sealed off and attacked from sea, land and air. Cherbourg, the only port, would be mined to prevent the further landing of supplies, aircraft and artillery would pound the port to rubble, and German panzers, backed by tactical air power, would be brought up to reduce the bridgehead and drive the Allies – or rather the British – back into the sea. Not being interested in a re-run of Dunkirk, the British naturally demurred and the Americans – especially the JCS – were deeply disappointed.

Since the Americans as yet had no troops in the European Theatre of Operations (ETO), only the British could carry out Operation SLEDGEHAMMER, and, to put it mildly, the British were extremely reluctant to attempt it. They had some experience of fighting the Germans, bitter experience the Americans currently lacked, and were well aware of the limitations created by a lack of air superiority over the Channel and a shortage of landing craft.

Besides, there were other priorities. The first of these was to wind up and win the current campaign in North Africa; to that end the British wanted a commitment of British and American troops in that theatre – a plan that became Operation GYMNAST, later Operation TORCH, the Anglo-American landings in Tunisia and Algeria in November 1942.

The British also believed that the next but concurrent task was to defeat the U-boat menace in the North Atlantic, where German submarines were currently sinking hundreds of thousands of tons of shipping every month. Only when the submarine menace had been defeated could Operation BOLERO, the build-up of US forces in Britain, really get under way. However, the British were not entirely negative; they allowed that, all being well, a landing in France, Operation ROUNDUP, could take place in the spring or summer of 1943 and would enjoy the fullest support from the British. Operation SLEDGEHAMMER in 1942, however, was simply not on.

Even so, the pressure to mount SLEDGEHAMMER continued with the arrival in the UK of Vyacheslav Molotov, the Russian Foreign Minister, charged to press the need for a Second Front on Winston Churchill. Having failed to change Churchill's mind, Molotov then departed for Washington. There he enjoyed a warmer reception and much support for his demands; Molotov returned to London convinced that a Second Front in 1942 was now part of Anglo-American policy, and had to be disillusioned all over again.

Churchill again demurred and to avoid any possibility of misunderstanding – a vain hope, as it turned out – handed Molotov an aide-memoire setting out the British position:

> We are making preparations for a landing on the Continent in August or September 1942. As already explained, the main limiting factor to the size of the landing force is the availability of special landing craft. Clearly, it would not further either the Russian cause or that of the Allies as a whole if, for the sake of action at any price, we embarked on some operation which ended in disaster or gave the enemy the opportunity for glorification at our discomfiture. It is impossible to say in advance whether the situation will be such as to make this operation feasible when the time comes. We can therefore make no promises in the matter but provided that it appears sound and sensible we shall not hesitate to put our plans into effect.[1]

Given the Soviets' ability to read what they wanted into any statement, it might have been better to answer Molotov's demands with a flat 'No', but one of the hard lessons of history is that the facts do not always speak for themselves. The facts here were irrefutable – a cross-Channel invasion in 1942 was beyond the capability of the Western Powers – but the Russians and the Americans were not to be dissuaded and a bitter argument duly developed. So it was that the JCS even went to the point of declaring that if the British did not comply, the USA would switch their main effort to the Pacific, a course warmly advocated by Admiral Ernest King and the many Anglophobes in Washington.

By 1942 any American admiration for Britain's lone stand against the Axis Powers – a view largely based on Churchill's speeches, the winning of the Battle of Britain and the British public's refusal to give up the fight even under the nightly pounding of the Blitz – had largely disappeared; deep-rooted, long-standing American Anglophobia was back in the saddle. It has to be remembered that in American history it is the British, not the Germans or the Japanese, and certainly not the Italians, who are the traditional enemy. This attitude dates back to the American Revolution and the War of 1812, and to a US conviction that the British secretly despised Americans and were jealous of American success and prosperity.

It is interesting to note that there is no British equivalent of Anglophobia and little evidence that the British felt anything for the Americans but friendship, though it is fair to add that many British commanders felt that the American generals had a lot to learn about this war and might be a little quieter while they went about learning it. However, when people are determined to take offence or find a reason for complaint, they usually find no difficulty in doing so. When the British dug their heels in over Operation SLEDGEHAMMER, all the Anglophobic animosities surfaced yet again.

In such circumstances one way, perhaps the only way, to convince the Americans that a cross-Channel attack in 1942 was simply not on was to try it. By doing so, the British, as with the construction of the Mulberry harbours, 'could let the difficulties argue for themselves'.

Mountbatten, the new head of Combined Operations, was believed to have considerable influence in Washington, where he now took up a role in the SLEDGEHAMMER argument. During his stay in the USA in the autumn of 1941 while HMS *Illustrious* was being repaired, Mountbatten had made the acquaintance of many of the movers and shakers in Washington and apparently made a considerable and favourable impression. This being so, in June he was despatched to the USA, there to gently explain to the US President the difficulties of mounting a cross-Channel assault in 1942.

The employment of Lord Louis in this role is hardly surprising. Mountbatten was rich, good-looking and a war hero, covered with glory from his recent exploits in the Mediterranean. He was also a British aristocrat and the US President Franklin D. Roosevelt, for all his republican sentiments and detestation of the British Empire, dearly loved a Lord.

Moreover, there was something deeply 'American' about Mountbatten. He could get along with anyone, was open and approachable and saw difficulties as problems to surmount rather than reasons for failure or delay. In short, he was not at all the average American's idea of the average Limey, and as a result they took to him right away. After he returned to the UK and took up his post at Combined Operations in 1941, the Americans quickly followed, and by the summer of 1942 a visit to Combined Operations Headquarters (COHQ) had already become an obligatory outing for any visiting US official or military commander.

This fact did not escape the notice of Winston Churchill. He saw that as far as the Americans were concerned, Mountbatten's views commanded respect, though the British commanders' attitude to him was tinged with a certain amount of caution, for Mountbatten was one of those worrying individuals best known as a 'loose cannon'. Be that as it may, he was duly despatched to Washington and apparently convinced the US President of the difficulties surrounding SLEDGEHAMMER. This task may not have been as difficult as it appeared; Roosevelt was firmly in support of 'Germany First' and was also well aware of the reasons underpinning the pressures to switch the US effort to the Pacific.

Churchill valued Mountbatten's 'get up and go' attitude and in March 1942, before this trip to Washington, Mountbatten was promoted from mere 'Adviser' to Director of Combined Operations and given the tri-Service ranks of Vice-Admiral, Lieutenant-General and Air Vice-Marshal. He was also placed on the UK Chiefs of Staff Committee and therefore on the Anglo-American Combined Chiefs of Staff Committee (CCS).

Winston Churchill thereby ordered a destroyer captain with no amphibious experience to the highest councils of the war in the teeth of opposition from, among others, General Sir Alan Brooke, later Lord Alanbrooke, the CIGS and head of the Chiefs of Staff Committee.

In his diary for 28 March 1942, Brooke records:

> A difficult COS [meeting] to handle. We were discussing ways and means of establishing a new Western Front. I had propounded a theory that a Western Front, to be of any use, must force withdrawal of forces from Russia. That it was impossible with the land forces at our disposal to force the Germans to withdraw land forces from Russia; but that we might induce them to withdraw their air forces. But to do this a landing must take place within our air umbrella, namely in the vicinity of Calais or Boulogne. Mountbatten was still hankering after a landing near Cherbourg where proper air support is not possible. Finally I think we managed to convince him.[2]

Apparently not, however, for on 8 April, prior to that visit by General Marshall, SLEDGEHAMMER surfaces again: 'Very difficult COS attended by Paget [C-in-C, Home Forces], Sholto Douglas [AOC-in-C, Fighter Command] and Mountbatten; subject, how to assist Russia through action in France. Plan they had put up was a thoroughly bad one!'

Brooke gives no details of this 'bad plan' but clearly the meetings with General George C. Marshall in April were equally difficult, Brooke recording: 'A momentous meeting in which we accepted their proposals for offensive action in Europe in 1942 perhaps and in 1943 for certain. They have not begun to realise the implication of this plan and all the difficulties that lie ahead of us.'

Commenting on another meeting with Marshall on 15 April, in which

SLEDGEHAMMER was clearly the main item on the agenda, Brooke writes:

> My meeting with Marshall this afternoon was an eye-opener. I discovered that he had not studied any of the strategic implications of a cross-Channel operation. He argued that the main difficulty would be to achieve a landing. I granted that this would certainly present great difficulties but that our real troubles would start after the landing. We should be starting with forces initially weaker than the enemy and in addition his rate of reinforcement would be at least twice as fast as ours.[3]

No meeting of minds there, then; and throughout the spring and summer of 1942, US pressure for SLEDGEHAMMER did not go away. Brooke's diary records further discussion on 5 June on the need for a lodgement or a raid, and again on 10–11 June and during the visit of Churchill and the British Chiefs of Staff to Washington between 18 and 26 June. There were further arguments on 1 July and another debate in London with Marshall and Admiral King on 21 July, when King advanced his former idea – if the British would not invade France in 1942 then why not transfer all of the US efforts to the Pacific? On the following day the US Chiefs presented a memorandum to their British colleagues, calling for an attack on Cherbourg as an essential preliminary to an attack – ROUNDUP – in 1943.

Fortunately, this relentless pressure got the Americans nowhere. Just for once the British proved adamant and stood their ground, making the point that other issues clearly had priority, not least the need to defeat the submarine menace in the North Atlantic, without which the build-up of US forces in the UK for any invasion was sure to be costly. The Americans could scream as loudly as they liked for SLEDGEHAMMER and threaten to move their efforts elsewhere, but the British were simply not going to do it. This combination of common sense and stubbornness eventually carried the day and on 24 July the US Joint Chiefs of Staff abandoned SLEDGEHAMMER in favour of the North African landings, Operation TORCH.

But the pressure on the British Chiefs of Staff and the Prime Minister to do *something decisive* on the coast of Occupied Europe remained. The unions, the Soviets and the Americans might be fended off individually, but collectively the weight of their influence was enormous. By July the bleak start to the year was beginning to brighten somewhat. The German summer offensive in Russia was not achieving all that had been hoped. Arthur Harris had taken over at Bomber Command in February and got a grip on the bomber offensive with the first 1000-bomber raid on Cologne. In the North Atlantic, while the submarine menace remained strong, the British escort groups, with better training and more ships, were holding their own and the Royal and Canadian Navies would effectively win the Battle of the Atlantic by May 1943.

As for the struggle in North Africa, the Eighth Army, if driven back into Egypt, had managed to hang on there; two months after Dieppe General Montgomery won the decisive victory over Rommel at El Alamein. But in listing this more hopeful scenario we run ahead of events. Very little of this was apparent when Combined Operations HQ started planning for the Dieppe Raid in the late winter of 1941–2.

PLANNING RUTTER

APRIL–JULY 1942

My own feeling about the Dieppe raid is that there were far too many authorities with a hand in it; there was no single operational commander who was solely responsible for the operation from start to finish, a Task Force Commander in fact.

FIELD MARSHAL VISCOUNT MONTGOMERY OF ALAMEIN,
MEMOIRS (1958)

ESTABLISHING THE CORRECT command structure is essential to the successful outcome of any military operation. This applies with particular force in amphibious operations where many additional problems – weather, tides, coastal difficulties like rocks and shoals, outdated charts, sandbars, beach gradients, the landing of troops over open beaches and supporting them thereafter – will have to be factored in.

Amphibious operations are obviously more difficult than purely land-based operations but this does not mean that the normal command process, the prior need for a careful 'commander's estimate' or 'appreciation of the situation' before a plan is prepared, can be abandoned. The normal command requirements remain in place but they have to be supplemented by a further consideration of the difficulties raised when landing a force on a hostile shore.

This being so, the command structure governing amphibious operations in 1942 needs to be carefully considered. The plan for RUTTER/JUBILEE arose from such a command structure, and it is at least arguable that the numerous flaws in the plan arose in part from the flaws in the command. Command is not easy, so to outline how such planning tasks might be arranged and give an example of good practice, it might be as well to consider the command structure employed at RAF Bomber Command, an organisation which mounted raids on the enemy almost every night.

The man in charge of these nightly bombing operations was Air Chief Marshal Sir Arthur Harris, AOC-in-C (Air Officer Commander-in-Chief) of Bomber Command. Like all the other Service chiefs, Harris worked to a series of directives issued via the Air Ministry from the Chiefs of Staff but enjoyed considerable latitude in how he carried these directives out. The Chiefs told Harris what to do; they did not tell him how to do it. The essential point is that Harris was in charge; Harris, and Harris alone, decided what Bomber Command would do.

The operational process began every morning at Bomber Command Headquarters near High Wycombe in Buckinghamshire when, during a group session usually described as 'Morning Prayers', the results of the previous night's operations would be analysed and the current state of the Command – losses, aircraft available, crew state and so on – assessed with a view to further operations later that day. If all was well and after consultation with his weather adviser, Mr Spence, Harris would select the 'Target for Tonight' and pass a brief order to his staff – 'Berlin, tonight' or 'Essen . . . wipe it out.'

A preliminary order to that effect would then go out to the Groups and Squadrons so that the aircraft could be fuelled and bombed up. Meanwhile Harris's staff worked out the many practical details for the forthcoming operation: the route to the target and back, any diversions, the target-marking routine – the latter obtained from the No. 8 (Pathfinder) Group – as well as weather-dependent take-off time and communications information; all this would be handled by Air Marshal Saundby, Harris's SASO (Senior Air Staff Officer), who would sign off the operational order on which later that day the bomber squadron's crews would be briefed for their attack.

All these steps having been completed, the squadrons would take off at the given hour, assemble into the bomber stream and set off for the target, which, hopefully, they would obliterate. This routine took place on a daily basis over five years of war, and with such daily practice the staff at Bomber Command got very good at it. But the secret of their success lay in the clear command structure and the establishment of efficient operational routines.

Such a happy state of affairs did not exist at Combined Operations Headquarters, where the first and most obvious difference lay in the role of the man in charge. As we have noted, even the title of this appointment could vary; the man at the head of Combined Operations might be the 'Adviser' or the 'Director' or 'Chief'. Each title would indicate a change of role and illustrates a fundamental problem: was the head of Combined Operations a 'Force Commander' like Harris, able to mount operations on his own authority – again, like Harris, within the remit of his instructions from the Chiefs of Staff – or was his role purely advisory?

At COHQ the situation appears blurred. The commander's role changed from time to time and largely depended on the current situation and the character and perseverance of the individual concerned. Combined Operations certainly had its own 'private army' in the shape of the Commando units, which could be used for small-scale raids without prior approval from above – but the Commando units could not be moved unless the Royal Navy was willing and able to provide the ships and men to transport them. Anything larger than a small raid involving, say, five hundred men, meant careful negotiation with the other Services and the possibility – or certainty – of interference.

This lack of clarity over the precise function of the Combined Operations command had infuriated Sir Roger Keyes. He had been given a clear brief by the Minister for War, Winston Churchill, and ordered to raid the enemy coast with frequency and vigour, only to discover that his plans to do just that were frustrated by the Chiefs of Staff. This led to his dismissal in October 1941 and the appointment of Mountbatten to this hot seat but, as already described, initially as 'Adviser', not 'Director' or 'Chief'.

When Mountbatten understood that his role at Combined Operations was purely 'advisory' he was less than pleased. His first and very understandable reaction was to ask for his immediate return to the command of HMS *Illustrious*. This request Churchill rejected, saying, 'What could you hope to achieve there, except to be sunk in a bigger and more expensive ship next time?'

According to the history of Combined Operations, Churchill then gave Mountbatten a private briefing, instructing him to start 'a programme of raids of ever-increasing strength', from the North Cape to the

Bay of Biscay.[1] But, Churchill added, 'your main object must be the re-invasion of France'. This briefing, coming as it did from the Prime Minister and Minister of War, gave Mountbatten the idea that his brief freed him from the direct control of the Chiefs of Staff.

Churchill then listed a number of tasks that Mountbatten and Combined Operations must undertake: selecting the bases from which the invasion must be launched, creating the Training Centres for the assault troops, bringing in other Services to create a proper inter-Service organisation to produce and refine the techniques of modern assault, and much more. Broad as this was, there was nothing here that offered Mountbatten an active command, but Mountbatten could be persistent; giving advice that might be ignored was not his idea of a fulfilling assignment in the middle of a world war. He continued to press for an expansion of his responsibilities until, in early March 1942, Churchill gave way.

The elevation of Mountbatten to the epicentre of military affairs on the COS Committee did not please the CIGS, General Alan Brooke, who wrote in his diary on 5 March 1942:

> Mountbatten's inclusion in the COS was a snag. There was no justification for this move. His appointment as Chief of Combined Operations was excellent and he certainly played a remarkable role as the driving force of this organization. However, the holding of this appointment was no reason for his inclusion in the COS, where he frequently wasted both his own time and ours . . . I enjoyed Dickie's presence on the COS, in spite of the fact that at times he was apt to concern himself with matters outside his sphere . . . The title of Chief of Combined Operations was also badly chosen, since every operation we were engaged in was a combined one. *It was certainly not intended that he should direct combined strategy* [author's italics] – his job was to evolve the technique, policy and

> equipment for the employment of the three Services in combined operations to effect landings against opposition.[2]

From this it appears that, whatever Mountbatten's title or personal inclinations, Brooke continued to see Mountbatten's role as purely advisory or at best administrative. This was not how Mountbatten saw it; neither did he see it as in line with the brief he had received from Winston Churchill, who was Brooke's political master and who as Minister of War could override the wishes of the COS. This vagueness over the role of the CCO created a gap in the command structure that Mountbatten was able to exploit later, on JUBILEE.

With some aspects of the command structure and Mountbatten's wily character at least partially revealed, we can now move on to the planning of Operation RUTTER, the original Dieppe Raid. The process appears to have started in January 1942, shortly after the Vaagsø Raid, when the Combined Operations staff drew up a 'Target List' of operations they hoped to mount in the coming year.

The targets chosen were nothing if not varied and highly ambitious. Apart from the attack on St Nazaire, for which the Navy were pressing, other targets included the Belgian port of Ostend, an attack by the Guards Division on Alderney – a proposal which Brooke hastened to block – a raid on Bayonne and one amazing proposal, an attack on German Headquarters in Paris; this latter lunacy was only abandoned at the end of June. The list of targets also included most of the cross-Channel ferry ports from Calais to Le Havre, including the port of Dieppe. According to Captain John Hughes-Hallett, the Naval Adviser at COHQ, Dieppe had no particular significance at this time; it was simply a possibility among many others. It appeared, he wrote later, 'that Dieppe was a small seaport and it would be interesting to capture it for a time and then withdraw. It had no particular military significance but was about the right size for a divisional attack.'[3]

The interesting factor here is that, apparently, none of these 'target ports' were properly evaluated with a view to assessing the difficulties involved in carrying out any particular raid. According to the Canadian author Brian Loring Villa, 'The evidence that the British planners knew perfectly well that the operation had virtually no hope of success has been almost hidden from view in later efforts to justify the raid *ex post facto* as having produced a rich harvest of important lessons.'[4] There is merit in this statement but the real lessons of Dieppe arise not only from what happened on the beaches but in the flawed processes of the planning stage.

Loring Villa picks up this point later, stating that 'one approach to the mystery of Dieppe is to explain it in terms not of some hidden motive but rather of drift'. As is surely becoming apparent, there is ample evidence of drift over Dieppe, even at the early stages of planning when the Target List was being reduced to a few of the more likely possibilities. Dieppe is moving into the target frame, and by early April 1942 the other possibilities had been rejected and Dieppe selected as the most likely target. But at no point had the proposed operation been subjected to a detailed analysis of its aims and the likelihood of achieving them, a process referred to in the jargon of 1942, and for many years afterwards, as 'making an appreciation of the situation'. This process is worth examining because it is fundamental to the next step, devising a viable plan. According to the then current Service journal:

> The term 'appreciation of the situation' means nothing more than an orderly sequence of reasoning leading logically to the best solution to the problem. Military appreciations may deal with tactical, strategic, administrative or other problems.
>
> Appreciations may be produced for one of two reasons:
>
> *a.* By a commander who wishes to clear his brain of conflicting detail and come to a balanced conclusion.

b. By a junior officer as a brief for his commander.

Although the same process of logical reasoning is used as in a full appreciation, a shortened version probably includes only the following headings:

a. Aim.

b. Factors affecting the aim.

c. Own courses.

d. Plan.

All this is very logical but it appears that no such prior 'appreciation' was made of the Dieppe operation, certainly not for RUTTER. When the second attempt, Operation JUBILEE, came up for discussion and the Ground Force Commander, General Hamilton Roberts, suggested that this time a proper appreciation was called for, his request attracted only abuse from his naval colleague, Captain John Hughes-Hallett, who wrote disparagingly of 'the preoccupation with appreciations and all that sort of rot'.[5]

This attitude reveals a great ignorance among naval officers like Mountbatten and Hughes-Hallett concerning the requirements of military and amphibious operations. Perhaps appreciations were unnecessary at sea with the enemy warships in plain sight, but on the beach or further inland, they are a prerequisite for success and a means of avoiding disaster. Importantly, they do not constitute a commitment to proceed; if the appreciation concludes that the task is impossible or fraught with excessive hazards, it can be abandoned before forces are committed and egos get involved. Had RUTTER and later JUBILEE been analysed in the straightforward terms demanded by an appreciation, there is every chance that the Dieppc Raid would not have been carried out.

Instead, the next stage of planning became the preparation of an Outline Plan, which in the usual practice of the time could be submitted to the Chiefs of Staff. The Outline Plan for RUTTER was as follows:[6]

1. Intelligence reports indicate that Dieppe is not heavily defended and that the beaches in the vicinity are suitable for landing infantry and armoured fighting vehicles at some. It is also reported that there are forty landing barges in the harbour.

2. It is therefore proposed to carry out a raid with the following objectives.
   A. Destroying enemy defences in the vicinity of Dieppe;
   B. Destroying the airfield installations at St Aubin;
   C. Destroying the RDF [radar] station, power stations, dock and rail facilities and petrol dumps in the vicinity;
   D. Removing invasion barges for our own use;
   E. Removal of secret documents from the divisional headquarters at Arques;
   F. To capture prisoners.

Intention.

3. A force of infantry, airborne troops and armoured fighting vehicles will land in the area of Dieppe to seize the town and vicinity. This area will be held during daylight while the tasks are carried out. The force will then re-embark.

As the Chiefs were normally more concerned with higher matters, the evaluation of the plan would usually be handled by someone lower down the pecking order, and in the case of RUTTER it went first to General Sir Bernard Paget, General Officer Commanding (GOC) Home Forces, and was passed by him to his subordinate, Lieutenant-General Sir Bernard Montgomery, then GOC-in-C South-Eastern Command, from whose command the landing force would be taken.

The Canadians became involved at the end of April. The Canadian Corps formed part of Montgomery's command but there is some dispute about exactly how the Canadian commitment to the Dieppe operation actually came about. While insistent that one distinct force must provide the main landing contingent, Montgomery later denied that he had personally chosen the Canadians. This he said was 'a high-level, political decision', a comment that points the finger at General Paget.

On the other hand, Lieutenant-General Harry Crerar, commanding the Canadian Corps, stated later that he was summoned to Montgomery's Headquarters on 27 April 1942, told of the plan to raid an as yet unidentified enemy port and asked if he wanted the job. 'You bet,' replied Crerar. This was that long-awaited chance of action and Harry Crerar could not let it pass by.

This casual offer and acceptance still needed higher authority. Montgomery – or Paget – therefore made a formal offer to General McNaughton, stating that Crerar had accepted participation in principle and had proposed the 2nd Canadian Division for this task. McNaughton telegraphed the proposal to his Government in Ottawa and the request was approved, provided the Outline Plan met with the approval of the COS. This approval came on 15 May, thus committing the 2nd Canadian Division to participation in Operation RUTTER.

Operation RUTTER was no small-scale undertaking or simple Commando raid and differed in various ways from the eventual JUBILEE operation. For example, the RUTTER plan called for the use of troops from Brigadier James Hill's 1st Parachute Battalion for the elimination of the coastal batteries; for JUBILEE, paratroops were replaced by Commandos in order to remove at least one weather variable, the need for good visibility and low winds when dropping paratroopers.

On the matter of size, RUTTER/JUBILEE was always big. Apart from three Commando units and two brigades of the 2nd Canadian Division, JUBILEE employed 250 ships and craft and 50 squadrons of the RAF, mustering 800 fighters and some 100 light or medium bombers. A raid on this scale was much larger than anything previously attempted and well beyond the normal remit of Combined Operations. This fact was reflected in the command structure and it could be argued that this increase in size also meant a decline in competence. The Commando units involved at Vaagsø and St Nazaire had known what they were doing – they had been carrying out raids of one kind or another for two years and spent the interim on hard training and exercises. When the force increased in size, a new command structure was set in place, one that neither had this experience nor made any real attempt to get it.

Once the Outline Plan was approved the final plan for the attack could be prepared. To this end three 'Force Commanders' were appointed by the Chiefs of Staff: a Naval Force Commander, in the case of RUTTER Rear-Admiral H.T. Baillie-Grohman; an Air Force Commander, Air Vice-Marshal Trafford Leigh-Mallory; and a Ground Force Commander, Major-General Hamilton 'Ham' Roberts of the 2nd Canadian Division. Their task was to draw up the final plan for the operation and be responsible for their respective Services thereafter.

The effect of this 'Force Commander' structure, as Montgomery noted in the epigraph to this chapter, was that no single person was actually in charge of the entire operation; RUTTER was commanded by a Triumvirate, each with his own remit, with no one person directly responsible for all of it. Triumvirate control was common practice in the British Services at this time, not least because no Service officer wished to place himself under the command of an officer from another Service. Inevitably this led to 'command by committee' and presented endless opportunities for 'passing the buck'.

This was only part of the problem. The theory was that since a Combined Operation involved all three Services, each Service should have a say in the planning, provide the necessary expertise and ensure that the operation got the necessary amount of support in terms of men, ships and aircraft. This seems reasonable, but the snag was that the three Force Commanders had split loyalties and were inevitably concerned not simply with Combined Operations and the task in hand, but also with their own Service interests.

For example, when it became apparent that the land forces at Dieppe needed a capital ship, an 8in-gun cruiser or a battleship for bombardment purposes, Rear-Admiral Baillie-Grohman was tasked to obtain one from Admiral Sir William James, the naval officer in charge at Portsmouth. The Admiral quickly told him that the Royal Navy had no intention whatsoever of sending a capital ship into mid-Channel in broad daylight where it could be attacked and probably sunk by the Luftwaffe. As a loyal naval officer, Baillie-Grohman was obliged to accept this decision, and duly sold it to his colleagues on RUTTER. He thereby committed the landing forces to making a landing supported only by the 4in guns of a few small Hunt-class destroyers, rather than providing the heavy gun support the troops actually needed.

Had Baillie-Grohman been wearing his Combined Operations hat firmly, he might have told the Port Admiral that 'without heavy gun support, this operation is not viable and must be cancelled' or advised his colleagues in the Triumvirate that the operation should be called off. That would still have taken a joint decision by all three or some firm, even adamantine, resolution on the part of one of them.

To his credit, Mountbatten, who was closely involved in the planning, did not give up on the need for a heavy-gun warship for this operation. He went in person to see the First Sea Lord, Admiral of the Fleet Sir Dudley Pound, and asked for a battleship. He got the same answer as Baillie-Grohman: risking a capital ship off the French coast was not an option the Admiralty would even consider.

Much the same situation affected Air Vice-Marshal Leigh-Mallory. Here again, the landing forces needed a heavy air bombardment of the port and the headlands before the troops landed – and especially if they were to be denied the support of heavy naval guns – but for various reasons, not least the threat to French civilian lives, Leigh-Mallory was told by his superiors that, following a directive from the Prime Minister's office, a heavy raid on Dieppe by RAF Bomber Command would not be permitted. Leigh-Mallory accepted this decision and sold it to his colleagues. As a result, the only air support supplied to the troops making the frontal assault at Dieppe was a short and totally inadequate strafing of the headland defences by cannon-armed Hurricane fighters.

Two people could – and probably should – have called off the operation at this point. They were Lord Louis Mountbatten, the Chief of Combined Operations and the adviser on such operations to Home Forces, and Major-General 'Ham' Roberts of the 2nd Canadian Division. Mountbatten could have told the Chiefs of Staff that without adequate air and naval support he simply could not advise a landing. Roberts could have stated that as his Division was gradually being stripped of all necessary support, the Canadians would be facing a disaster even as they went ashore, and he was not prepared to carry out the operation.

Both men knew the reality of the situation but neither would go as far as to take sole responsibility for cancelling the Raid. Mountbatten was totally committed, having no other operation in hand, and clearly believed that, with luck, RUTTER still had every chance of success. As for Roberts, as we have noted in a previous chapter, the Canadians were desperate for action and Roberts would do nothing that might damage that prospect and deny his men the chance to show what they could do. Even had Roberts declined to take his men ashore, it would probably have made no difference. The Raid would have gone ahead anyway, either under a new Canadian commander or with the Canadians simply removed from the plan and replaced by the Royal Marine Division, which was also available and equally hungry for action. So two more steps were taken on the road to disaster on the beaches.

The basic decision the planners now had to make was a choice between a frontal assault on Dieppe town and no frontal assault at Dieppe but a series of attacks on the flanking beaches, after which the port would be surrounded from the landward side. Dieppe is set in a large gap in the chalk cliffs of the *pays de Caux*, and offered a pebble beach, about a mile long and split by the mouth of the River Arques, as a frontal landing area. Behind the beach lies an open promenade and the town, and the beach is completely overlooked by the two headlands, the eastern and western, the latter dominated by a medieval castle. The western side of the wide, flat promenade was occupied in 1942 by the Casino building, which in August the Germans were in the process of demolishing.

Here was the first problem, one related to the ground. If the planners opted for a frontal attack on Dieppe, this steep, sloping pebble beach, those headlands and that wide promenade presented considerable difficulties to the landing force; an enemy established on the headlands could quickly turn the offshore waters, the beach and the promenade into one vast killing ground. One way around that problem was to abandon the idea of a frontal attack entirely and make a flanking attack on some nearby beaches east and west of the town. The problem with that option was it allowed no convenient landing place for the Churchill tanks that were such an integral part of the operation. They represented a great leap forward; no raid so far had employed armour, but apart from the Dieppe seafront the only other place along this coast where (or so it was believed) tanks could be successfully landed was on the wide beach at Quiberville, eight miles away to the west and on the far side of two rivers, the Scie and the Saâne. There were two snags with that option. Firstly, the bridges over those rivers might not sustain the weight of the tanks; secondly, the time taken for the tanks to roll up to Dieppe would surely diminish the essential element of surprise and leave the landing forces without support for hours.

Therefore, very early in the planning phase, two proposals were on the table at COHQ, both presenting difficulties and both attracting support. Anxious to avoid the clear dangers inherent in a frontal assault, Mountbatten pressed for the flanking option, landing the tanks and a battalion of infantry at Quiberville, two more battalions at Pourville two miles west of Dieppe and another battalion at Puys one mile east of Dieppe, with – for RUTTER – Hill's parachute troops assaulting the coastal batteries at Berneval five miles east of Dieppe, and at Varengeville, three miles to the west. The second option approved of flanking attacks but also wanted the frontal assault on Dieppe.

The problem for COHQ was that they were not in direct charge of the final planning process. In accordance with now established practice, this had been delegated to the three Force Commanders and HQ Home Forces – in effect to General Montgomery – all of whom were firmly in favour of a frontal assault. The reasons for this enthusiasm were those given above – the difficulty of finding a place to land tanks, those inter vening rivers, the distance between Quiberville and Dieppe, their assessment of the strength of German forces in Dieppe and the promise of naval and RAF support. The German forces, or so the Force Commanders believed, presented no particular obstacle to a forceful landing as there were only 1400 of them and most of those were 'second-rank' troops, with no real support available inside eight hours. In this assessment, as in much else, the planners were wrong.

In 1942, the German defenders of north-western France were deployed in a fashion that would not change much before D-Day, 1944. Under the overall command of Field Marshal Gerd von Rundstedt, the Normandy–Picardy sector was occupied by Army Group 'B', which consisted of two armies, the Seventh and Fifteenth, with units of the Fifteenth Army positioned north of the River Seine, covering Dieppe.

The Fifteenth Army, three Corps strong, was commanded by Colonel-General Curt Haase. The 302nd Division of the LXXXI Corps, which was responsible for the coast around Dieppe, was commanded by another, unrelated Haase, Major-General Konrad Haase. The 302nd was charged with defending some 80km of coast and was, allegedly, not a first-class formation, being ill equipped, undertrained and largely composed of non-German soldiers, including Poles and ethnic Germans from newly occupied territories in the East. Finally, the 302nd was said to be under strength. British Intelligence reports in mid-summer 1942 estimated that the 571st Regiment of this division had only a small brigade of troops in or close to Dieppe.

This harping on about the 'poor quality' of the soldiers defending Dieppe was another example of wishful thinking by COHQ and the Force Commanders. By now, three years into this war, one in which the British could list only one decisive victory – and that over the Italians at Beda Fomm at the end of 1940 – it was a little late for comforting comments that German soldiers, even 'second-grade' soldiers, were not fully capable of defending their positions strongly when ordered to do so. A wise planner would assume that these troops would provide a formidable opposition to the landing force unless previously battered by heavy naval gunfire or bombing.

As the events of 19 August were to show, the Dieppe defenders proved more than adequate to stop the landing in its tracks, not least because these men were in pillboxes or bunkers, impervious to the totally inadequate weight of fire brought against them and well equipped with artillery, mortars and machine-guns with which to flay the Canadians on the beaches. It also appears that the individual soldiers fought well and that their snipers in particular were very effective.

As for the defending armament, this included three batteries of 150mm heavy coastal guns situated close to the coast and a hazard to offshore shipping. All were given codenames by the British: Battery 'Hess' at Varengeville, 'Rommel' at Dieppe and 'Goebbels' at Berneval. Under the RUTTER plan the first and last were to be attacked by paratroopers and eliminated before the landing force appeared offshore, and Battery Rommel would be overrun when the town fell.

Dieppe town was surrounded on the landward side by a belt of wire and mines containing three batteries of guns, 100mm or 200mm calibre, with two more batteries outside the wire. The headlands overlooking

Dieppe harbour and the beach supported pillboxes and trenches and some 75mm guns, with plenty of machine-guns and mortars; more of these deadly, quick-firing weapons were deployed on the promenade.

Caves dug in the cliffs contained heavy machine-guns and the exits from the promenade were blocked with concrete cone-shaped bollards, strong enough to stop a tank. The sum total of the Dieppe defences was enough to turn the beach and promenade into a killing ground unless those defences and the defenders could be reduced by heavy fire. A similar defensive arrangement – pillboxes, bunkers, machine-guns, mines and artillery – covered the landing areas at Puys and Pourville where the landing beaches were equally or, certainly at Puys, even more restricted. These defences were currently being expanded by workers from the Todt Organisation, based in Dieppe while working on the Atlantic Wall, the German defensive line of guns, mines and barbed wire that was supposed to run from Norway to the Pyrenees.

Any notion that the defences and defenders of Dieppe were inadequate and unable to resist an assault can be quickly dispelled. Set in that narrow notch in the high chalk cliffs, Dieppe was naturally defensible and to its natural advantages the Germans had added a great deal of wire, plenty of automatic weapons and guns and a considerable garrison. Nor was this all: reinforcements were on hand, including a full panzer division, 10th Panzer, which was based at Amiens, less than 80km away.

It remains debatable how much of this was known to the RUTTER planners. Enigma information would not have revealed the details of the defences or deployments, but would have advised the planners of the presence of the 302nd Division and 10th Panzer. Aerial photography should have displayed the extent of the defences on the headlands. Indeed, they must have done so as the planners were fully aware that unless these were reduced, the troops coming ashore immediately below would get a hot reception.

However, the general impression gained from studying the various planning meeting minutes is one of optimism: the German defenders were a poor lot, not expected to put up much resistance, and where defences could not be seen it was assumed they did not exist. Indeed, the final plan for RUTTER, sent to the CCS on 9 May, blithely comments, 'Dieppe is not heavily defended and some of the beaches in the vicinity are suitable for landing infantry and armoured fighting vehicles.'

By that date it was too late to change the plan. On 18 April General Montgomery approved the central assault, suggesting that the notion of flanking attacks alone had been abandoned. However, a week later, on 25 April, this frontal assault proposal came under attack from Mountbatten who, as related, had been in the United States explaining the problems of SLEDGEHAMMER. On his return, he reviewed the RUTTER plan and commented later:

> I came out strongly against the frontal attack but the Home Forces planners stuck to their guns, maintaining that a heavy bombing attack of maximum intensity immediately before the attack and followed by low flying aircraft attacks, would counter-balance the risks of a frontal assault.

The planners' claim is highly debatable even with the promised support. In the event, the heavy bombing attack, though briefly approved by Churchill, was finally cancelled on 5 June when strong pressure from Home Forces forced COHQ to yield on this point also. And still the plan went ahead: the frontal assault on Dieppe, without strong air or naval support, was duly approved by the Chiefs of Staff and the stage was set for a disaster.

General Roberts had selected two 2nd Division brigades for RUTTER. The 4th Brigade, commanded by Brigadier Sherwood Letts, consisted of battalions from the Province of Ontario, one each from the Royal Regiment of Canada, the Royal Hamilton Light Infantry and the Essex

Scottish; like many of his colleagues, Brigadier Letts had fought in the First World War, winning the Military Cross.

The 6th Brigade, commanded by Brigadier William Southam, contained the French-Canadian Fusiliers Mont-Royal from Quebec, the Cameron Highlanders of Canada from Alberta and the South Saskatchewan Regiment. Armoured support came from the 14th Canadian Tank Battalion, a unit generally known as the Calgary Tanks. Much of the detailed planning – when and where and how the Canadian troops landed and what they did once ashore – was carried out by one of Roberts's staff officers, Lieutenant-Colonel Churchill Mann. Churchill Mann had little amphibious experience but claimed that the plan was 'a most fantastic conception of the place most suited to land a strong force of AFVs [armoured fighting vehicles]'. He evaluated the plan for Roberts and concluded that it was not only viable but that the part calling for a frontal assault on Dieppe had 'the advantage of simplicity'; he 'recommended acceptance of the outline plan'.[7]

As mentioned, for the actual Raid, Operation JUBILEE, the task of eliminating the coastal batteries was given to the two Army Commandos while the Royal Marine 'A' Commando, which had been committed to RUTTER, was tasked with entering Dieppe harbour, capturing the invasion barges anchored there and sailing them back to England. This last task, comments General Julian Thompson, is 'a classic example of a planning officer dreaming up a task for lack of finding anything better since there was no possibility of these craft being of any use to the British'.

For JUBILEE, No. 3 Commando, commanded by Lieutenant-Colonel John Durnford-Slater and landing on Yellow Beaches 1 and 2 at Berneval, were tasked to knock out the Goebbels battery east of Dieppe. No. 4 Commando, commanded by Lieutenant-Colonel Lord Lovat, were to land on Orange Beaches 1 and 2, west of Dieppe, and knock out the battery at Varengeville. The Royal Marine 'A' Commando were still committed to the task of capturing the forty or so German invasion barges moored in Dieppe.

The Royal Regiment of Canada was to land on Blue Beach at Puys, take the village and move on to the eastern headland of Dieppe, knocking out the defences there before the main assault arrived on the beach below.

The South Saskatchewan Regiment and the Cameron Highlanders of Canada were to land on Green Beach at Pourville, west of Dieppe; once ashore the Saskatchewans would take the village and move up to the western headland overlooking Dieppe, while the Cameron Highlanders, landing half an hour later, would push up the valley of the River Scie to attack the German airfield at St Aubin.

With the coastal batteries reduced and the two headlands secure, the Essex Scottish and the Royal Hamilton Light Infantry, supported by the Calgary Tanks, would land – half an hour after the flanking attacks – on the one-mile-long shingle beach in front of Dieppe (codenamed 'Red Beach' for the Essex Scottish and 'White Beach' for the Hamiltons), occupy the town, push inland and to the flanks and link up with the battalions from Puys and Pourville.

The last Canadian battalion, the Fusiliers Mont-Royal, would remain afloat as Force Reserve. H-Hour for this attack was 0450hrs. When all had been achieved – within the space of a single tide – the entire force would withdraw back to sea through Dieppe and return to the UK.

The details of what happened on these particular beaches will be fully described in subsequent chapters and the flaws in this plan will be fully revealed by what happened to the troops sent ashore. Even at this stage, however, the tactical errors are multiplying like some uncontrolled virus; that decision to attack the Dieppe beach is typical of the major planning failure, an apparent inability to think the plan *through*. Clearly, the headlands had to be cleared or the forces up there silenced before the central landing began – but what if the flanking troops failed to reach the headlands? Where was the alternative plan in the event of any failure or delay? Military operations rarely run exactly to plan or stick to timings with the regularity of an American Greyhound bus.

In any event, the minute the Canadians stepped ashore at Puys and Pourville, all the German forces in Dieppe would be on the alert and manning their positions, and they were being given a full half-hour to prepare before the frontal assault came in at Dieppe in full daylight. This delay would leave the main assault fully exposed. Granted, there was a choice of difficulties, but either a heavy bombardment of the headlands or a landing in the dark at the same time as the flank attacks was a better option than the one the planners chose.

On 13 May, with the RUTTER plan approved, the landing forces moved to the Isle of Wight for assault training. They were in full occupation of the island by 20 May when, as a security measure, it was sealed off and all traffic with the nearby mainland stopped. This training, which involved plenty of physical activity, bayonet fighting, street-fighting drills and lots of live firing and grenade throwing, went very well.

The same cannot be said for the landing exercises. The first of these, YUKON 1, carried out on the south coast, was a total disaster. Some landing craft crews got lost, others landed the troops late, and the actual landing was followed by general chaos among the units ashore. None of this should be taken as unusual or even unexpected: amphibious operations were and are often fraught with error, as Brigadier Peter Young, then of No. 3 Commando, would readily confirm:

> Describe a typical World War II landing operation? Well, it would be pitch dark, with no lights permitted. There would be a sea running, so most people would be sea-sick. It would take twice as long as we thought it would to get the chaps into the landing craft and then half the landing craft would disappear in the darkness and never be seen again. When the rest of us embarked, we would bounce around for a while and then be landed on the wrong beach

> and while we were working out where we actually were we would be shelled by the Royal Navy . . . and that was on a good day.[8]

The errors that were to affect some of the RUTTER landings should therefore be taken as typical, but YUKON 1 on 11 June was such a shambles that the date of the operation was put back to July. On his return from the USA Mountbatten demanded that the entire exercise should be run again. YUKON 2 was much more successful and Operation RUTTER, so long in the planning, was set for the first favourable weather opportunity between 2 and 8 July. The men were duly embarked in their transports and the entire fleet assembled in Yarmouth Roads, awaiting the arrival of calm seas for the crossing and light winds for the paratroopers.

Unfortunately, the weather did not improve. If anything it deteriorated and as the days after 2 July ticked away, spirits began to fall among the invaders and at COHQ. The final blow came on 7 July when a force of German aircraft appeared over Yarmouth and bombed the assembled shipping. They did no actual harm; the few bombs that struck the ships failed to explode, but the Germans had seen the invasion fleet and taken knowledge of its existence and its probable purpose back to Occupied France. Even so, it might have been possible to proceed with RUTTER, but the weather remained unsettled. Therefore, later on 7 July, Operation RUTTER was cancelled and the men and ships dispersed. That seemed to be the end of the matter but less than two weeks later Operation RUTTER, now codenamed Operation JUBILEE, was back on again.

REMOUNTING JUBILEE

22 JULY–18 AUGUST 1942

The time has come when I must be informed more precisely about the military plans. Who made them? Who approved them? Did the General Staff check the plans? At what point was the VCIGS informed in the CIGS's absence?

WINSTON CHURCHILL TO GENERAL ISMAY,
DECEMBER 1942

ONE OF THE GREAT mysteries of the Dieppe Raid concerns the question of who actually authorised the remounting of RUTTER as Operation JUBILEE, the landing of 19 August 1942, or indeed whether JUBILEE was ever officially authorised at all. The preceding chapters have revealed both the basics of planning military operations and, shall we say, a slight weakness in the command and planning functions at COHQ. None of this explains how a major amphibious operation, involving two brigades of Canadian infantry, a regiment of tanks, more than 200 Royal Navy warships and transports, landing craft and squadrons of RAF aircraft, could be launched without a definite operational order. Any competent authority will state categorically that it could not be done.

And yet according to many historians and other authorities that is exactly what happened. This contention is supported by the fact that there is no definite paper trail running from the Chiefs of Staff to the Force Commanders directing them to re-form the RUTTER force and carry out the slightly revised version, Operation JUBILEE. As proof of this belief we can refer to the epigraph at the opening to this chapter, part of a series of questions from Winston Churchill to his representative on the Chiefs of Staff Committee, General Sir Hastings Ismay, in December 1942. Four months after the Raid, Churchill was demanding an explanation for the decision to launch JUBILEE and threatening an immediate Court of Inquiry if a sound explanation was not forthcoming. Sixty years later, the world is still waiting.

Analysing the decision process has to begin with the cancellation of RUTTER on 7 July. On 8 July, as the downcast, disappointed Canadians began to drift back to their camps, General Montgomery, who had always been lukewarm about the raid, recommended that the operation should be cancelled for good. Coming from such a source, this seems a definite proposal, but the very suggestion raises a question. If the men were on their way back to barracks and the landing ships dispersing to their home ports, surely the raid had *already* been cancelled for good? The man who cancelled it was Admiral James at Portsmouth, who had the final decision on whether or not the RUTTER force should sail. Yet Montgomery's suggestion introduces the point that the Raid might still be remounted, unless someone higher up the command chain declared otherwise.

Montgomery would have passed that suggestion or that possibility to his superior at Home Forces, General Paget. There is no evidence that Paget ever acted on the suggestion or passed it on to the Chiefs of Staff, and specifically to his superior officer, General Sir Alan Brooke, the CIGS, who was in the Middle East with Churchill for much of this time. Neither is there any evidence that the COS discussed this proposal. However, there is some evidence that Mountbatten pressed the COS for the RUTTER forces to be held in readiness until a final decision was taken. From this we can reasonably affirm that while RUTTER was indeed called off on 7 July, the option to remount the operation remained on the table.

At this point more of those extraneous factors, so common in this story, intrude yet again. It was becoming clear that the ill-conceived cross-Channel operation SLEDGEHAMMER would not happen, and the arguments that surrounded it have created yet another Dieppe myth, that RUTTER/JUBILEE was mounted to demonstrate to the Americans that a cross-Channel operation was simply impossible – in other words, the Dieppe Raid was laid on to fail. As tends to happen with such myths, the plot grew deeper over time; for example, given the engrained US belief in British timidity, according to one myth the use of Canadian troops on RUTTER/JUBILEE was a cunning British ploy. To the British, the Canadians were not unlike Americans, while to the Americans they were at least not British; any failure in the operation could not therefore be blamed on the well-known British reluctance to get stuck in.

There are only two snags with this particular myth. First, there is not a scrap of evidence of any such intention; the Canadians were employed at

Dieppe by invitation and with their own eager consent. Secondly, SLEDGEHAMMER was cancelled on 24 July in favour of Operation TORCH, the North African landings, and a full month before JUBILEE was launched.

On the other hand, with Mountbatten as Chief of Combined Operations and a member of the CCS, it seems most unlikely that the Dieppe Raid, the major, indeed the only, Combined Operations venture in 1942 after St Nazaire, did not present opportunities for experimentation to members of the CCS. If SLEDGEHAMMER was not on, as the British stoutly maintained, then perhaps another operation could serve as a substitute?

This was not to shelve SLEDGEHAMMER as a ludicrous idea – an objective study of the facts should do that – but to demonstrate that the British were as keen to carry the war to the enemy as anyone else. Besides, to cancel one operation – SLEDGEHAMMER – might be seen as justifiable. To cancel two, the second being RUTTER, might seem craven.

Here we have two cross-Channel operations – SLEDGEHAMMER and RUTTER/JUBILEE – and one man directly concerned with the latter, Vice-Admiral Mountbatten, sat on the CCS Committee, which was deeply concerned with the former. It is beyond belief that these two operations were not brought up for discussion by the British Chiefs of Staff or the Combined Chiefs and their competing problems at least discussed – yet there is no written evidence to show that the CCS considered JUBILEE as any compensation for the loss of SLEDGEHAMMER. One should not make too much of this, but the point remains: stopping RUTTER after cancelling SLEDGEHAMMER would have been at best unpalatable, and remounting it made that much more desirable.

At the time of RUTTER's cancellation Churchill and Alan Brooke were about to depart for Egypt to visit the Eighth Army, there to sack General Sir Claude Auchinleck, who had failed to bring about the desert victory Churchill so urgently required. From Cairo the Prime Minister and his military advisers would fly to Moscow for an uneasy confrontation with Marshal Stalin. Stalin was totally disenchanted with the efforts of his Western Allies, who had failed to deliver that 'Second Front' the Soviets had been demanding impatiently for the last year. Compared with what was happening in Russia in the summer of 1942, a landing of some 10,000 men on the coast of Occupied France was not much to offer, but it would have been evidence of effort. One can therefore take it that Churchill was less than happy about the abandonment of RUTTER, which sent him naked to the Moscow conference table.

As for General Montgomery, the next man in the frame, he was also on the move. Although the news was yet to break, Montgomery was in line for the post of British commander on Operation TORCH, the Anglo-American landings in North Africa, an operation that the Americans had finally accepted as a 1942 alternative to SLEDGEHAMMER. Montgomery was in North Africa before JUBILEE was launched and as the world now knows, fate had another destiny in line for Monty: within four months of RUTTER's cancellation, he had taken command of the Eighth Army and smashed Rommel's forces at El Alamein. Though a number of historians have attempted to list Montgomery among the Dieppe culprits, his part in the debacle really ends with his proposal in July that the operation be permanently shelved, and at that point he disappears from this story.

So too does the Naval Force Commander for RUTTER, Rear Admiral Baillie-Grohman. Like Montgomery, the Admiral had never been keen on RUTTER, showed no enthusiasm for holding the ships and troops in readiness for renewal, and quickly requested a posting to another command. This left the other Force Commanders for RUTTER in post, Air Vice-Marshal Trafford Leigh-Mallory and Major-General 'Ham' Roberts.

Leigh-Mallory's interest in the Dieppe Raid was entirely confined to the possibilities it offered for bringing the Luftwaffe to battle, so he was broadly in favour of renewal and would give the air support to which he was already committed. As for Roberts, for all the reasons already described he wanted to go ahead and renew, but with certain reservations. These surfaced on 9 July in a letter to Mountbatten, signed by Baillie-Grohman and Roberts, which raised the point that RUTTER had been planned without any prior 'appreciation' and implied, if not actually suggested, that if the operation were to be remounted, then it might be a good idea to carry out a proper 'appreciation' first. This was a sound suggestion but it came a little late in the day and served only to arouse opposition at COHQ, where enthusiasm for remounting the raid was rapidly gaining ground.

On 11 July, Mountbatten and Hughes-Hallett met Baillie-Grohman and Roberts to discuss remounting, and the contents of the letter. According to Hughes-Hallett the meeting rapidly developed into a row, with Hughes-Hallett, a naval captain, even threatening the two Force Commanders, his superiors in rank, with an official inquiry if the cancellation of RUTTER was not reversed. This threat did not play well with any of the Force Commanders, including Leigh-Mallory, who supported his naval and Canadian colleagues in their bid for a proper appreciation. No decision was reached on this point before the meeting broke up, and apparently no appreciation was ever made. Pressure was brought to bear on Roberts to withdraw his objections, Baillie-Grohman was cut out of the command set-up and Leigh-Mallory seems to have lost interest in further argument; JUBILEE, a clone of RUTTER, now needed only official sanction to go ahead.

The process of launching RUTTER has already been explained and the same process should have applied to JUBILEE; the final authority lay with the Chiefs of Staff and the War Cabinet or at least with the CIGS, General Sir Alan Brooke. Had any of these authorities made the decision to remount the raid, surely a paper trail would exist and a great mystery would never have arisen? One answer to this mystery comes from

Mountbatten, who stated that, in the interests of security, the decision was verbal and no written order to remount the raid was ever given.

Well, perhaps. Now let us see what actually happened, as far as it is possible to do so, for such hard evidence as exists is widely fragmented and spread about among the official sources. Sources for this part of the story come from files in the Liddell Hart Archive at King's College London,[1] the Hughes-Hallett papers in the Imperial War Museum and various Cabinet papers in the National Archives at Kew.

A number of the papers involved arise from those concerns expressed by Churchill in December 1942 and the research he ordered into the Dieppe Raid while preparing to cover this operation in the *Hinge of Fate* volume of his history of the Second World War in 1950. The correspondence can be found in the Ismay Papers in the Liddell Hart Archive.[2]

The sum total of it all is contradictory – there is no clear evidence that JUBILEE ever received official approval and certainly not in writing. However, this research shone some light into the thorny question of how the Raid came to be remounted, and under that fitful light one fact emerges with some clarity: the pressure to remount RUTTER came almost entirely from COHQ, with the slender balance coming from the Prime Minister.

Churchill's involvement can be analysed first. Eight years after the Raid, when writing to General Ismay in August 1950, he again asked who took the decision to revive the Dieppe operation:

> . . . nothing in the papers I have now seen or my own record explains who took the decision to revive the attack after it had been abandoned and Montgomery had cleared out. This is the crux of the story. Surely the decision could not have been taken without the Chiefs of Staff being informed? If so, why did they not bring it to my attention, observing that I did not leave the country until July 30

> or 31? It was a major decision of policy and if the decision was made after I left the country was the Defence Committee or the War Cabinet informed? How did all this go?

Churchill is clearly baffled on this point and is alleging that he knew nothing about the revival of the plan when he left for Cairo on 1 August. He continued to maintain this position but in a later exchange Ismay refutes the claim, reminding the Prime Minister that on 17 August he had sent a cable to London, asking for news of Operation JUBILEE:

Reflex 137/ 17 August – Message from Churchill, 'Please report if/when JUBILEE takes place?'

Ismay duly replied: (Tulip 170) 'Owing to weather, JUBILEE postponed to first light 19 August.'[3]

In 1950 therefore Ismay raised a very valid query: if Churchill knew nothing of the relaunching of RUTTER, then how did he know of this new codeword and that RUTTER had become JUBILEE before the operation was launched? The inference of Ismay's query is that Churchill had apparently forgotten that he knew of the relaunch of RUTTER as JUBILEE *before* he left the UK and approved of this intention. Indeed, in a letter to his research assistant, General Sir Henry Pownall, Churchill stated that he had supported the RUTTER operation but: 'I was not consulted about the resumption as I was away. I am sure I would have been most worried but I think I had already started for Cairo when the decision to renew the operation was taken. Certainly I heard about it and did not oppose it . . .'

This is about as far as Churchill was prepared to go – that he had heard about the plan for renewal *and did not oppose it.* In such circumstances the plan would go ahead, but who was driving it in Churchill's absence? It cannot have been General Sir Alan Brooke for he was with Churchill in the Middle East, so the search turns to the COS Committee, which, in the absence of the CIGS, would be attended by the Vice-Chief of the Imperial

General Staff – VCIGS – General Sir Archibald Nye, with one of the other Service chiefs in the chair.

Then the trail becomes confusing. In 1950, General Nye, in a letter to Ismay, stated that 'he had no idea that the operation was on until reports started to flow in from the scene of the action'. That was on the morning of 19 August 1942. Nye was clearly less than pleased about being kept in ignorance of JUBILEE and years later expressed his anger strongly to Ismay.

From this it appears that the senior officer at the War Office in the absence of General Alan Brooke had not been informed of this major amphibious operation and therefore could not have authorised it. But how could this be? As mentioned above, any search for the answer on that point leads to Mountbatten who – or so it appears – had already requested the COS for authority to relaunch the Raid, *before* Nye slipped into Alan Brooke's chair at the War Office, but had also suggested that 'in the interests of security', only a limited number of people should know about this decision and no minutes about the operation should be taken, a very strange proposal indeed.

The security limits excluded many members of the Chiefs of Staff Committee, including, apparently, the VCIGS, General Nye. The decision not to take minutes of the meetings would account for the absence of a paper trail and bolster Mountbatten's assertion that he received verbal authorisation to mount the Raid. The notion that the COS Committee was insecure is an intriguing one, but an examination of the records tends to suggest that this is what happened: knowledge of the decision to mount JUBILEE was restricted to the Force Commanders, the Canadian Commander, General McNaughton, Mountbatten and some of the senior staff at COHQ.

Concerns over security were one of the paramount objections to remounting the Raid. After RUTTER was abandoned the troops were dispersed and drowned their sorrows in the south-coast pubs, where the news that they had been hanging about in the Solent for the last week, preparing to assault Dieppe, was soon common knowledge. Indeed, Lieutenant-Colonel Lord Lovat, then in Scotland with No. 4 Commando, relates that 'lavatory rumours' of the cancelled raid had even been heard up there, and Major-General Houghton confirms that this information was common knowledge in the Isle of Wight where the 'A' Commando were based. Were the Canadians to disappear again, it might occur to enemy agents that the Raid was on again, so in the early stages of mounting JUBILEE a number of steps were taken to counter this notion; most notably the invasion fleet remained dispersed along the south coast and did not reassemble at Yarmouth or Cowes.

As for the fact that JUBILEE was a virtual replica of RUTTER, opinions varied on whether or not that was part of the deception or a decision made simply to save time, by using a plan that already existed. The evidence would suggest that keeping Dieppe as the objective was one of the very few good ideas. The groundwork had been done, the objectives had been studied and the plans laid; very poor plans perhaps, but plans nevertheless. Even on security grounds, using the same target was not a bad idea; the Germans might consider that going for Dieppe again was such lunacy that the British would never attempt it. The Germans were certainly aware that Dieppe had been targeted and they worked even harder at the port defences, but there is no evidence whatsoever that they were informed that the port had been targeted yet again for JUBILEE, in spite of a great deal of anecdotal evidence from Canadian prisoners later that their captors had declared that the raid had been anticipated.

So far as the evidence takes us we can assume that Churchill and Brooke knew of the *proposal* to relaunch the raid and at least did not oppose it. We can also assume that the COS Committee, or some of them, were also aware of the proposal and also knew that their masters, Churchill and Alan Brooke, were not opposed to it either. So who put the actual relaunch proposal forward with a request for at least verbal

A view across the harbour of modern-day Dieppe, seen from the eastern headland. The castle is on the horizon, beneath the cloud. *The Travel Library*

A modern-day view across Red and White Beach, taken from the castle. *Images of France*

Operation Rutter: Canadian troops disembarking from landing craft during a training exercise before the raid on Dieppe. *Library and Archives Canada PA 113243*

Major-General John Hamilton 'Ham' Roberts, commander of the 2nd Canadian Division and Ground Force Commander for the Dieppe Raid, subsequently blamed by posterity for his role in Operation Jubilee. *Crown Copyright PA 153531*

Lord Louis Mountbatten, Chief of Combined Operations, inspecting Canadian soldiers in training at a Combined Operations centre, 1942. *IWM A13222*

Air Chief Marshal Sir Trafford Leigh-Mallory, Air Force Commander for the Dieppe Raid. *IWM CH 11985*

HMS *Calpe* laying a smokescreen off Dieppe. The smokescreen offered additional protection to the Allied forces since it helped conceal their movements from the German forces. *Library and Archives Canada PA 116301*

A Douglas Boston aircraft of the RAF taking part in the Raid on Dieppe. *Library and Archives Canada PA 183771*

Troops of the Cameron Highlanders of Canada in landing craft prior to the Raid on Dieppe. *Library and Archives Canada PA 113245*

Light naval craft of the Royal Navy covering the landing at Dieppe. *IWM A 11234*

The French coast comes into sight, as seen from the bridge of one of the destroyers covering the Raid. *IWM A 11222*

Landing craft approach the shore under the cover of a smokescreen during Raid. *IWM A 11231*

Lieutenant-Colonel Cecil Merritt, commander of a light battalion of the South Saskatchewan Regiment who mounted the assault on Green Beach to the west of Dieppe, seen here talking to two of his officers during training for Combined Operations, July 1942. Merritt was awarded Canada's first VC of the war for his courageous actions in leading his men several times across the bridge at Pourville as it was swept by German machine-gun fire. *IWM H 21373*

The King talking to Major Pat Porteous VC while inspecting Lord Lovat's Commandos, 22 May 1944. In the rank of Captain, Porteous won his VC in 'F' Troop of 4 Commando during the Dieppe Raid, leading his men in a charge on a gun-pit even though hit twice in the arm and leg. *IWM H 38759*

Lieutenant-Colonel Lord Lovat, commander of 4 Commando, who mounted the assault on Orange Beach at Varengeville, to the west of Dieppe - seen with his troops at Newhaven after the Raid. *IWM H 22583*

Monty chats to Lieutenant-Colonel Durnford-Slater in 1943. Durnford-Slater was the commanding officer who led 3 Commando's tenacious assault on Yellow Beach at Berneval. *IWM E 26179*

Landing craft burning on the beach after the raid on Dieppe. *IWM HU 1906*

Burnt-out tanks and landing craft lie strewn across the beach. Of the 24 landing craft that took part, 10 managed to land a total of 24 tanks, all of which were lost. *IWM HU 1905*

Allied troop casualties have been covered with blankets. Background right is a landing craft, in front, a light reconnaissance tank, to the left, a heavy tank. *IWM HU 1808*

German soldiers examine Churchill tanks abandoned by Allied soldiers as they evacuated. Fourth in the British series of infantry support tanks, the Churchill first saw action at Dieppe. *IWM HU 1902*

A British destroyer rescuing soldiers from the water after their landing craft had sunk. *IWM A 11238*

Wounded soldiers being helped aboard a destroyer by an RNVR surgeon. *IWM A 11225*

Two of the landing craft – one containing a Bren carrier – come alongside a destroyer after returning from the beaches. *IWM A 11228/11229*

Allied prisoners rest by the roadside, guarded by Germans, 19 August 1942. *IWM HU 1894*

Above and below: Allied prisoners being marched through the streets of Dieppe, 19 August 1942. *IWM HU 1897/1890*

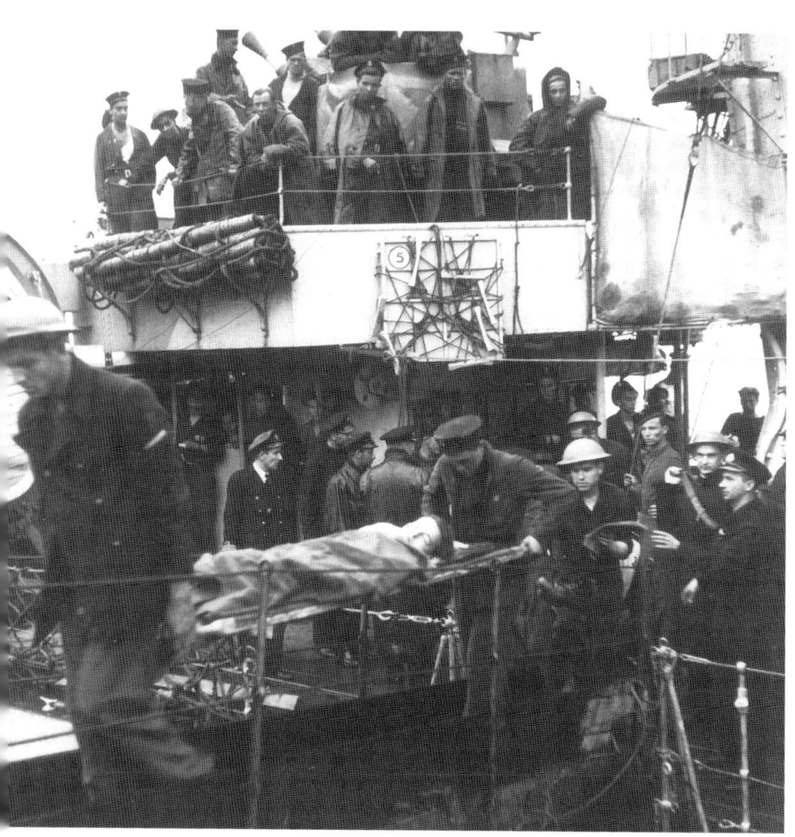

A wounded Canadian soldier being disembarked from a Polish destroyer at Portsmouth on return from Dieppe. *IWM H 22637*

An LCP craft returning to Newhaven after the Raid. *IWM H 22605*

An American soldier receives a light for his cigarette from a compatriot at Newhaven on his return from Dieppe. This was the first time that American troops had seen action in Europe during the Second World War. *IWM 22580*

Captain Jock Anderson of the Royal Regiment of Canada, cup of tea in hand, recounts his experiences to Brigadier Tees after disembarking at Portsmouth. *IWM H 22638*

The arrival back from Dieppe: G.L. Mieus, INS correspondent, with two sailors at Newhaven. *IWM H 22631*

The Canadian War Cemetery at Dieppe. *IWM HU 16310/16307*

approval? General Nye, the VCIGS, and General Ismay, Churchill's representative on the COS Committee, claim that they were not even informed, yet alone consulted, though Ismay certainly knew that the relaunch proposal was on the table.

The finger therefore points inexorably at Mountbatten, who, at a COS meeting in December 1942, stated that he had taken the responsibility to relaunch the raid – and this December response is indeed minuted. However, in 1950, in response to Churchill's demands for an explanation to include in the *Hinge of Fate* volume, Ismay contacted Mountbatten and asked that very question again. Getting an answer proved difficult, and Mountbatten passed most of the questions on relaunching the Dieppe Raid to his former colleague at COHQ, John Hughes-Hallett. The sum total of Hughes-Hallett's reply was that in a private conversation with Mountbatten, Churchill had stated that he regarded the cancellation of RUTTER as 'tantamount to a defeat' and 'the Chiefs of Staff had approved the decision to remount the operation'.

As the Canadian author Brian Loring Villa points out, these replies were solely based on conversations Hughes-Hallett had held with Mountbatten in 1942.[4] Hughes-Hallett was not on the COS Committee or privy to the alleged conversation with Churchill, so in providing his old commander with these replies and explanations, he was simply quoting Mountbatten back to Mountbatten. It is necessary to state, yet again, that there is no documentation, even in the Cabinet papers, to support the claim that the relaunch of the raid had COS approval.

The Ismay Papers record some interesting exchanges between Pownall and Churchill in 1950. For example, that 'there is both interest and controversy in Canada and Mountbatten has taken all the responsibility, which is surely more than he need bear'. Evidence to support this noble gesture by Mountbatten has proved hard to find but Pownall continues:

According to my recollection, we had prepared this large descent as

> a specimen raid on a grand scale. The op was cancelled after all 10,000 men embarked had been told about it. I was not consulted about the resumption but I had heard about it and did not oppose it. There is no doubt that Mountbatten pressed most strongly for it and I expect you will find that the War Cabinet gave him their assent. Monty declares that he never accepted the slightest responsibility for the military side of the op after the first attempt was cancelled.

On 22 March 1950, Ismay wrote to Churchill: 'My general impression is that it was not one of our most creditable ventures because the underlying object had never been clearly defined; nor, so far as I can remember, was the chain of responsibility. I do not, in fact, think that we deserved success.'

In this comment we have confirmation of two major errors, a failure to define the aim, and a failure to establish a clear command structure – both of which would make failure almost inevitable. This point clearly occurred to Churchill, as seen by his letter to Ismay in August 1950 quoted on p. 113. Seeking clarification on the crucial point of how the Raid was authorised, on 9 August 1950, Ismay wrote to Mountbatten, who had become somewhat elusive, asking for clarification but adding or hinting that he was 'absolutely clear that at least the COS must have been informed and given approval'.

On 10 August, before Mountbatten replied, Ismay wrote to Churchill that 'nothing was put on paper. Nye [the VCIGS] had no idea the op was on until reports started to flow in from the scene of the action,' but then adds, 'you yourself must have approved the idea in principle before you left England on August 2,' and asks how otherwise could Churchill have known about the JUBILEE codeword?

The next significant communication is a long memorandum from Mountbatten, who 'gave orders that nothing was to be put in writing and only two or three senior officers should be informed about it for the present'. He also claimed that he 'broached the matter with the COS *and having obtained their concurrence* [author's italics] I went personally to the Prime Minister and obtained his approval. The Defence Committee were neither consulted nor told about it. The approval came entirely from the Prime Minister and the COS.'

In short, Mountbatten claims that he got his authority – verbal authority – from both the COS and the Prime Minister. The problem with this is that we have to take Mountbatten's word for it, at least up to a point. There is no paper trail from the COS and, as the above correspondence reveals, if Churchill gave his approval he had forgotten that fact by 1950 – admittedly eight busy years after the event and when there is a small body of evidence to suggest that he did in fact know of the plan to resume the operation in August 1942 'and did not oppose it'.

There is no real need to proceed further with this search for a paper trail. Historians have been searching for written authorisation for six decades and failed to find any paper that gives the appropriate high-level authority for launching JUBILEE; one may safely assume that if it still existed they would have found it. This being so, we are forced to speculate, partly – as above – by using such sources as exist, and partly by considering what actually happened in August 1942 and in the following months.

First of all, in spite of all the theories and lack of evidence, it is indeed inconceivable that an amphibious operation of such magnitude could have been launched without the authority of the COS Committee. The entire process of decision-making, including the writing and issue of plans – and the final plan for JUBILEE runs to some two hundred pages – begins with that authorisation. We must therefore accept Mountbatten's claim that he had at least verbal authority to relaunch the raid from the Chiefs of Staff. Indeed, the subsequent after-action report on JUBILEE contains a sub-heading on a 'New Directive to the Chief of Combined Operations', which covers the planning for the raid and concludes that 'it was under this directive that the Chief of Combined Operations launched the Raid'.[5] The difficulty is that this report was written at COHQ, under Mountbatten's personal direction.

However, the claim of verbal authority is supported by subsequent events and the actions taken by Mountbatten's superiors. It has to be remembered that JUBILEE was a disastrous failure and failures usually require scapegoats – a role subsequently filled by Major-General 'Ham' Roberts. Had Mountbatten launched this disastrous raid without official sanction he would have been pole-axed, driven from office, his reputation in ruins, his career at an end. The CIGS, General Sir Alan Brooke, who was no fan of Mountbatten, would have quickly seen to that and it would have been his duty to do so.

None of that happened. Mountbatten's wartime career continued to flourish with his subsequent appointment to the post of Supreme Allied Commander, South-East Asia. There he was able to claim much of the credit for the defeat of the Japanese in Burma. In the postwar world Mountbatten was the last Viceroy of India and a leading figure in military and naval circles for several decades, ending his career as Chief of the Defence Staff, the effective head of the entire military establishment, Navy, Army and Air Force. None of this could have happened had he lost his head in 1942 and launched a catastrophic operation without the proper authority.

Besides, Mountbatten was not a fool. He was well aware that the Dieppe Raid was a high-risk undertaking even if all went well. Should all not go well, he needed official authorisation to cover his back and he would not have moved without it. Granted, he might have been more open about it but that was never Mountbatten's way; 'Dickie' not only had a talent for intrigue, he actually enjoyed it.

The Dieppe Raid was relaunched because the cancellation of RUTTER was a great disappointment to all concerned and left COHQ with no operations in hand. However, the possibility of reinstating the Raid remained on the table and when Mountbatten and Hughes-Hallett – 'a real fire-eater' according to that astute Royal Marine officer, General Houghton – declared that it could be done, they found plenty of people willing to listen and no one violently opposed. Montgomery and Baillie-Grohman had departed and Roberts was quickly browbeaten into agreement by his superiors.

In such circumstances it is hardly surprising that the idea of a relaunch gained at least tacit approval from the COS, for what had they got to lose? The proposal gained momentum, the forces were remustered, the ships prepared, the plan tinkered with – and eventually the troops sailed from the south-coast ports for their rendezvous with destiny; as with many tragedies there is something inevitable about the Dieppe Raid.

The decision to launch JUBILEE was taken on 22 July. This was also the time when the Americans finally agreed to abandon SLEDGE-HAMMER in favour of the North African landings, Operation TORCH.[6] This happy conclusion to months of argument may have diverted the Chiefs of Staffs' attention from what was currently being put in train at COHQ. However, there was plenty of time – more than a full week – for Churchill and Brooke to learn about this intention to remount before they left for the Middle East on 2 August. The remount proposal was still at the planning stage and a lot of work had to be done before the operation was actually 'on'. First of all it was necessary to find a new Naval Force Commander to replace Baillie-Grohman; the choice fell on Captain John Hughes-Hallett, even though he was junior in rank to the others in the Triumvirate, and on the staff at COHQ. On the other hand he knew all about the planning for RUTTER and needed no time to read himself in on the plan for JUBILEE.

The JUBILEE command and control set-up was put in place at this time and their posts during the Raid decided. The Naval and Ground

Force Commanders – Hughes-Hallett and Major-General Roberts – would embark in the destroyer HMS *Calpe*, which would act as headquarters ship and be equipped with extra radio sets for communication with the rest of the invasion fleet, the troops ashore and the UK. According to one account, the communications equipment included the provision of two carrier pigeons; this set-up was fully duplicated on HMS *Fernie.*[7]

HMS *Fernie* would also carry some American observers, including Brigadier-General Lucian Truscott from General Eisenhower's newly established Headquarters and the Chief Operations Officer of the 2nd Canadian Division, Lieutenant-Colonel Churchill Mann. Should anything happen to Roberts or HMS *Calpe* be sunk, Colonel Mann, who had played a major part in planning the small but vital details of the Canadian assault, would assume command of the landing operation.

This duplication of the command and communications set-up was very sound but, as we shall see, did little to help matters when the landings went awry. As for the last two commanders, Mountbatten and Air Vice-Marshal Leigh-Mallory, they would be based at Fighter Command's No. 11 Group Headquarters at Uxbridge, close to London, again (or so it was hoped) in constant radio contact with Roberts and Hughes-Hallett on *Calpe.*

Then the plan had to be revised somewhat; RUTTER had been defeated by the weather and in an attempt to remove one potential weather snag, the paratroopers were replaced by Nos. 3 and 4 Commandos for the attack on the batteries. This change again took a little time, for the Commandos had to examine their orders and work out how they were to get ashore, climb the cliffs and assault the batteries. Meantime the Canadians were reassembled and began to move to their eventual embarkation ports, still unaware that the Raid had been remounted.

Durnford-Slater and Lovat, the commanding officers of Nos. 3 and 4 Commandos, knew what they were doing. Just to begin with they insisted on some alterations to the plan, notably that they could land before the main Canadian force, under cover of full darkness, and carry out their tasks without reference to events on their flanks; the Commando operations at Dieppe would not be under the direction of Churchill Mann. The Commandos also absorbed fifty officers and men of the 1st US Ranger Battalion, which had recently completed training in Scotland and wanted some experience of Commando operations. These US troops were distributed between the two Commando units and did good work during the Raid.

The introduction of Commandos also required more landing craft and this in turn led to a further decision, that No. 3 Commando, the Puys force of Canadians and some other units would not cross the Channel in transports and then trans-ship to assault craft but go all the way across in their assault landing craft. This promised to be vastly uncomfortable for the troops but it saved a certain amount of time during the landing phase.

When these various changes and additions were being made the final plan for JUBILEE was put in place. As stated, this was essentially the same as the RUTTER plan, but before we follow the troops to sea, it would be as well to briefly review what was supposed to happen when this force reached the coast of France, if only to stress that JUBILEE was always a high-risk operation, with tight margins between success and failure.

The first point to underline is that surprise was essential; if the invasion fleet was spotted when closing the coast, the entire enterprise was doomed. In a bid to avoid landing in daylight, the landing time for the flanking attacks had been set for 0450hrs, in the immediate pre-dawn period, a time referred to in many accounts as 'nautical twilight'. This 'twilight' covers that time when the sun is still below the horizon but the sky is beginning to grow lighter; it lasts about three-quarters of an hour before full dawn. This was too dark for observed naval shellfire, so the flanking attacks would be relying for their security entirely on darkness and surprise. High tide at Dieppe was at 0403hrs.

At 0520hrs, half an hour after the flanking attacks had gone in, and when the large coastal batteries had been attacked by the Commandos and the flanking battalions were, one hopes, firmly established ashore and heading for the two headlands overlooking the port, the main, frontal assault on the Dieppe beach by Canadian tanks and infantry would go in. By that time it should be full daylight and this attack could be supported by naval gunfire from the 4in guns of the supporting destroyers and a steam gunboat, HMS *Locust* – which also carried the Royal Marines of the 'A' Commando – and a few minutes of strafing from the ground-attack fighters of the RAF using cannon and rockets; the inadequacy of this support has already been exhaustively explained.

This plan, so carefully worked out, contains a number of other flaws, some of them quite basic. The main flaw was that there was no provision whatsoever for action in the event of failure – if the attack stalled, if the enemy reacted strongly and held the invaders on the beach, if there was any major hold-up of any kind, no arrangements were in place either to call the attack off or to divert part of the landing forces to some other beach. The only order concerning the abandonment of JUBILEE stated that if the raid was not called off by 0300hrs on 19 August, it was to proceed, whatever subsequently happened. The JUBILEE plan lacked any kind of flexibility and since in war something always goes wrong, not least because the enemy forces are totally devoted to making things go wrong, this lack of a fall-back position was a grave and fundamental error.

The second major flaw concerns the arrangements for the withdrawal. The withdrawal is always the trickiest part of any amphibious operation other than a full-scale invasion, when the problem of the logistics of maintaining the troops ashore arises instead. The fact that there was no logistical provision for Dieppe is further confirmation that this was only a big raid. This entire operation was to be completed within one tide – a matter of a few hours, six to nine at the most.

According to the final plan, some of the forces ashore (the Calgary Tanks and the Cameron Highlanders) would meet up near Arques or at the St Aubin airfield, some distance inland from Dieppe, and then pull back to the port. Having completed their tasks, all the troops ashore would withdraw through the town and be taken off from the Dieppe beaches or from the harbour, in craft which had been been waiting offshore in a boat pool throughout the operation. What the Germans would be doing during this withdrawal phase was not closely examined but in the third year of the war the planners should – must – have known that the enemy would not be quiescent under this attack. Their rapid response at Vaagsø and St Nazaire was current proof of that.

As we shall see, a great many of the casualties on JUBILEE were incurred during the withdrawal phase. This is hardly surprising and the failure to take the high possibility of casualties during the withdrawal into account is another indication that the planners either did not know what they were doing or failed to factor withdrawal problems into their plans.

The first and most obvious problem was that as soon as the invaders stopped advancing and started to fall back, the defenders would press closely on their heels; that is standard military practice, to follow up the retreating foe and attempt to turn his retreat into a rout. The invaders would also be encumbered with wounded and probably with prisoners, and would inevitably be in some confusion with no clear idea what craft they should get into when they reached the beach, always assuming the craft were there. There was also the matter of re-embarking the tanks, an inevitably lengthy process – and all this was to be done off the main Dieppe beach, under the two headlands, which presented a problem on landing and would surely present an even greater problem during the withdrawal if the Germans were able to reoccupy them and bring the beach again under fire.

None of these points seemed to have been bothering the Force Commanders on the morning of 18 August when the troops boarded their landing craft and awaited the order to sail. The Churchills of the Calgary Tanks were already embarked on the LCTs moored in Newhaven harbour, where the Cameron Highlanders of Canada and No. 3 Commando were boarding their Eurekas. Meanwhile the rest of the JUBILEE force filed aboard the transports at Shoreham, Southampton, Gosport and Portsmouth, under the interested eyes of civilians and Service personnel. The assault troops had yet to be informed where they were going this time, but many must have guessed that Dieppe was, yet again, their destination.

This was high summer when the long days were extended by the use of Double Summer Time, all clocks being advanced by two hours from Greenwich Mean Time. It was therefore still broad daylight when the first of the invasion fleet, HMT *Princess Astrid* with the Royal Regiment of Canada, embarked, cleared Portsmouth harbour and set course on a smooth sea for the hostile coast of France.

On board HMS *Calpe*, the Naval Force Commander, Captain John Hughes-Hallett, who had been involved in all this for months, recorded 'an understandable feeling of relief'.[8] The planning stage, the endless discussions, the meetings and the worries were now at an end; the die was cast and for better or worse, within a few hours Operation JUBILEE was finally going to take place.

'Of course I was aware,' he wrote later, 'that there were shortcomings in the plan, particularly the lack of heavy supporting fire, but the moment of sailing was no time for jogging back and I put my fears behind me.'[9] And so they sailed.

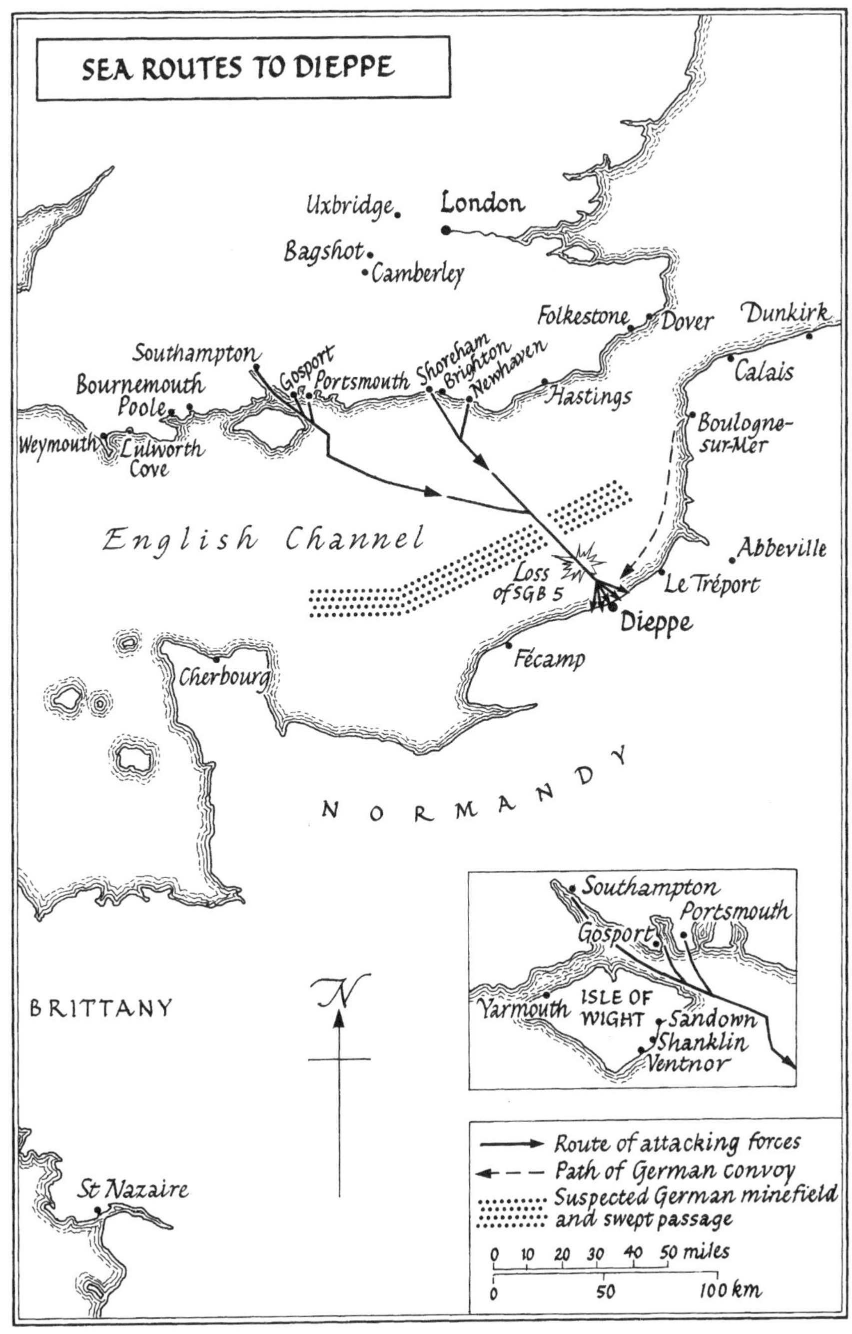
SEA ROUTES TO DIEPPE
Uxbridge
London
Bagshot
Camberley
Folkestone
Dover
Dunkirk
Calais
Southampton
Gosport
Portsmouth
Shoreham
Brighton
Newhaven
Hastings
Bournemouth
Poole
Weymouth
Lulworth Cove
Boulogne-sur-Mer
English Channel
Abbeville
Loss of SGB 5
Le Tréport
Dieppe
Fécamp
Cherbourg
NORMANDY
BRITTANY
N
St Nazaire
Southampton
Portsmouth
Gosport
Yarmouth
ISLE OF WIGHT
Sandown
Shanklin
Ventnor
Route of attacking forces
Path of German convoy
Suspected German minefield and swept passage
0 10 20 30 40 50 miles
0 50 100 km

YELLOW BEACH 1 AND 2

BERNEVAL

Probably my best operation. I took eighteen men ashore, did the job we had to do and brought eighteen men back.

Major Peter Young, No. 3 Commando

LED BY STEAM gunboat (SGB) No. 5, No. 3 Commando sailed from the Sussex port of Newhaven at 2030hrs on 18 August. The Commando was to cross the Channel already embarked in their assault craft – Eurekas or LCP (L)s – and twenty-three of these, arrayed in four columns, each craft capable of carrying twenty-five fully equipped soldiers, followed SGB 5 out of the harbour. Two support craft, a landing craft flak (LCF No. 1) equipped with anti-aircraft guns and a motor gunboat, ML No. 346, shepherded this convoy from astern.

Lieutenant-Colonel Durnford-Slater of 3 Commando, Captain Roy Murray of the US Rangers and the Force Commander for Yellow Beach 1 and 2, Commander D.B. Wyburd, RN, were all embarked on SGB 5, which was well equipped with communications and in radio contact with the two Force Commanders on HMS *Calpe*. Once clear of the harbour, SGB 5 increased speed to 10 knots, which, as Commander Wyburd later admitted, soon proved too fast for most of the Eurekas. As a result, the convoy began to straggle, a number of craft then developed engine trouble and four of the Eurekas, carrying over a hundred men, were forced back to Newhaven. The rest pressed on, gradually re-forming into their columns, and by 2359hrs nineteen of the Eurekas were back on station, through the Channel minefield where gaps had been carefully swept earlier that night, and closing on the French coast.

This German minefield lay like a great barrier across the Channel, running east to west from the Pas de Calais to Le Havre. It was designed to offer German coastal convoys a supposedly safe passage down the narrow gap between the minefield and the French coast. Only 'supposedly', for the shallow-draught craft of British Coastal Forces, fast, heavily armed gunboats and torpedo boats, crossed this minefield on a nightly basis, to patrol the far channel and engage German shipping. These engagements out at sea and their visible effects – explosions, gunfire, tracer bullets, fires and flares – were therefore a very common sight off the French coast and would arouse no particular interest in the German sentries or coastal gunners. Nor was the minefield much of an obstacle to the Eurekas. It was more of a threat for the large transports in the JUBILEE convoys – the HMT *Glengyle* and converted cross-Channel ferries like the *Princess Astrid*, which drew more water – which were led by groups of minesweepers from Portsmouth, which cleared two channels through to the far side of the field.

The Germans on the Channel coast were more alert than usual on the night of 18–19 August, for orders had been received putting all the coastal garrisons on a high state of readiness. This was partly because of orders from von Rundstedt's OKW, the German General Headquarters, stating that the German successes on the Eastern Front made the possibility of some action in the West a distinct possibility, partly because the calm seas and moonlight made some Commando activity likely and – possibly – because of some intelligence on the cancellation of RUTTER. For all these reasons the German troops were on the second stage of readiness – Threatened Danger – which put them on stand-by, boots on and weapons to hand. In such circumstances any sudden flare-up offshore would be noted and reported and result in the various outposts going onto full alert. Just such a flare-up was in the offing.

By 2359hrs on 18 August, a problem was revealing itself on naval radar screens at Dover and along the south coast of Britain. A German convoy was making its way down the swept channel, heading south and west from Boulogne and apparently set on a collision course with the British landing craft making for Yellow Beach 1 and 2 at Berneval.

This German convoy was tracked by the radar at Dover and Portsmouth and a warning of its presence and two signals were sent to Roberts and Hughes-Hallett on HMS *Calpe*, one at 0127hrs and another at 0244hrs. Neither was received by *Calpe* or by either of the two escort destroyers, HMS *Brocklesby* and the Polish warship *Slazak*, that had taken up their position on the eastern side of the JUBILEE fleet. HMS *Fernie* picked up the 0244 signal but assumed that the other escorts had also received it, and took no steps to pass the warning on to any of the other stations, including the Yellow Beach force commanders on SGB 5.

From this incident, two questions arise. When the signals were not acknowledged by *Calpe*, why were they not sent again or some efforts made to pass the information to the Force Commanders by some other channel? This information was vital and greater efforts should have been made to ensure its delivery. Secondly, why were the signals not repeated to the commanders on SGB 5, which was clearly not on a direct signals link with the Dover station but to whom this information was, if anything, even more vital? Communications problems plagued Allied operations throughout the Second World War but few steps were ever taken to allow for the possibility – even probability – that the messages were not getting through. Once again, one sees signs of complacency or inexperience among the Force Commanders and the effects of this particular example were to be far-reaching.

The outcome of this communications failure was that No. 3 Commando, blissfully unaware of the enemy convoy, sailed on through the night until 0347hrs, when a sudden burst of starshell bathed them in light and revealed their craft to the German convoy escorts. The surprise seems to have been mutual but the Germans were the first to react and one of their escorts, a submarine chaser, UJ 1404, opened a heavy and accurate fire on SGB 5.

Charles Hustwick was a Special Service Brigade signaller attached to No. 3 Commando, and embarked in a Eureka for the JUBILEE operation:[1]

> The night before the raid we were shown a model of the area to be attacked. It all looked rather grim, with high cliffs and minefields to negotiate before getting to the objective. Training started with everything to be done at speed; a great deal of running was involved. We boarded Eureka landing craft with fast engines and

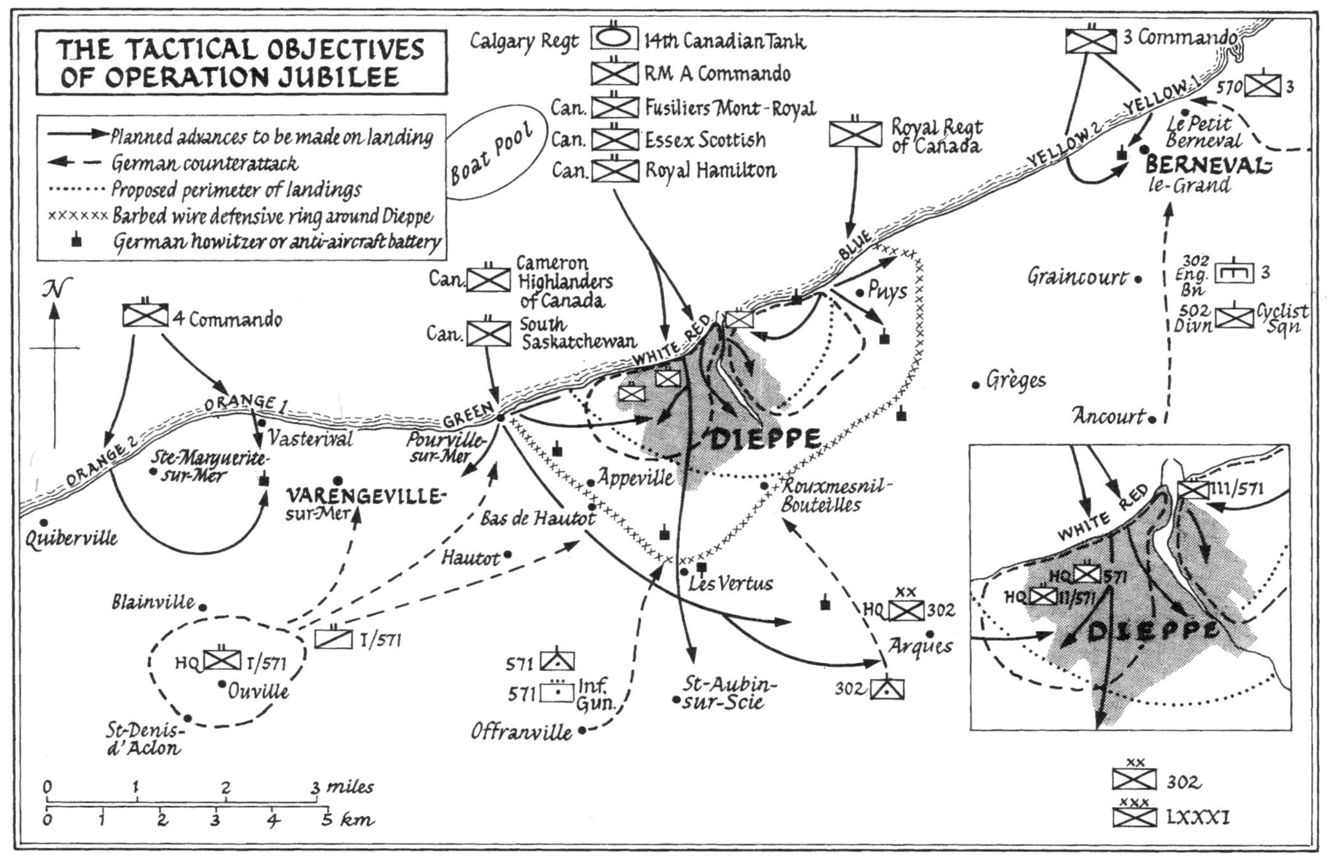
THE TACTICAL OBJECTIVES
OF OPERATION JUBILEE
Planned advances to be made on landing
German counterattack
Proposed perimeter of landings
Barbed wire defensive ring around Dieppe
German howitzer or anti-aircraft battery
Boat Pool
Calgary Regt
14th Canadian Tank
RM A Commando
Can. Fusiliers Mont-Royal
Can. Essex Scottish
Can. Royal Hamilton
Royal Regt of Canada
3 Commando
570 3
YELLOW 1
YELLOW 2
Le Petit Berneval
BERNEVAL-le-Grand
Can. Cameron Highlanders of Canada
Can. South Saskatchewan
4 Commando
N
ORANGE 1
ORANGE 2
GREEN
WHITE
RED
BLUE
Puys
DIEPPE
Graincourt
302 Eng. Bn
3
502 Divn
Cyclist Sqn
Grèges
Ancourt
Vasterival
Ste-Marguerite-sur-Mer
VARENGEVILLE-sur-Mer
Quiberville
Pourville-sur-Mer
Appeville
Bas de Hautot
Hautot
Rouxmesnil-Bouteilles
Les Vertus
Blainville
I/571
HQ I/571
Ouville
St-Denis-d'Aclon
571
571 Inf. Gun.
Offranville
St-Aubin-sur-Scie
HQ 302
Arques
302
III/571
HQ 571
HQ II/571
302
LXXXI
0 1 2 3 miles
0 1 2 3 4 5 km

additional fuel drums strapped to their top-sides. I don't think there were more than twelve chaps in our boat, so there was plenty of room, and the passage through the Channel minefield, which had been cleared by the Navy, was uneventful until nearing the French coast. Then a star-shell went up and there we were, bathed in glorious light.

My Number Two, Signalman H.H. Lewis and I were actually having a pee over the side when this happened and all hell then let loose. We had been caught by enemy armed trawlers who were escorting a convoy into Dieppe and they opened a heavy fire upon us. However, our flotilla was now dispersed over a wide area, smoke and the smell of cordite was everywhere, and a heavy curtain of fire was coming from the shore where the enemy had been alerted. We were sitting ducks and fanned out in all directions, taking cover in the darkness until the firing died down.

After some argument between our Adjutant and the coxswain of our boat, we made our way back to the Steam Gunboat which was supposed to be protecting us. A grim spectacle she was, full of holes like a colander. The bridge had been destroyed, the steering gone and only one gun was still firing. We were hoisted aboard and the Adjutant and the CO of No. 3 Commando, Lieutenant-Colonel Durnford-Slater, got into our landing craft to try and find the HQ ship, HMS *Calpe*, with the overall Commanders aboard.

I was a signaller so I knew that we had no means of letting the powers that be know what a disaster our effort had been. There was no wireless communication as the radio on board the gunboat had been destroyed, and with no steering to speak of the gunboat was going around in circles.

The Germans' success in knocking out SGB 5's radios was their most useful achievement. After a few minutes SGB 5 was stopped in the water, steam belching from a score of shattered pipes, her wireless aerials down and some 40 per cent of her crew casualties. Even so, SGB 5 could still fight, so while the Eurekas scattered and the Landing Craft Flak hastened up to join in the fray, SGB 5's gunners quickly opened fire on the German warships starkly illuminated on the surface of the sea.

One German vessel, UJ 1441, was quickly riddled with shellfire and also had her radio antenna shot away; another, a minesweeper No. 4014, received a shell on the bridge wheelhouse, which killed or wounded several of the crew, and the UJ 1404, the ship that first engaged the British convoy, was raked by the guns of LCF No. 1, set on fire and blown up with all hands. It was soon apparent that the German escort captains had bitten off more than they could chew, and they made haste to break off the action and disappear into the night after their departing charges.

The damage, however, had been done. Chaos now reigned among the Eurekas, which had been taken completely by surprise and had therefore scattered to seek safety in the darkness. Several had been abandoned during this brief, fierce engagement; one Eureka, the naval coxswain and his two-man crew having been killed, was steered all the way back to England by a 3 Commando NCO, Sergeant Clive Collins, using a hand-held prismatic compass; Collins brought his Eureka safely into Newhaven six hours later.

The problem facing Durnford-Slater was this: he had no communications with the Force Commanders and no means of rounding up the scattered craft containing his unit; SGB 5 was stopped and dead in the water. Granted, half a dozen Eurekas, containing about 150 men, had returned to the stricken mother ship and were bobbing about nearby, but this was hardly enough to carry out the Commandos' task.

This sudden eruption of fire out at sea seems to have caused little concern to either the rest of the landing force or the Germans. The latter were well used to flare-ups at sea and seemingly assumed that this was just such an action, while the two escorts, HMSs *Brocklesby* and *Slazak*, assumed the firing was from shore batteries and continued their patrol, guarding the northern flank of the assault fleet. Only the men in the Yellow Beach craft fully realised how badly their plan to attack the German battery at Berneval had been compromised.

The first requirement was to assess the extent of the damage and see what force remained. Commander Wyburd quickly ascertained that of the nineteen Eurekas which had been travelling in SGB 5's wake half an hour before, only five were now present; those missing had not been sunk, but those not abandoned were widely scattered and failed to rejoin. This being so, and with the precious hours of darkness slipping away, Wyburd and Durnford-Slater had to face the fact that their landing at Berneval would have to be abandoned.

Their next task was to convey that decision to the Force Commanders on *Calpe* and advise them that the Goebbels battery would probably be in action against the assault fleet as soon as it grew light and bear down particularly on the craft taking the Royal Regiment of Canada into Blue Beach at Puys. Having no wireless, the two officers trans-shipped into a Eureka and set off to find Roberts, unaware that further away on that dark sea, steps to continue the Yellow Beach landings and attack the Goebbels battery were still in hand.

The man chiefly responsible for getting the Yellow Beach operation back on track was Lieutenant Alexander Fear of the motor gunboat ML 346. Having taken part in the action against the German escorts, ML 346 had moved away from the circle of burning ships and set about rounding up any Eureka that had fled the action. Five were eventually found – containing a total of 106 very willing men, including six US Rangers – and these followed Lieutenant Fear towards his particular objective, Yellow Beach 1, east of Berneval.

Nor was this all. Also out there, still heading for the enemy coast, was a solitary Eureka (LCP 15) commanded by a young naval sub-lieutenant, Henry Buckee. This craft contained eighteen men of No. 3 Commando

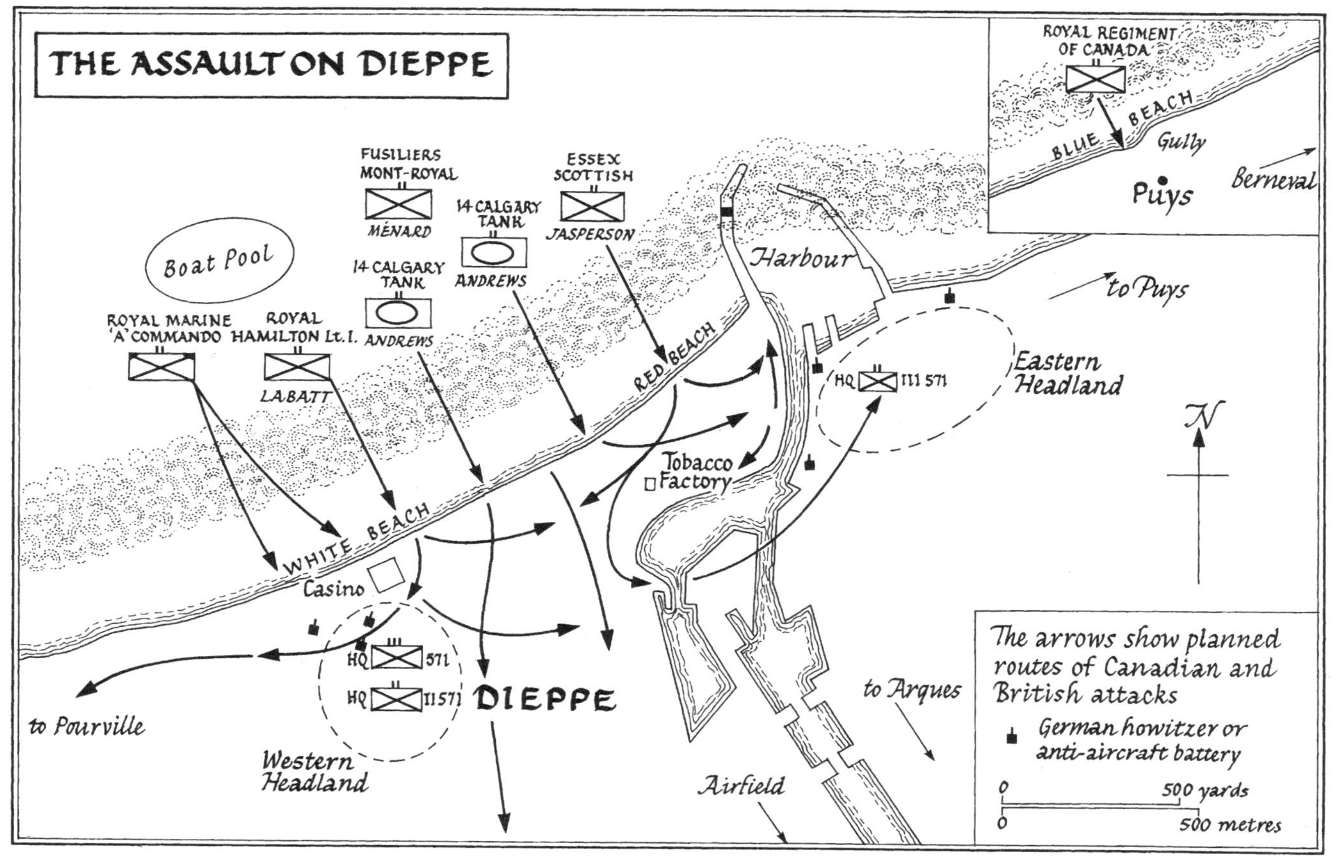
THE ASSAULT ON DIEPPE
Boat Pool
ROYAL MARINE 'A' COMMANDO
ROYAL HAMILTON Lt. I.
LABATT
FUSILIERS MONT-ROYAL
MÉNARD
14 CALGARY TANK
ANDREWS
14 CALGARY TANK
ANDREWS
ESSEX SCOTTISH
JASPERSON
WHITE BEACH
RED BEACH
Casino
Tobacco Factory
Harbour
HQ
III 571
Eastern Headland
to Puys
ROYAL REGIMENT OF CANADA
BLUE BEACH
Gully
Puys
Berneval
HQ
571
HQ
II 571
DIEPPE
to Pourville
Western Headland
Airfield
to Arques
The arrows show planned routes of Canadian and British attacks
German howitzer or anti-aircraft battery
0
500 yards
0
500 metres

commanded by Major Peter Young, a veteran of the Guernsey, Lofoten and Vaagsø raids. LCP 15 had already had its full share of excitement that night; Buckee had been in position directly astern of SGB 5 when the action started and it took some violent evasive action to get his Eureka clear of the stricken gunboat and away into the safety of the darkness.

That done, Buckee and Young conferred and found themselves in full agreement. It was now just starting to get light, at least enough to reveal the line of the French coast, and indicating a point on the coast as the probable site of Yellow Beach 2 west of Berneval, Buckee declared that his orders, 'were to land his troops even if there is only one boat left'. Major Young was, if anything, even more determined. 'My orders,' he said, 'are to land even if we have to swim.' This proved unnecessary; Commando soldiers always appreciate a dry landing and at 0445hrs, five minutes ahead of schedule, Buckee put Young and his men ashore, dry shod, on Yellow Beach 2, where Buckee offered to moor his craft offshore and join Young's force for the attack, an offer Young gratefully declined.

What Peter Young was proposing to do here has to be appreciated. As far as he knew, the eighteen men he had with him were the effective strength of No. 3 Commando; where the rest of the unit was he did not know. Several hundred men were supposed to carry out this attack on the Goebbels battery but since they had vanished, Young proposed to land, go to the battery and see what he could do with a section of eighteen men; that his men would inevitably be outnumbered many times over did not feature in his calculations:

> No, I can't say I was bothered about it. I did not know what we could do but there was the coast and I thought we should go ashore and see what the score was . . . all the chaps seemed keen to have a go, so we went ahead and like a lot of seemingly-desperate ventures, it came off . . . probably just luck but then I have always been lucky . . . I got through the war without a scratch, you know.[2]

While Buckee and his sailors prepared to wait offshore, Young duly mustered his men for the assault on the Goebbels battery. His total of eighteen men included two officers, Captain John Selwyn and Lieutenant Buck Ruxton. This small platoon possessed a range of weaponry which included a Bren gun, six Tommy guns, assorted rifles and pistols and two mortars, one 3in and one 2in. This seemed barely adequate to subdue the gunners and garrison of the German battery, but the first problem was to get off the Berneval beach, up a narrow, muddy, chalk gully, choked with wire and probably mined; fortunately, the enemy were not about.

Getting off the beach and up the cliff took about half an hour, clawing their way up on the pegs and stakes the Germans had used to secure the wire to the chalk, avoiding the path for fear of mines. Once at the top and having caught their breath, Young's force was reorganised into three parties, each under an officer, and they set off at the trot towards Berneval guided by the sound of firing from the massive 170mm guns of the Goebbels battery, which had just opened fire on the offshore shipping. By now they also knew that they might not be alone, for from the top of the cliffs they had seen another group of Eurekas closing the coast to the west – Lieutenant Fear's small flotilla heading for Yellow Beach 1.

This was a desperate venture and Young later admitted that at this stage of the proceedings some of his men were less than keen on this attack:[3]

> My experience is that if you set an example and carry on as if you know exactly what you are doing, the buggers will follow you perhaps only out of curiosity or the innocence of their hearts. At Dieppe I remember telling them that two bricks or nine feet of standing corn would stop a bullet; this was probably complete nonsense but it cheered them up at the time and we pressed on to the target, up the road and at the double. They quickly perked up – they were a very good bunch.

The road to the battery led through Berneval village and here the party came under fire from a machine-gun sited further up the road, forcing them to take cover in the churchyard. They entered the church in the hope of firing on the German position from the tower, but this proved impossible, as there were no stairs or any other means of climbing the tower. This being so, Young led his men into the cornfields surrounding the battery, from where they brought the Germans serving the guns under effective fire from the Bren, rifles and tommy guns and, until they ran out of bombs, the 2in mortar.

Young and his men kept up this distracting, harassing fire on the German battery for the next hour and a half; their fire proved so galling to the enemy that eventually the Germans manhandled one of the great guns round and fired a dozen rounds at their tormentors. This action delighted Major Young:

> We were far too close to them so they could not depress the gun sufficiently to hit us – or anyone within a mile of us – but while they were firing at us they were not firing at the offshore shipping. They must have fired half a dozen shells into the countryside before they realized they were wasting their time and gave up. So we had no problems at all until we began to run out of ammunition.

It was full daylight and well after 0700hrs when Peter Young decided to break off the action and pull out, sending Captain Selwyn back to the beach to contact Lieutenant Buckee and call in the landing craft. Buckee was still waiting patiently offshore and at 0745 the evacuation began. This was none too soon, for German infantry had arrived at the battery and were attempting to outflank the Commandos lurking in the cornfields. Stopping to fire at the enemy and keep him back, the Commandos withdrew without undue difficulty until they got to the cliff top, when German marksmen began to fire on the descending men and Buckee's single landing craft, now closing the beach. Fire from Lieutenant Fear's gunboat, ML 346, forced the Germans back from the cliff edge and the embarkation continued with only one man wounded.

This is not to say that the re-embarkation was easy. The tide had gone out and when the men entered Buckee's craft, their extra weight drove it firmly aground. Weapons were thrown overboard in an attempt to lighten the load but in the end Major Young, Lieutenant Ruxton and a Bren gunner were obliged to get off; thus lightened, Buckee got his craft free and pulled it off the beach using a kedge anchor over the stern. He then headed out to sea, pulling Young and the other two behind on ropes until they were in deep water – this part of the withdrawal was under heavy rifle fire from the cliff top, fire which wounded one of the landing-craft crew. Once out at sea, Young and his men transferred to ML 346 for the run back to Newhaven and disembarked there at 1045hrs, Major Young 'pleasantly tight after dining on coffee, whisky and rum'.

'I was lucky enough to see a lot of action during the war,' said Peter Young later, 'but I think the best operation of all was the Dieppe Raid – I took eighteen men ashore, did the job and brought eighteen men back . . . you can't do better than that.' For their actions at Berneval Major Young and Lieutenant Buckee were later awarded the DSO.

Meanwhile, what of the men in the five landing craft heading for Yellow Beach 1? Lieutenant Fear had led them to the coast but it took time to get there, and by the time they closed Yellow Beach 1 at around 0530hrs it was broad daylight and, according to one account, German soldiers standing on the cliffs were watching the landing craft come ashore. The number of defenders hereabouts was not large and consisted of a ten-man section armed with rifles and automatic weapons, some Luftwaffe personnel from the radar station at Berneval and a machine-gun detachment from the Goebbels battery. Nor was the beach a problem: with the tide well in, the landing party had little open ground to cover before reaching the shelter of the cliffs, there were no mines and if the only way off the beach was choked with wire, at least the gully was not covered by fire and the wire could be cut, albeit slowly.

The landing craft still came under fire as they closed the beach and two naval crewmen were killed before the craft grounded, the men streaming across the rocks and sand to huddle under the shelter of the cliffs, out of sight of the Germans above, who were by now under machine-gun fire from ML 346. This firefight between the ML and the Germans went on for about half an hour while the Commandos cut a path through the wire and made their way up the gully. This task was made difficult by a German machine-gun, which sprayed bullets down the gully until it was put out of action by a well-directed grenade flung by Corporal Hall.

Meantime, there were further diversions on the beach. About half an hour after the first Eurekas landed another one made its way in, bringing another twenty-five men to the muster. Shortly after that a larger ship came drifting in; this turned out to be the 200-ton German coaster *Franz*, a survivor of the offshore battle. The *Franz* was promptly engaged by ML 346, set on fire and driven ashore; shortly after that, the gully having been cleared, the Commandos were able to reach the top of the cliff and prepare for their assault on the Goebbels battery.

The best estimate of this party's strength at this time amounts to 120 British Commandos and six United States Rangers, the latter commanded by Lieutenant Edwin Loustalot. Leaving a naval detachment on the beach, this force, commanded by Captain Geoff Osmond of No. 3 Commando, swept through the hamlet of Le Petit Berneval, wiping out a machine-gun post and killing several of the Luftwaffe men. Osmond knew exactly where he was and had a clear route to the battery, which, freed from Peter Young's attention, was now engaging the offshore shipping; if these men of 3 Commando could bring these guns under fire yet again, the effects on the assault fleet would be very beneficial.

Unfortunately, the Germans were now fully alert and well aware that

British Commandos were landing along the coast. A strong detachment of around battalion strength had already been despatched from Dieppe under the command of a Major Blücher with orders to engage the Commandos at Berneval and drive them into the sea. Major Blücher's force headed for the Goebbels battery and when the Commandos arrived they met with a stiff resistance and repeated flanking attacks.

'It was a complete shambles,' records Sergeant Wally Dungate. 'We did the best we could with what we had but we were not up to strength and half our gear had been lost. As a result we had not moved very far when the Germans attacked.'[4]

With German numbers increasing and resistance stiffening, it was clear that this detachment of No. 3 Commando was not going to achieve very much and should withdraw as quickly as possible. It was some time after 0700hrs and the Commandos were pulling back to Yellow Beach 1 while a series of Verys lights signalled the withdrawal to the Eurekas waiting offshore. The landing craft duly came in, only to be greeted with an accurate and heavy hail of mortar and machine-gun fire from the cliff top, which the guns of ML 346 were unable to quell. Forcing their way in and beaching, the craft were then bombarded with 'potato-masher' hand-grenades hurled down from the cliff top.

Even worse for the landing-craft crews was the fact that, apart from the Naval Party, the beach was empty. The withdrawal signal had been made too soon and while they were waiting for the Commandos to arrive these craft suffered a considerable amount of damage. The Naval Party embarked on LCP No. 157, which promptly ran aground on the rocks. When LCP No. 1 went in to help pull it off, it too ran aground; with the tide ebbing fast both craft were now firmly stuck a few hundred yards offshore, fully exposed to enemy fire from the cliff top. Unable to float off, crews and passengers were rescued by another LCP, No. 85. No. 157 was abandoned while LCP No. 1 managed to drag itself off the rocks and returned to the scanty shelter of the beach. There they waited for another half-hour, under attack from grenades, machine-gun and rifle fire, but no Commandos arrived back on Yellow Beach 1.

Shortly before 0800hrs, the officer in charge of the LCPs, Lieutenant Dennis Stephens, having lost another landing craft, No. 42, whose entire crew had been killed by fire from the cliffs, decided that the Commandos were not going to return and that his best course of action was to save what was left of his small flotilla and withdraw out to sea. Leaving No. 42 abandoned on the beach, No. 157 blazing and No. 81 sinking, Lieutenant Stephens withdrew, having lost half his craft in the last hour while waiting to withdraw the troops.

In fact, though Stephens could not know this, the men of No. 3 Commando were still in action and still attempting to withdraw, challenged now by a large cycle detachment of German troops from Dieppe who had managed to enfilade the path leading down the gully from the cliff top to the beach with machine-gun fire. The only way to reach the beach was by making a mad dash over open ground to the shelter of the gully. A number of men were killed attempting this dash, among them the US Ranger officer, Lieutenant Edwin Loustalot, who thereby became the first US officer killed in action in the European theatre.

Those who got down to the beach faced a great disappointment: only beached, derelict or burning craft awaited them, and still the rifle fire and stick grenades came down from up above. Various means were tried in an attempt to attract attention and recall the landing craft; a Union Jack flag was pinned to the chalk cliff with bayonets in the hope it would be spotted by some offshore craft. One or two men stripped off and volunteered to swim out and try to contact any landing craft waiting offshore; another man swam out and boarded the abandoned LCP No. 42, but found it in a sinking condition, riddled with machine-gun fire.

There was no way off the beach and that fact gradually dawned on the survivors. Captain Osmond, who had been wounded seven times, including one hit which shattered his right arm, decided there was no

YELLOW BEACH 1 AND 2

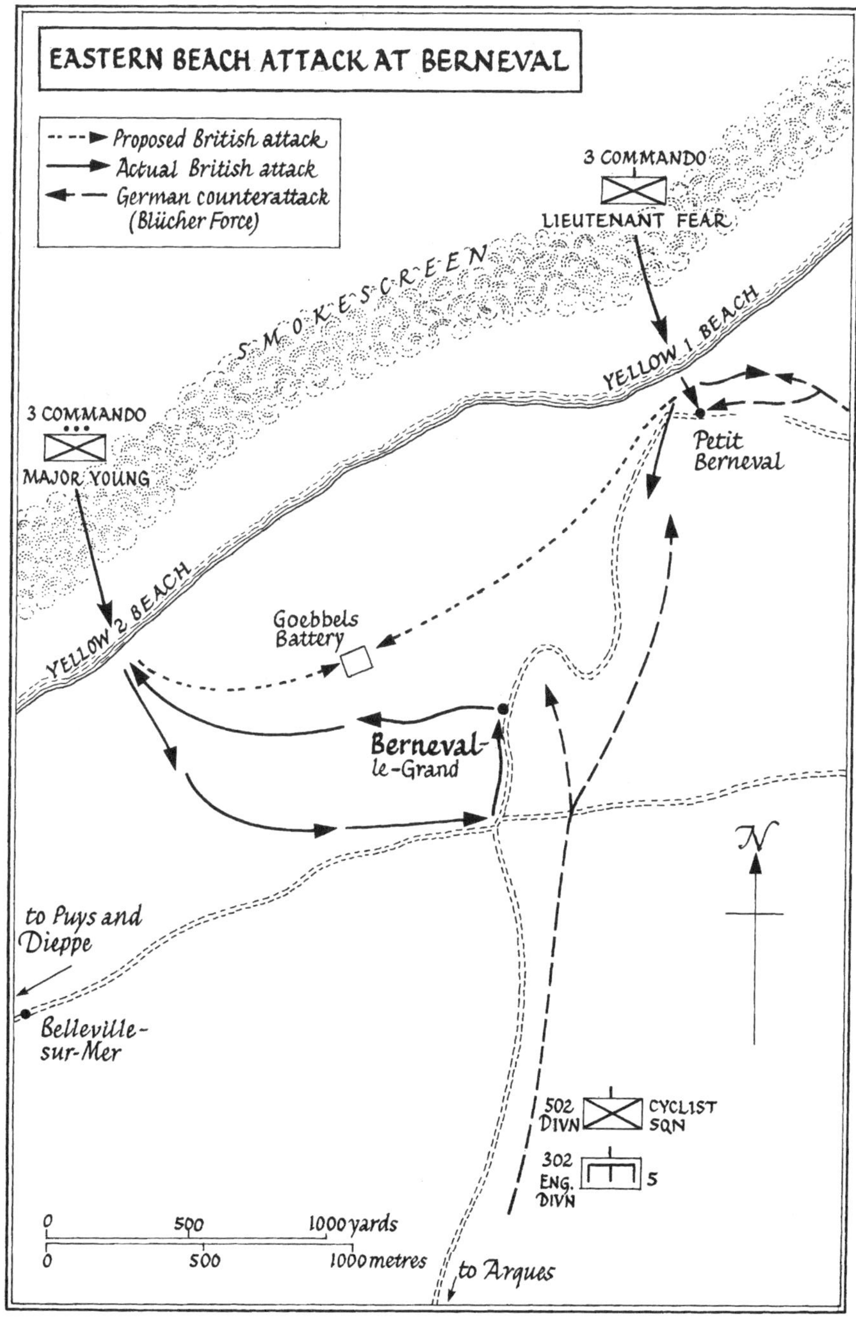

option but surrender and ordered his men to lay down their arms.

Getting this order out proved difficult. Some Commandos were still on the cliff top; others had taken shelter in caves, and everywhere, where they had ammunition, the Commandos continued to fight until, with German troops now swarming everywhere, further resistance was clearly pointless. By 1030hrs all resistance at Berneval was at an end and the survivors from Yellow Beach 1 passed into three years of captivity.

Charles Hustwick, the Brigade signaller and one of those who got back to England, recalls the end of this operation:

> After bobbing about in full daylight off SGB 5, we were eventually taken on board an RAF rescue launch and, after picking up a fighter pilot from the water, we arrived back at Newhaven around 13.30 hrs on the 19th. I don't really know what the survival figures of 3 Commando were but at breakfast the following morning there were treble helpings for all.[5]

Losses in No. 3 Commando had been severe, mostly among those who landed on Yellow Beach 1, and most of those casualties had been incurred during the withdrawal. The total casualty figure, killed, wounded and missing, came to 140 men – about one-third of the unit. Of the 126 men who landed on Yellow Beach 1, 37 were killed and 82 were taken prisoner, many of them wounded. Only one man got back from Yellow Beach 1, a corporal who swam out to sea and was picked up by a passing ML. Of the twenty-three landing craft that set out from Newhaven carrying No. 3 Commando, only four returned undamaged.

As for Colonel Durnford-Slater and Commander Wyburd, they finally reached HMS *Calpe* at around 0700hrs. Durnford-Slater was quite unaware that many of his men had actually got ashore and that Peter Young's party had done a great deal to keep the Goebbels battery from engaging the assault fleet; indeed, Durnford-Slater did not know what his men had been doing that day until he returned to Newhaven that night. Even had he known this cheering news, it is not likely that the information would have lightened the mood among the Force Commanders on *Calpe* which was, said Durnford-Slater, 'one of the deepest depression'.

No. 3 Commando did very well at Dieppe, displaying a resilience and aggression typical of the very best Commando soldiers. The outstanding element in their conduct was a dogged refusal to accept defeat and a determination to press on with the task. When their convoy was disrupted and their force much reduced, they still had officers and men willing and eager to get on with the job and carry the war to the enemy. One can only wonder at what this fine unit would have achieved had it got ashore intact. To their achievement can be added the tenacity and devotion to duty of their landing-craft crews, the men on the LCP Eurekas, most notably Lieutenants Fear, Buckee and Stephens, who stayed offshore, often under fire, and did all they could both to support the landing parties and to bring them off afterwards.

We can now leave the remnants of No. 3 Commando, some sailing back to England, others trudging into captivity, and go to the other end of the landing area where the second Army Commando unit, Lord Lovat's No. 4 Commando, is assaulting the western battery.

ORANGE BEACH 1 AND 2

VARENGEVILLE

At the other end of the battle, on the extreme western flank, the Commando intervention had gone completely right.

BERNARD FERGUSSON,
THE WATERY MAZE, P. 176

WHILE PETER YOUNG and the men of No. 3 Commando were engaged with the battery at Berneval, twelve miles away to the west, on the far side of Dieppe, No. 4 Commando, just 250 strong and commanded by Lieutenant-Colonel Lord Lovat, were about to mount a similar attack against the six-gun coastal battery, codenamed Hess, at Varengeville.

This action against the Varengeville battery, the one part of the Dieppe operation that went 'completely right', repays close and particular study. This will reveal that experience, careful planning and a close attention to the problems inherent in the task are the prime ingredients of success. Lovat concentrated his mind on the problems of reaching, attacking and withdrawing from the battery. All this paid off, but he also cleared his path towards the creation of a viable plan from the moment he arrived at Combined Operations. The Commando plan evolved in a very different fashion from the overall JUBILEE plan and deserves separate consideration.

Colonel Lovat's involvement with JUBILEE began shortly after the cancellation of RUTTER, when an urgent signal summoning him and John Durnford-Slater to London arrived at the Commando training grounds in Scotland. Lovat's account of this visit to COHQ is full of illuminating details and it is clear that the Scots Commando colonel was not impressed. Lovat records his initial impression of the Richmond Terrace offices as:

> . . . a beehive, swarming with red-tabbed officers, filled with every branch of the Services, some of the powder-puff variety, who looked elegant in silk stockings. There was said to be a fair proportion of drones among the inmates. Signing a pass allowed the visitor, having stated his business, to sit around talking to pretty WRENS, or out on the terrace when it wasn't raining. As a port of call, Combined Ops was not favoured by the serving officer.[1]

Lovat and Durnford-Slater made their way to the office of Major-General Charles Heydon, Mountbatten's Chief of Staff, where they were briefed on the Commando phase of the upcoming operation but not on the actual destination. They were to destroy two coastal batteries before the main landing took place and on leaving Heydon's office would be provided with intelligence information, air photographs and models of both target areas, but no maps. They would also be given a general appreciation, the general intention and the method by which the operation would be carried out. They were to study all this, then go away and think about the problem before returning with a plan.

This briefing is interesting, for from it one gathers that COHQ *had* done an appreciation of the situation, or at least of those targets chosen for Nos. 3 and 4 Commandos. This is not in itself surprising for, as related, preparing an appreciation is normal military procedure, even when the targets have been selected and cannot be changed. It merely adds to the wonder that something similar was not done, or so it appears, for the main Canadian landings.

The Commando colonels duly went off to review the available information and left COHQ having obtained two useful concessions: first, they would each evolve their own plan and, second, they would land before daylight, whatever the main landing force did. Before leaving, the colonels met General Heydon again and disconcerted the Chief of Staff considerably by telling him that they had already worked out that the target of JUBILEE was Dieppe, mainly because the name 'Dieppe' was written on the back of the air photos supplied as part of the intelligence, a slip of which the Chief of Staff was apparently unaware.

A few days later, having presented his plan for the attack on the Hess battery – codenamed Operation CAULDRON – to Heydon, Lovat rejoined his Commando at Weymouth where the unit was put through a long series of landing exercises and rehearsals at Lulworth Cove, operating from LCAs launched from the transport *Princess Astrid* and using an accurate model provided by the RAF for briefings.

Here again, there is some cause for wonderment. Heydon had in his office two of the most experienced amphibious soldiers in Britain, which at that time meant the world. Why were they not invited to look over the JUBILEE plan, if only to see if they could spot any snags? The security risks were minimal and their advice could have been invaluable, but it was neither requested nor, apparently, offered.

From all this it appears that the Commandos at least were very well briefed and supplied with both air photographs and models of their objective, giving them accurate information on the enemy positions they would have to overcome.

> We knew the range and distance to be covered to every target and learnt every fold and feature set out on the ground. The demolition squad could blow gun breeches in their sleep. Wireless communications were tested and counter-tested. Every weapon was fired over measured marks; Bren gunners, Tommy gunners and riflemen blazed away on short range practices. The 2in mortar men became so accurate they could drop 18 out of 20 shots in a 25ft square at 200yd.[2]

'Our success at Dieppe was largely due to the training we did beforehand,' says James Dunning, then Sergeant-Major of 'C' Troop. 'My Troop was to go in under the unit second-in-command, Major Derek Mills-Roberts. "Mills Bomb", as we called him, was a very good, quite fearsome officer; some of the men were far more afraid of him than they were of the Germans.'[3]

Clearly, No. 4 Commando, already trained to a hair, then underwent yet another intensive training programme, specifically geared to the task they would face in France and based on the intelligence information they had received from COHQ. It is therefore hard to believe that the men of the 2nd Canadian Division were any less well informed about the opposition they would face when they went ashore, not least about the extent of the German defences. However, knowing about a problem is one thing; acting on that knowledge is something else again.

A further sign of operational experience is demonstrated by the fact that No. 4 Commando also practised the tricky matter of the final withdrawal:

> First as a drill, then with stretcher cases, then in the face of fierce opposition and finally under cover of smoke. All officers and NCOs inspected the layout to the coastal defence systems. The men were splendid and I was well pleased.[4]

Maps of the ground finally arrived on 16 August and the Commando duly left Weymouth for Southampton where they would join the *Prince Albert* transport for the crossing. At Southampton they were seen off by Lord Mountbatten in person; the full strength of the unit was just 252 officers and men, including five soldiers from the US 1st Ranger Battalion.

Like Durnford-Slater, Lovat had split his assault force into two sub-units. The first of these, under Major Derek Mills-Roberts, would land on Orange Beach 1, below the Pointe d'Ailly lighthouse, climb a narrow gully and advance past the western edge of Varengeville to within a few hundred yards of the battery; from there they would give covering fire on the battery during the main assault. The second group, commanded by Lovat himself, would land a little further west, on Orange Beach 2 near Quiberville, and advance inland, first up the valley of the River Saâne before turning east to assault the battery from the south. This point should be noted: by selecting two landing points, Lovat gave his plan flexibility, for if anything went wrong at one of them, he could switch his forces to the second or entrust the attack to the balance of his force.

The timings for this operation were very precise. Mills-Roberts's force was to engage the battery at 0615hrs and keep the defenders' attention fully occupied while Lovat's force moved into position. At 0627hrs, Spitfires would strafe the Hess position with cannon fire and at 0630hrs Lovat would put up three Verys flares and his group would assault the battery from the rear, covered by a smokescreen laid by Mills-Roberts. If all went well, a confused enemy should put up little organised resistance.

The Hess battery, manned by the 813th Army Artillery Troop, lay on the southern edge of Varengeville, about a kilometre from the beach, and consisted of six 150mm guns embedded in gun-pits 25ft in diameter and some 6ft deep. These heavy gun batteries were part of a long series of defensive works currently under construction as part of Hitler's Atlantic Wall, a complex of guns, minefields, barbed wire, beach obstacles and infantry which, Hitler hoped, would deter and perhaps defeat that invasion of France which was now inevitable following the US entry into the war in December 1941.

The typical heavy-gun battery – the intention was to establish over two hundred of them down the western coast of Occupied Europe – had a range of eleven miles and a high rate of fire, quite enough to make the task of disembarking troops offshore risky if not impossible for any invasion fleet. This work had only recently begun with the building of battery positions around the major ports in the Pas de Calais, but at Dieppe the defences were clearly well in hand, with the heavy-gun batteries in position and many of the infantry pillboxes and trenches established.

Two years later the heavy-gun batteries in Normandy, at Merville, on the Pointe de Hoc and at Longues, would pose a problem for the D-Day planner and, as at Varengeville, had to be taken out by *coup de main*, at Merville by the men of the 9th Battalion, the Parachute Regiment, the Pointe de Hoc battery by the US Rangers and the Longues battery by the accurate fire of the cruiser HMS *Ajax*. Such assets were not available at

Dieppe, where the Hess battery at Varengeville was taken with the bayonet and grenades.

The Hess battery was protected by infantry, machine-guns, mortars and barbed wire. The garrison, including the gunners and their infantry support, numbered at full strength something in excess of two hundred men. All were contained within a belt of mines, concrete defences, a pair of anti-aircraft cannon mounted on a tall flak tower to give covering fire, and a complex series of trenches. A further German detachment, numbering seventy-seven men, was stationed at the Pointe d'Ailly lighthouse. The Germans had had two years to work on the Hess defences and they had made a thorough job of it.

No one got much sleep on the *Prince Albert* that night; Mills-Roberts records eating breakfast at 0115hrs, and the men, fully armed and equipped, faces blackened with camouflage cream, were ready to embark in their LCAs by 0200hrs. One hour later, as their landing craft prepared to move towards the coast, the JUBILEE force passed the point of no return; if nothing went wrong, and no signal to abort the operation had been received before 0300hrs on 19 August, the troops would go ashore, no matter what happened thereafter.

The Commandos boarded their seven landing craft seven miles from the shore. They were then organised into two columns, one for each beach, and led towards the coast by the landing officer, Lieutenant-Commander Hugh Mulleneux, in a motor gunboat, MGB 312, shepherded from astern by SGB 9 commanded by Lieutenant Peter Scott, son of the famous British explorer known as 'Scott of the Antarctic' and later a famous naturalist. The task of these small ships was to escort the landing craft ashore and provide any necessary close-fire support during the landing phase. They would then shepherd the LCAs back to the offshore boat pool, out of range of the coastal guns, where these craft would wait until the time came to re-embark the troops after the attack.

The approach was easy, largely thanks to the fact that the Pointe d'Ailly lighthouse was still flashing, common practice when German convoys were anticipated at Dieppe. However, the approach of the craft was not without incident: shortly after the two columns divided for the final approach to the shore, Lovat's craft had to make a sudden shift to starboard to avoid three darkened German ships, heading east up the coast from Dieppe.

'We didn't see any of that,' says Sergeant-Major Dunning. 'It only affected the other group, but we did see the fires and flares to our left where No. 3 Commando had run into a coastal convoy. Otherwise it all went as planned and we had a dry landing on a shingle beach, right on target, near the two gaps in the cliff.'

Mills-Roberts's party, eighty-eight men in all, landed exactly on time at 0450hrs, just before dawn, and proceeded to examine the two steep exits off the beach. The left-hand gap was judged impassable, being choked with wire, but the right-hand one, though also wired and probably mined, seemed possible if the lower part of the wire was removed with Bangalore torpedoes. Using these meant abandoning any hope of surprise, but time was pressing and the wire was duly blown. After that the Commandos made their way up the gully, keeping carefully to the sides, 'avoiding the path like the plague; it was sure to be mined'.

Fortunately the explosion of the Bangalores failed to arouse any opposition or alert the enemy. Mills-Roberts's party reached the top without delay and set off for the battery position about a kilometre inland, one group pausing to cut the telephone wires linking the battery with the German naval force at the lighthouse. Everything was going very well for Mills-Roberts's group: they were ashore, undetected, en route for their objective and had time in hand; it was now around 0545hrs and Lovat's assault on the battery was not due until 0630hrs. They were also on hand when the enemy reacted to the news that the assault fleet had been sighted offshore and opened fire.

This fact was announced to Mills-Roberts when a great blast of noise came from up ahead as the Hess battery guns fired ranging shots at the shipping; it was now growing light and the assault craft assembling offshore were gradually being revealed to the German battery observers. It was still not 0600hrs and it would be some time before Lovat's assault party could be in position to assault the battery. Mills-Roberts then received a report from the beach that the Dieppe convoy were already in sight of the shore and apparently within range of the Hess battery, which was starting to drop shells among the ships. Six salvoes from the battery had already been fired in rapid succession and the guns were starting to get the range; this firing had to be stopped without delay.

Mills-Roberts therefore decided to attack the battery with the force he had on hand. Forcing their way through the woods, his party made their way to a point overlooking the battery, about a hundred yards from the perimeter wire. Like Peter Young at Berneval, they began to engage the enemy with platoon weapons – rifle, Brens and mortar fire – and had an immediate piece of luck. A 2in-mortar crew, commanded by Sergeant-Major Dunning, dropped a bomb into the centre of the battery – right among a pile of shells and explosives.

'It was a lucky shot,' says James Dunning, 'and we were all pretty surprised at the result, but it certainly helped us beat down their fire.'

The mortar bomb produced 'the father and mother of bangs' and caused a number of casualties, and the battery ceased firing while the gunners attempted to put out the resulting fire, all the while under attack from Mills-Roberts's well-trained snipers and steady bursts of Bren and mortar fire.

The Commandos now came under attack from German mortars and heavy machine-guns. A firefight developed between the two sides which had the effect of keeping the German gunners away from their guns. Then at 0628hrs a burst of white Verys lights from behind the battery told Mills-Roberts that the rest of No. 4 Commando were in position and about to launch their attack. Mills-Roberts's group promptly deluged the battery with smoke and, right on time, a squadron of RAF ground-attack fighters swept over the battery, raking its position with cannon fire. Then Colonel Lovat's group went in with the bayonet.

Lovat's contingent, the larger part of No. 4 Commando, carried in four LCAs, landed on Orange Beach 2 at Quiberville, exactly at H-Hour, coming ashore opposite two pillboxes set at the eastern side of the River Saâne. Their landing was not entirely unopposed; the LCAs were spotted close to the shore, illuminated with starshell and briefly raked with fire from an outpost on the nearby cliffs. Fortunately, the steel sides of the LCAs, unlike the wooden ones of the Eurekas, were impervious to this fire and the unit incurred no casualties on the run-in to the beach. When the troops got ashore, though, the weight of fire grew heavier.

The troops had a dry landing and the two pillboxes were rushed by the first men ashore and put out of action with grenades. Lovat recalls that Orange Beach 2 was 'quite a nasty beach, steep shingle with wire on the top of it'. This barrier looked like turning the beach into a killing ground, where the landing party would be caught between the wire and the water, and the Commandos were anxious to get off it as quickly as possible.

More machine-gun fire was now raking the beach and mortar bombs were falling on the pebbles. This fire killed or wounded about a dozen men, including Captain Gordon Webb of 'B' Troop who, though hit in the shoulder by a mortar fragment, continued to lead his men across the wire. There was no time here to place Bangalores. The wire was crossed by men hurling themselves on it to provide a path for their comrades or by throwing over coconut matting, brought along for just such a purpose. Another half-dozen men were lost in the process but it got No. 4 Commando off the beach quickly and with minimal casualties. The unit regrouped on the far side and set off at the double up the right bank of the Saâne (the sides of a river are decided by the direction of flow), leaving the wounded behind under the care of medical orderlies.

Once on the move, Lovat's group made good progress, running along the bank of the river for about a mile before swerving left into the Blanc-Mesnil le Bas wood, which lay just to the rear of the Hess battery. 'We ran the whole damned way, stopping now and again to regroup, but nobody was out of breath and we had no laggards.' Lovat's men were being drawn on by the sound of mortar explosions and rifle and Bren-gun fire from up ahead, and paused only a moment to fix bayonets before moving forward again.

Their first encounter, deeper in the wood, was with a platoon of enemy soldiers which was forming up for a flank attack on Mills-Roberts's party; these were taken in the rear and quickly disposed of with bursts of Tommy- and Bren-gun fire. That done, snipers went forward to engage the enemy, among them a US Ranger, Corporal Franklin D. Koons, who found a good position in a barn overlooking the battery and picked off several Germans running about in the open. This was the crux of the battle for the Hess battery, with Lovat's men forming an assault line on the edge of the orchard close to the perimeter wire and going in hard when Lovat fired a white Verys flare to start the attack.

The bayonet charge on the guns at Varengeville was a truly desperate venture. Lovat had around 150 men, three 'Fighting Troops', for this attack, of which two, 'F' and 'B', actually charged the gun-pits 'with fixed bayonets, yelling like banshees' – and they had 100 yards of open ground to cover before reaching the battery – which was protected against just such an attack by a thick belt of barbed wire and defended by men backed up with machine-guns and mortars. Mills-Roberts recalled later:

> The assault had gone well; it had not been expected from that quarter. The enemy had been looking to their front and to our fire group facing the battery. Of the two assault troops, the right hand one had been lucky but the left hand troop had met accurate

> machine-gun fire, lost all its officers and been badly knocked about. Captain Porteous took over and led the charge . . .[5]

The garrison, fully alert and aggressive, opened a heavy fire on the assault wave, killing two Troop officers with a single grenade, which wounded several other men. But No. 4 Commando was not to be stopped now. There was nothing scientific about this attack: it was an old-fashioned bayonet charge in which the issue would be settled with close-quarter fighting and cold steel . . . and events became somewhat confused.

A German on the flak tower is shot by a Commando and falls sixty feet to the ground, turning in the air 'like an Indian in a Western picture'. Boston Havocs – some accounts say Spitfires – screaming low over the battery, raking the ground with cannon fire before the advancing troops. Sergeant-Major Bill Stockdale, half his foot blown off, sitting on the ground but still firing his rifle. Men falling or running in all directions, Germans being shot down, shouts and screams on every side, bayonets glinting in the smoke, and always the chatter of machine-gun fire and the crump of mortar fire. In short, chaos.

Amid this chaos one man's actions stand out, those of Captain Pat Porteous of 'F' Troop, the Troop attacking the guns. As the attack went in, Captain Porteous was wounded, a bullet passing through his hand and lodging in his arm. Undeterred, he pressed on, closed with the man who had shot him and bayoneted him. He then led his men on a charge against the nearest gun-pit, where he was hit again, in the leg this time, and knocked to the ground. Captain Porteous got up and, supported by Troop Sergeant-Major Portman, pressed on, killing the crew in one gun-pit before moving on to the next.

The outcome is contained in the citation for Captain Porteous's Victoria Cross: 'though shot through the side he continued to the final objective where he collapsed from lack of blood'. Porteous stayed at the head of his men as they shot and bayoneted their way through the gun position, finally falling into one of the gun-pits.

The final attack on the battery lasted only a few wild minutes. After that the Commandos fanned out to mop up any surviving enemy, search the buildings and destroy the guns; the entire operation, from landing to wiping out the battery garrison, had taken just over two hours. The enemy's guns were blown up by the Commando assault engineers, who placed explosive charges in the breeches and muzzles, the ends of the barrels splitting open 'like bananas'. With this done, the barracks thoroughly looted and all the buildings set on fire, the Commando prepared to withdraw.

The defenders had been quickly overwhelmed by the force and speed of this attack but they had put up a stiff fight; thirty of the garrison had been killed and the same number wounded before the survivors surrendered, and others had been killed or wounded in the surrounding woods. No. 4 Commando lost twelve men killed, twenty-one men wounded and thirteen missing in this classic Commando operation. Most of the wounded recovered and were back with the unit in a matter of months; the wounded men on the beach at Quiberville had to be left to the enemy, who treated them well.

The Commando withdrew to the sea via Mills-Roberts's landing beach at Varengeville, where the unit's 3in mortars were positioned and firing back inland, keeping the now advancing enemy away while the unit embarked. The tide was now ebbing and the men had to wade out to the landing craft, in perfect order, where possible rejoining the craft that had brought them ashore. As for Lovat, he was full of delight at the success of this operation and, as the LCAs pulled away, had his signaller send a triumphant message to Mountbatten: 'Hess battery destroyed, all enemy gun crews finished with the bayonet – is this OK with you?'

In fact, quite a large number of the enemy had managed to escape into the woods and there was a rather less happy ending to the story of No. 4

Commando in the JUBILEE operation. Lovat wanted to report his success personally to the two Force Commanders and transfer his severely wounded men onto the destroyer, so he directed his craft to head for the command ship. However, when they arrived alongside HMS *Calpe* they found boatloads of wounded men on the same errand and the decks of the destroyer already covered with stretchers bearing dead or wounded.

This was Lovat's first intimation that other parts of Operation JUBILEE had not gone as well as his own attack at Varengeville. 'We put seven or eight of our wounded on *Calpe*, which was a mistake,' he wrote later, 'because she was already full of wounded men and very lucky not to be sunk.' This rendezvous would have been sometime after 0900hrs, but the fact that the JUBILEE operation was turning into a disaster had not yet been fully grasped by the Force Commanders.

The No. 4 Commando LCAs circled HMS *Calpe* for about ten minutes, keeping constantly on the move as German fighters and medium bombers were starting to appear off the beaches, bombing and strafing. No further orders came from General Roberts and eventually a staff officer appeared on deck and, calling out to Lovat with a loud hailer, told him that the Commando 'might as well go home'.

The seventy-mile journey back across the Channel was made in LCAs, which arrived in Newhaven at around 1600hrs in the afternoon. The men's excitement subsided as weariness took over and Colonel Lovat's elation at his unit's success was gradually dampened as the realisation dawned that he must spend the next day or two writing sad letters to the relatives of those who had died. Spirits picked up again at Newhaven, where the unit disembarked to cheers from the crowds, excited questions from the press and some muttered advice from Brigadier Robert Laycock that discretion was called for when recounting their success as 'the Canadians have taken losses'.

These cheers for the returning Commandos were well earned: No. 4 Commando had pulled off the only complete success of the Dieppe Raid and one of the best-organised Commando operations of the war, while No. 3 Commando succeeded in denying the enemy guns the chance to concentrate on the offshore shipping for more than two hours at a time when every minute counted.

This success of No. 4 Commando at Varengeville requires some analysis but clearly begins with the initial plan. The Commando colonels declined to be bound into the overall Force Commanders' plan, a refusal which indicates that they must have seen it. They insisted on landing under cover of darkness, having studied the intelligence information and decided on the right tactics for each situation. It is interesting that Lovat made careful preparations to get his men off the beach quickly. His methods – laying out thick coir matting or having some men in leather jerkins trained to throw themselves across the wire and so make a path for their comrades – were quite simple, yet effective in getting the troops off the death-trap of the beach quickly and with the minimum of loss.

Both Commando units elected to land on two beaches rather than one and to split their force for the attack. Commanders generally frown on splitting their force in the presence of the enemy but here it made good sense, providing the attackers with an element of flexibility; if one party got into trouble or some unexpected circumstances arose, the other party could intervene. This division of the force proved of great benefit to both Peter Young and Mills-Roberts, who were able to take a decisive role in the operation when the need arose.

Thorough training and previous experience clearly paid off, not least in the withdrawal phase when the enemy were kept back from the re-embarkation area with 3in-mortar fire from the beach and then by Bren-gun fire from gunners in the LCAs. This is not something that can be arranged when already under fire; the tactics for withdrawal have to be built into the operational plan so that the men involved know what they have to do and are ready to get on and do it without further instruction.

Experience, careful, detailed planning and tough, realistic training all played a great part in the success of No. 4 Commando. The aggression and sheer guts displayed by people like Captain Pat Porteous backed these assets, but courage alone is not enough in battle. The Canadians landing on the other Dieppe beaches about this time also showed a great deal of courage, but that did not stop matters there going disastrously wrong.

BLUE BEACH

PUYS

It would have been difficult to discover anywhere on the coast of Europe a less favourable place for an assault landing.

Regimental History,
The Royal Regiment of Canada

ACCORDING TO THE revised plan for flanking attacks before the main landing, the strategy for the Dieppe landings called for the gradual envelopment of the port and the defenders' positions before any landing took place on the shingle beach fronting the promenade and the town centre. There is nothing inherently wrong with this strategy; had it worked it should have seen a gradual reduction and final elimination of German resistance on the headlands overlooking the central beach. The problem was that this strategy depended on total success attending the flank landings. If those attacks failed, the main landing would be a disaster.

Total success was not achieved on 19 August 1942. The landing of the Royal Regiment at Puys saw an accumulation of errors adding up to a disaster. 'Faulty intelligence, human frailty and a complicated, rigid operational order, all combined to reduce a trained, eager, disciplined battalion to a scattered litter of men.'[1]

This statement is very true, but the mistakes committed at Puys were even more fundamental, not least in the planners' failure to realise the difficulties of getting off the beach and up the single gully that gave access to the cliff top. The success of the Royal Regiment at Puys in either task depended entirely on surprise; that in turn depended on the cover of darkness attending at least the first stages of the landing.

When darkness was lost the Puys landing should have been called off; without it the operation was impossible. As we shall see, the failure to build a cut-off point into the plan underpins many of the disasters that attended the Dieppe Raid. Similarly with the gradual elimination of naval support. A support asset – be it a battleship or a heavy bombing raid or, as at Puys, the cover of darkness – was declared essential, but when that asset was later denied or lost, the raid went on anyway, with grimly predictable results.

At Puys there was a further failure. Having studied the landing beach and brooded over the difficulties, Lieutenant-Colonel Catto, CO of the

Royals, suggested to General Roberts that the cover of darkness asset could be abandoned if it was replaced by a heavy bombardment of the beach and cliff top just prior to the assault. Roberts declined this request, stating that a bombardment was unnecessary, as there appeared to be no barbed wire on the beach and the exits were therefore clear. Catto demurred, stating that his experience on the Western Front in the First World War had shown him that German defensive positions were always heavily wired, and there was no reason to doubt that wire entanglements existed on Blue Beach.

Roberts's response to this statement was the same dusty answer that the General had himself received about the entire operation: if Catto was afraid to lead his men ashore he would be replaced by another commander. This was a stupid answer; Catto was entirely within his rights to point out the possibility of further obstacles confronting his battalion and he was, if anything, underestimating the difficulties.

Fixed defences, like barbed wire and minefields, are not a serious obstacle to well-trained troops; unless they are covered by fire, they can be quickly cleared. It follows that any such obstacles will be covered by fire from machine-guns and mortars, which can be deployed against the sappers clearing these obstacles and the troops held up in front of them. The presence of wire was therefore a good indication that machine-guns and mortars would cover the beach at Puys and need to be reduced by bombing or shellfire. But since no wire was shown on the aerial photographs, Roberts chose to believe that it did not exist. And so, with the assault force already compromised, we can turn to the landing itself.

While the coastal batteries were being eliminated or harassed by the men of Nos. 3 and 4 Commandos, the Canadians were making two flanking assaults east and west of Dieppe. Both went awry, most notably the one in the east, where the Royal Regiment of Canada was tasked with making an assault on the village of Puys (or Puits), a resort hamlet a mile east of Dieppe, between Berneval and the main port. The Royals had to clear Puys and then turn west along the cliffs to overrun German positions on the eastern headland – codenamed 'Bismarck' in the Canadian plan – overlooking the port.

The main task sounds simple, given that the distances were not great and the enemy judged inferior. In fact this task was fraught with difficulty, and the problems the Royal Regiment faced simply added to the men's conviction that they were, in some senses, a 'hard-luck' battalion. They had had more than their share of 'cock-ups' and errors in training, especially on the YUKON 1 exercise when their landing craft got lost and landed them both late and in the wrong place. While waiting in the Yarmouth Roads before the start of RUTTER, the Royals had been on board the landing ship struck by bombs. Had they known what awaited them on Blue Beach, this feeling, that someone 'had it in for them', could only have increased.

It does not require hindsight to say that the landing on Blue Beach never had a chance; the ground was difficult, the enemy alert and the plan inflexible. The margins in terms of time were simply too tight, there was only one way off the beach, which had not been secured by the time the main force came ashore, and it would take only the slightest amount of opposition to stop the battalion in its tracks. Everything had to go absolutely right on Blue Beach for the landing to have any kind of a chance; in the event nothing went right.

The beach at Puys was just the first problem. First of all, it was an obvious place for a landing. It was the only break in the cliffs for miles east of Dieppe and the only point for a flank landing if an attack was made on the main port; the enemy had therefore taken steps to defend it, with four concrete pillboxes containing heavy machine-guns which enfiladed the beach from the east. Then there was the beach itself, only 200 metres long, extremely narrow, and overlooked by high cliffs. From the tide-line to the sea wall was at best only a few hundred yards, fully exposed at low tide to anyone on the cliffs above. The beach at Puys – Blue Beach – was obvious but not easy; if the landing force was opposed, Blue Beach was a death trap.

Moreover, on the day and at the time of landing these existing limitations were compounded by the fact that landing was at high tide, which reduced the width of the beach to a mere 50 yards. The cliffs curve away to the east, exposing the beach below which could be covered by those concrete pillboxes on the cliffs, overlooking the beach and the seaward approaches. Unless the landing force could get off the beach *quickly* this stony strand at Puys was a killing ground. And getting off the beach would not be easy either.

At the back of the beach came a sea wall some 10 feet in height, crowned with a mesh of barbed wire. This wall protected the only exit from the beach, a narrow gully leading to the top of the cliffs, gradually widening as it climbed until it entered the outskirts of Puys. The gully was steep, mined and crammed with wire, and presented the attacker with another tactical problem the plan made no attempt to solve. Such a passage is like a bridge to the open ground above, and the only way to secure it was by attacking both ends at once; otherwise the troops attempting to climb up would be subjected to machine-gun fire and grenades tossed down from above, missiles to which they had no means of replying. To get off the Puys beach, the Royal Regiment needed to secure the gully, but how were they to do this when it could not be outflanked? The anticipated answer was the old one – darkness and surprise – and both were quickly lost.

Essentially, the Royal Regiment were in the position of a rush-hour crowd on a subway platform, attempting to get up the escalator to the street above. As everyone knows, that process always involves a certain amount of pushing and shoving and hanging about, but hanging about gets costly under machine-gun fire. If the Royal Regiment came ashore in a closed-up body, they would inevitably be held up at the sea wall and the gully entrance, fully exposed to fire from the enemy above, who would also engage their boats on the way in. This fire would continue while the wire was cleared, by which time the enemy would be in position at the top of the gully, where one man with a machine-gun could keep them at bay all day.

An assault battalion landing at Puys could only be sure of getting off the beach in good order if some other force had landed first, cleared the gully and held both ends of it. This might have been achieved by landing Commandos or paratroopers in the dark of the previous night, to clear the gully and knock out the pillboxes, but such a move was not contemplated in the plan. It was assumed that surprise alone would be sufficient – if only surprise could be achieved.

In the event, the defenders were on the alert. The defences at Puys were not heavily manned, being occupied by just two platoons of infantry mustering some ninety-four men, but these were equipped with Spandau heavy machine-guns and 81mm mortars, both of which far exceeded the Canadian platoon weapons in weight of fire; the belt-fed Spandau could not be quelled by the fire of the magazine-fed Bren.

Another answer to this dilemma might have been provided by the Canadian battalion's 3in mortars, which, as we shall see, were brought ashore with plenty of ammunition. The snag was that the beach below the cliffs was too narrow to permit the deployment of mortars, which need their barrels canted back at least sixty degrees to be even marginally effective; firing directly up a cliff face only invites the bombs to fall back on the mortar crews below.

The other option, to go out onto the beach so that the mortars could engage some of the enemy with high-explosive bombs or 'smoke out' the fire from the pillboxes, was not available either; first of all the tide was in and the beach under water and, secondly, moving out of cover would expose the three-man crews to machine-gun fire as they worked around the mortars in the open. Besides, the 3in mortar, the only heavy weapon available to the battalion, is an 'area-neutralising' weapon, only useful against troops in the open. A rain of bombs might have driven the Germans away from the cliff top; it was useless against troops in trenches or pillboxes.

Examine the options and one fact becomes clear: the Canadians landing at Puys needed support from the sea. Some support was available, from the destroyer HMS *Garth* and from MGB 316, the pilot craft that led the Blue Beach craft to the shore, but this support was never sufficient in either weight or quantity.

Secure in their concrete emplacements, the German infantry had nothing to fear and were in position to deny Blue Beach, and therefore the eastern headland, to any force General Roberts could send ashore. As a final blow, the German soldiers were fully alert. The night of 18–19 August had been selected for the weekly 'stand to' exercise laid on for the Dieppe garrison, and the men at Puys had been further aroused by the sight of tracers and gunfire from the 3 Commando action out at sea to the north; not an unusual occurrence perhaps, but nevertheless one that had the defending troops on the alert on the night of 18–19 August.

Taking everything into account, the landing beach at Puys was the sort of place any wise, experienced, amphibious soldier would stay well away from, for the sum total of the geographic limitations was to transform Blue Beach into a tight, congested killing ground. When this ground was crammed with a mass of Canadian infantry, unable either to move inland up that single exit or return to their landing craft, the result would be carnage.

However, given that the main task of the flank landings was to clear the way for the central assault at Dieppe, avoiding the beach at Puys was simply not an option. Having got ashore – and reached the cliff top – the Royal Regiment of Canada, 554 men commanded by Lieutenant-Colonel Douglas Catto, were charged first with swinging west to gain and secure the eastern heights overlooking Dieppe, overrunning and capturing any positions they encountered on the way.

In addition to their prime task, the battalion also had to destroy an anti-aircraft battery close to Puys, overrun the Army barracks at Les Glycines and capture the four-gun battery, codenamed 'Rommel', just inland from Puys. The Force Planners had ordered the battalion to turn these guns against the Germans in Dieppe and provided Colonel Catto with a detachment of gunners for the purpose. The gunners were also charged with removing the gun sights from some anti-aircraft guns sited close to Puys, instruments that were thought to be of revolutionary design.

The Force Planners – in this case General Roberts – had also provided a company of the Black Watch of Canada for flank protection, to screen Catto's men from an attack from the east as they assaulted the eastern headland. From this multiplicity of tasks one can conclude that a certain amount of hubris had affected the planners at Combined Ops HQ; any one of these major tasks would have absorbed the capacity of a single full-strength infantry battalion.

It will be noticed, however, that Colonel Catto's battalion was below strength; an infantry battalion in 1942 should have mustered over 700 men. The shortfall is accounted for by the fact that a number of rear echelon and staff personnel – drivers, clerks, cooks – had been left out of the battle; the landing force at Puys was made up of officers and men from the battalion's four rifle companies.

As if these various limitations and obstacles were not enough, the Royal Regiment also suffered from a scarcity of accurate intelligence. As we have noted, aerial reconnaissance had failed to reveal the existence of barbed wire on the sea wall or in the gully and, with all the other assets negated, the key to any successful landing at Puys was surprise. Surprise is often dependent on luck – the good fortune of having everything go exactly to plan – but luck was in short supply off Dieppe that morning, when the plan for landing the Royal Regiment went awry from the start. When matters go wrong in war they tend to go wrong at the beginning, and so it was here.

The battalion crossed the Channel in two cross-Channel ferries, the *Princess Astrid* and the *Queen Emma*. These ships stopped to unload the troops into LCAs, and at that point were ten miles off the French coast and slightly ahead of schedule when the first LCAs hit the water at 0300hrs. However, loading heavily armed troops into landing craft, then lowering and launching the LCAs, inevitably took longer than the planners allowed for. Time started to slip away and then there was a major error when some of the Royal Regiment craft formed up behind an escort boat, MGB 315, bound for another beach – an easy mistake to make in the darkness but a costly one in terms of time. Some fifteen minutes were lost before this error was sorted out and it was not until 0325hrs, one hour and twenty-five minutes before H-Hour, that the Royal Regiment, guided by Lieutenant-Commander Harold W. Goulding in MGB 316, set out for Blue Beach.

This initial delay was then compounded by the actions of Lieutenant-Commander Goulding who, in an effort to make up time, stormed off at speed towards the coast, leaving two slower craft, both Landing Craft Mechanised (LCMs), and some smaller craft, together containing about half the battalion, floundering in his wake and falling steadily behind.

It also appears that instead of heading directly for the beach at Puys (or fearing he might miss it in the dark) Goulding headed first towards the harbour entrance at Dieppe and turned north there, just short of the port, to cruise east along the cliffs for a mile or so to find Puys. This had the effect of spreading the assault craft out still further, causing further delay and attracting the attention of the shore batteries at Dieppe, which picked out the Puys craft with searchlights and starshell and then chased them up the coast with shellfire. At 0440hrs, five minutes before their landing time, the Blue Beach force was still two miles offshore and flares were already cascading from German positions on the cliffs ahead.

Here was the brief moment for one major decision – to call off the attack while the battalion was still together and intact. Surprise had clearly been lost. Had there been an alternative plan in place, directing Catto to proceed to some other location, a diversion might have been possible, but there was no alternative location, no 'Plan B' for Blue Beach. Lovat had an alternative beach and Durnford-Slater had an alternative beach, but there was no Blue Beach 2, no alternative east of Dieppe except the beaches at Berneval some miles away.

The plan called for the Royals to land on Blue Beach and nowhere else, so the only viable alternative was for Catto to contact Roberts and ask permission to call off the landing and put his battalion into Force Reserve. In view of the need to take the eastern headland and their previous exchange this was not a likely request for Catto to make, even had he wanted to at this stage in the landing.

So far everything that could go wrong had gone wrong, but these problems were nothing to those that struck the Royal Regiment as the first wave of landing craft neared the beach. The first wave of nine LCAs touched down nearly half an hour behind schedule and came into Blue Beach just as dawn was breaking, their approach in the grey light being watched with interest by the Germans on the cliffs above, sixty men commanded by Lieutenant Willi Weber. The time was 0507hrs, eight minutes before dawn; both surprise and darkness had been lost.

These Germans were not equipped with field artillery but they had a clear field of fire and perfect targets for their 81mm mortars and machine-guns, and they quickly opened fire on the approaching craft. Machine-gun fire lashed at the LCAs and mortar bombs began to fall among them when they were still offshore, killing or injuring a number of men in the craft. This fire came from four concrete pillboxes on the left of the beach, one disguised as a summerhouse, and from the eastern headland to the Canadian right. Only along the narrow base of the sea wall was there any kind of cover. 'This wall did not give us much protection,' records Corporal Ellis, one of the few men to reach it. 'It was enfiladed pretty effectively by a machine-gun buried into a concrete wall on the eastern slope of the gully.'

The first man down was Major G.P. Schofield, commanding the leading assault wave, and the first man out of his craft. He fell, badly wounded, on the ramp of his LCA; and again, with surprise clearly lost, this would have been a good time for Colonel Catto to call off the Puys landing entirely, with or without Roberts's permission. About half the Royals had gone ashore in the first wave and were now being cut to pieces on the beach; putting more men ashore would only add to the losses. However, there was still a chance that the gully was clear and a determined rush might get the rest of the battalion off the beach and into cover – and, finally, there was no time to stop the assault.

The boats were now surging hard for the beach and stopping them was impossible – the battalion had to try and get ashore. The full weight of enemy fire was reserved until the LCAs grounded on the pebbles, the bow doors were opened, the ramps kicked down, and the men sprinted out to the open beach. What happened then can only be described as a slaughter.

From the LCAs grounding on the beach to the sea wall was perhaps 50 metres, but very few in the initial assault wave of over 200 men got that far; most of them were cut down on the beach or fell back into the sea, or were killed on the landing ramp of their LCAs, raked with fire as they sprang from their boats. Within a few minutes (seconds in some places) Blue Beach was carpeted with dead and wounded men while the narrow bows of the landing craft were choked with those who had been shot down before even setting foot ashore. The dead and wounded blocked the way to those men in the rear of the craft, who had to climb over the bodies of their comrades just to get on the beach. Of the 250 or so men in the first nine landing craft to beach, representing about half the battalion, only a handful made it to the dubious safety of the sea wall. And the second wave was now coming in.

This consisted of two LCMs and four LCAs, and they came into Blue Beach in full daylight at 0530hrs, twenty minutes behind the first wave.

Those on board who dared to put their heads above the ramp could see the disaster that was taking place on shore. Blue Beach was already a shambles, covered with dead and wounded men and still under heavy fire. The shoreline was dotted with wrecked or badly damaged LCAs, while other craft, under fire from the cliffs, were attempting to haul off the beach and get back out to sea. A Canadian war correspondent, Ross Munro, embarked in one of the LCMs, recalls 'peering round the steel doors of the craft to see what was going on, but the craft was so crowded that I sat on a cartful of 3in mortar bombs'.

At this point one of the naval officers advised Lieutenant-Colonel Catto, who was in one of these LCMs, that, since something had clearly gone very wrong on Blue Beach, it would be as well to call off the landing and avoid adding more bodies to the slaughter ashore. Colonel Catto replied that he could not do that for 'Half my men are already there and I have to go in with the rest.'

Hindsight tells us that Colonel Catto should have called off the landing, abandoning the men on the beach in order to save those who had yet to go ashore, but that is not how things are done in a well-ordered battalion; comradeship, *esprit de corps* and duty take over. Those were Catto's men out there on that beach and he could not turn his back on them. And so the Royal Regiment of Canada went to its doom.

Ross Munro wrote later of what he saw when the ramp went down:

> I saw the slope, leading a short way to a stone wall littered with Royal casualties; there must have been sixty or seventy of them, cut down before they had a chance to fire a shot. On no other front have I seen such carnage. It was brutal and terrible and shocked you almost to insensibility to see the piles of dead and feel the hopelessness of the attack at this point.

This struck others too. There were instances of men refusing to leave their craft and being ordered out at pistol point, but these were the exception – and rather sensible exceptions in the circumstances. Other accounts tell of men rushing into the fire as if into heavy rain, turning back to shelter, then turning to try again, until they too were cut down. As Sergeant Legate recorded:

> We hit the beach and found the battle already in shape. The cross-fire coming at you made it impossible to move two feet from the wall or else you got hit. There was nobody around to look after the wounded and if there had been it was impossible to get near them. It turned out to be every man for himself.

The LCMs, drawing more water than the LCAs, grounded further off the beach; many men leapt into the water six or eight feet deep and had to drop their rifles or drag off their kit just to wade or swim ashore, all the time raked with fire. One or two of the landing-craft coxswains declined to land at all, dropping their ramps and opening the bow doors when their craft were some distance offshore, unloading the heavily encumbered infantrymen into deep water.

It is hard to blame them; the sights ashore would have daunted the most heroic. Shattered, bullet-riddled craft firmly aground, dead and wounded men on the beach, bodies rolling about in the waves, lashing tracer bouncing off the pebbles and, over all this, the battering sound of exploding mortar bombs, their shrapnel compounded by splinters from the pebbles. That memorable place of slaughter, the first day of the 1916 Battle of the Somme, can offer nothing more ghastly than what happened on the beach at Puys in 1942.

One of the mortar detachments, six men under Sergeant John Carroll, landed in deep water well short of the beach. One of the crew, Private Al Macdonald, tells what happened next:

> A splash and we were over our heads in deep water – not good when carrying heavy mortar parts. We could not get ashore like that and had to let it go. Then on the beach the first thing I saw was Johnny Carroll, he had been hit in the stomach and his entrails were hanging over his hands. I don't know how he could live in that condition but they got him back to England and he survived. I got ashore and started firing my rifle up the beach but before I got through one magazine I was hit three times in the arm, hand and leg, before I was able to get to the sea wall.

Within a few minutes the survivors of the second wave had joined those of the first against the sea wall. About this time, less than an hour into the action, a spontaneous move began to get off the beach and back onto any of the craft that were still offshore, some manned, some damaged and drifting. Most of those who landed and got back did so on the LCM carrying Ross Munro, the war correspondent, that had brought ashore the mortar detachments. This craft also contained the Naval Beachmaster for Blue Beach and it was his decision to abandon the landing that led to the withdrawal, the LCMs pulling off the beach and then turning west towards Dieppe, coming under machine-gun fire whenever they got anywhere near the coast; closing one of the destroyers, the first LCM unloaded the wounded and prepared to return to the UK.

All order had now been lost on Blue Beach where, in spite of the disasters that had struck the first two waves, a third wave was about to come ashore from the assault ship *Duke of Wellington*. This was the 'Edwards Force', that company of the Black Watch of Canada tasked to cover the eastern flank of the Royals during their move on Dieppe and those artillerymen who were supposed to take over the guns of the Goebbels battery. These men were only to go ashore when ordered in by Colonel Catto, but since no signal had been received, their commanders, Captain Hicks of the Royals and Lieutenant Jack Coyle of the

Royal Canadian Navy, blamed the 'fog of war' and decided to go in anyway.

Carried in five craft, the Edwards Force landed under the cliffs at the western end of the beach. They were raked with fire on the way in, but the curve of the cliff protected the actual landing from fire from the east; casualties were light, the only man killed being Lieutenant Jack Coulson, hit by machine-gun fire as he crossed the beach. The snag now was that the curve in the cliff also prevented the Edwards Force giving any help to the Royals pinned down on their flank; every time they moved out from cover, a hail of machine-gun fire and hand-grenades lobbed down from above cascaded about them. The Edwards Force had been put 'in the bag' from the moment they stepped ashore and took no further part in the action.

News of what was happening on Blue Beach was still not getting back to HMS *Calpe* or only doing so in a fitful and confusing fashion, since either the battalion's wireless sets had been drowned in the landing or their signallers had been quickly killed. Some contact was being maintained with the destroyer HMS *Garth*, which was patrolling offshore, darting in and out of the now-spreading smokescreen and attempting to bring some fire down on the cliffs and the eastern headland while dodging fire from the coastal batteries. *Garth* was sending some signals to *Calpe*, based on speculation or on what the sailors could see of the fighting ashore.

At 0535hrs, *Calpe* was informed that 'Doug had touched down' – 'Doug' being the codename for the entire battalion, taken from the forename of its Colonel, Douglas Catto. Silence fell until 0550hrs when the log records: 'No word from Doug'; and half an hour later, at 0620hrs, another signal was handed to Roberts telling him: 'Royal Regiment not landed.' All this while the battalion was ashore and being cut to pieces on the beach.[2]

According to some reports, the two signalmen in the Beach Signals Party had their set knocked out as they went ashore, Colonel Catto's battalion signaller was killed, and the Colonel's own set was shot from his hand into the sea. Thus the elaborate signals arrangements made before the landing did not survive the first few minutes of the assault. This left General Roberts unaware of what was happening to this battalion and rather more worried about the effect any delay by the Royals at Puys would have on the main assault on Dieppe.

As the morning wore on, the sounds of firing from the beach gradually faded out. At about 0700hrs the signaller still manning his set on the beach put out a message calling for an evacuation, presumably on the authority of some surviving officer. The man who should have been in charge on the beach was the Beachmaster, Lieutenant Warnecke, a naval officer, but the information here is confused; some reports have him on the beach, while others state that Warnecke was still on the landing craft and never went ashore. In any event, the return of the landing craft to the beach only led to further chaos and loss.

One landing craft duly closed the beach and scores of men left the shelter of the sea wall and attempted to get on board. An LCA could carry about thirty men and over fifty were scrambling over the sides as the LCA, now firmly aground on a falling tide, attempted to haul off the beach using the kedge anchor over the stern. The forward ramp and doors could not be closed as men were jammed in the entrance, and as water poured in the craft heeled over and sank.

All this time mortar bombs and machine-gun fire continued to rake the men around the boat until there were only half a dozen, some of them wounded; all decided to abandon any attempt to right the craft and swim out to sea in the hope of being picked up later by some passing boat – an option chosen, sometimes successfully, by other men from other beaches. Private Al Macdonald, the mortar man, remembers one such:

> I remember a fellow swimming away from the shore; he had a Mae West lifejacket on and some bugger with a machine-gun opened up

> on him and you would see the water boiling about him and he would stop. But as soon as the fire switched away from him he would start kicking again, going like hell for the open sea. The last I saw of him he was still kicking and almost out of range; I don't know who he was, but I hope he made it.

Colonel Catto was still trying to get his men off the beach, urged on by the fact that the Germans had now brought up more automatic weapons and some field artillery to engage any craft that emerged from the smoke offshore. With withdrawal now impossible unless these guns could be destroyed, the only way out was up the gully. Colonel Catto therefore ordered a search for some wire-cutting Bangalore torpedoes; any available torpedoes lay out on the beach and attempting to retrieve them was suicide, so the Colonel and his officers attacked these iron thickets with wire-cutters, attempting to snip a way through, all under sniper and machine-gun fire.

A gap was cut in the wire on the sea wall and a small group of some twenty men, led by Colonel Catto, crawled through it and got to the top of the cliffs. The gully widens as it climbs and a number of chalets and cottages gave Catto's party some cover as they drew near the top. They assaulted one of these cottages, killing some machine-gunners they found inside. More house clearing might have followed but another machine-gun then came into action from the village, concentrating its fire on the top of the gully, so no troops could get up from the beach. By 0800hrs, Catto found himself cut off from the bulk of his men, both physically and by radio.

By 0730hrs, apart from the smart crack of a sniper's rifle, most of the firing on Blue Beach had stopped. Then two more boats closed the shore. These were Eurekas, tasked to pick up any of No. 3 Commando still alive on Yellow Beach but which had come into Blue Beach by mistake. In they came under heavy fire, picking up a number of men in the water before pulling out, two crew members on one of the Eurekas being killed in the process.

The picture emerging from the signals logs is inevitably confused. At 0655hrs Hughes-Hallett, the Naval Force Commander embarked on *Calpe*, sent a message to MGB 316, the escort boat for Blue Beach, demanding a report on the situation ashore. Goulding had no real idea what was happening ashore, only that the craft were going in and there was the sound of heavy firing from the beach. Presumably he received the 0700hrs signal, since he sent in the landing craft, so it is hard to see why he then reported to Hughes-Hallett: 'The landing has been effected with light casualties and no damage to craft' – a claim wildly at variance with the facts.

Hughes-Hallett clearly found it hard to believe, for at around 0730hrs he summoned Goulding onto *Calpe* for interrogation, only to receive another equally encouraging report – actually an estimate – that by now the Royals must – surely – be off the beach and on the eastern headland. On the basis of this opinion, Roberts sent a signal via HMS *Fernie* to Leigh-Mallory and Mountbatten at Uxbridge, stating: 'Royal Regiment landed on Blue Beach. Doug landed three companies practically intact.'

This signal, timed at 0740hrs, became somewhat enhanced before *Fernie* passed it on. The signal sent to Uxbridge stated: 'Doug landed three companies intact at Blue Beach, 0740hrs, all going well.' This strange timing should have alerted someone, for it appeared to say that Catto had gone ashore successfully in broad daylight and two hours late.

The source of the next signal in the log, timed at 0817hrs, is even more confusing: '*Calpe* reports Doug three companies OK. Heavy fighting for fortified house. Took cover, no further news. No news of 4th Company.' It is not clear where *Calpe* got this information, which was anyway incorrect. The truth came in a desperate signal from HMS *Garth*: 'From Blue Beach. Is there any possible chance of getting us off?'

Some naval support was reaching Blue Beach, though far too late to do any good. Two LCGs – Landing Craft Guns – had begun cruising off-shore, closing to about 100m and engaging the houses and pillboxes; these craft were promptly engaged by artillery and shore batteries and forced to withdraw by around 0745hrs, returning to the main fleet lurking in the smoke off Dieppe with dead and wounded men on their decks.

Also in action was the gallant little *Garth*; in his after-action report the captain, Lieutenant-Commander J.P. Scatchard, records:

> I found throughout that the [German] fire was extremely accurate and it was impossible to go through the smoke and carry out a steady bombardment. It was a matter of going in through the smoke till close, squaring off and then retiring, then circling to come in again and repeating the manoeuvre. On each occasion we were straddled with shells and it became extraordinary that not more of us were hit.[3]

Garth kept up this tactic until around 0900hrs, by which time she had sustained a number of hits, lost a number of men and almost exhausted her stock of 4in ammunition; reporting to *Calpe*, Scatchard was ordered to take on board as many wounded men as possible and head for England.

Communications were now very difficult and the resulting picture is therefore confusing. Catto, at the top of the cliffs with a small platoon of men, was cut off from Roberts on *Calpe* but a signaller on the beach was in touch with HMS *Garth*, so it should have been possible to send messages back to the Force Commanders. But then, when attempting to assist the troops pinned down on Blue Beach, *Garth* fired a salvo that brought part of the cliff top down on the men lurking below, destroying all but one of the surviving signal sets in the process. The shore batteries then drove *Garth* back into the smokescreen and shore contact was lost yet again.

And that was the end on Blue Beach. The remains of the battalion surrendered at 0805hrs and a few minutes later the log of the German

571st Regiment reported: 'Puys in our hands. Enemy has lost about 500 prisoners or dead.'

This was an accurate assessment, and the final account for the Royal Regiment of Canada makes grim reading. From a fine battalion that mustered 546 men when the ramps went down – 26 officers and 520 men – only two officers and 63 men got back to England, representing a battalion loss rate of 88 per cent. Both of the officers, one of them Colonel Catto's brother Jack, were wounded, as were 31 of the 63 other ranks. Of those that got ashore, 209 were killed and 262 became prisoners of war, 103 of them being wounded before capture and 16 dying later in their prisoner-of-war camps.

Finally, what of Colonel Catto, last seen on the cliff top? Catto attempted to contact the men on the beach by shouting down from the cliff top, but there was no response. Then, detecting a German patrol moving against him from the centre of Puys, he decided to take the twenty-strong remnant of his battalion along the cliff towards the eastern headland overlooking Dieppe, where they might link up with the Essex Scottish battalion, which should now be ashore on Red Beach.

The Essex Scottish were not there, for reasons we shall shortly discover, so Colonel Catto then elected to lie up near the anti-aircraft battery that had been one of the battalion objectives. There he remained until he saw the remnants of his battalion being marched into captivity, and at 1600hrs he came out of cover, put up his hands and joined them. There was nothing else he could have done.

A disaster of this size almost defies analysis. Everything hinges on the initial plan and the belief that a flank landing at Puys was necessary to ensure the neutralisation of the German defences on the eastern headland. The planners then failed to realise that – for the various reasons already described – a landing at Puys was a high-risk undertaking with a strong possibility of failure.

There was no alternative plan, probably because no other beach existed to which a landing force tasked to clear the eastern headland could be diverted. And this brings us back, yet again, to the problem of support. If the landing at Puys was deemed so important, then every effort and every asset needed to ensure a successful landing there should have been provided. Yet in the end the support available to the troops on Blue Beach came down to the 4in guns of one destroyer and the small-calibre cannon of a motor launch. It makes one want to weep.

GREEN BEACH

POURVILLE

The Germans, knowing that an invader would only land at Pourville to attack Dieppe, had placed their first line of defence on the eastern heights.

TERENCE ROBERTSON,
THE SHAME AND THE GLORY, P. 274

TEN MILES TO the west of Puys, two Canadian infantry battalions, one each from the South Saskatchewan Regiment and the Cameron Highlanders of Canada, were tasked to go ashore on the beach at Pourville. There they were to take the western headland overlooking Dieppe and perform various other tasks; and there, as at Puys, they were to meet with disaster. The major difference was that at Puys matters went wrong during the landing; at Pourville the Canadian landing went seriously awry during the withdrawal.

This fact illustrates one of the problems with raiding operations. Raids fall into three parts – the landing, the execution of the mission and the withdrawal. Every stage of these proceedings is critical and fraught with hazard, and therefore requires prior planning and careful rehearsal. It is not possible to jack in the raid at some point, amble back to the beach and simply re-embark. Unless thoroughly quelled, the enemy, by now stirred into action, will see to that. Since these phases are, or should be, an integrated process, a successful withdrawal depends very largely on what has gone on during the landing and the execution. Not all of this can in fact be planned – operations of war rarely run exactly to plan and, as we have seen at Puys, a rigid plan is a recipe for disaster.

All the more reason, then, to establish the tasks of the operation clearly, while bearing in mind that at some point it may be necessary to pull back and withdraw, mission completed or not. The fact that the landing at Pourville went well initially should not be allowed to obscure this basic truth: a raiding operation is not over until the troops have been safely withdrawn, and the withdrawal phase requires as much planning and rehearsal as the other two.

The South Saskatchewan Regiment, the first battalion to land, was more fortunate than the Royal Regiment, at least in the choice of beach. The beach at Pourville was wide, allowing space to deploy, and if the sea wall behind it could be crossed, there was easy access to the village and the countryside beyond. The River Scie flows into the sea through Pourville

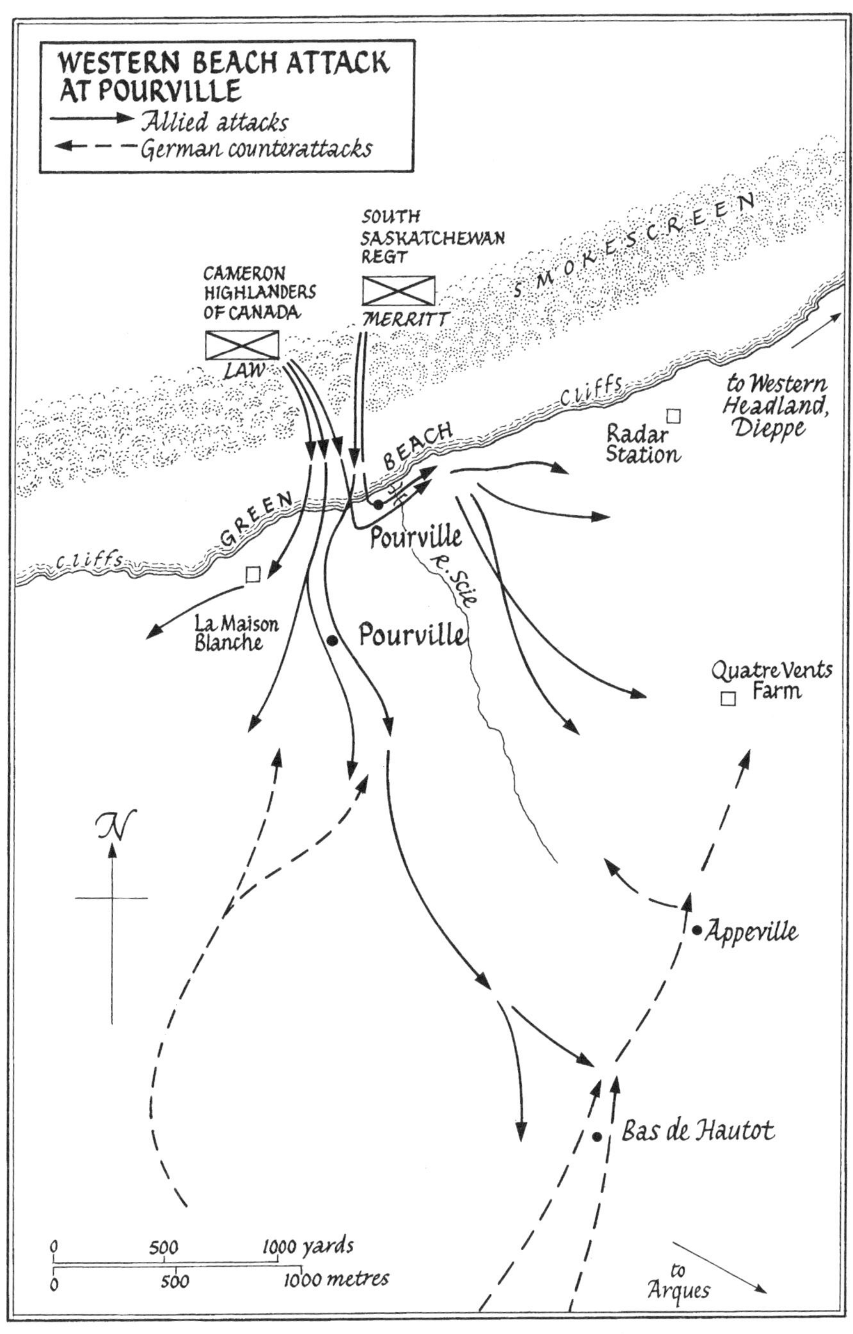

WESTERN BEACH ATTACK AT POURVILLE
Allied attacks
German counterattacks
SOUTH SASKATCHEWAN REGT
MERRITT
CAMERON HIGHLANDERS OF CANADA
LAW
SMOKESCREEN
GREEN BEACH
Cliffs
Cliffs
to Western Headland, Dieppe
Radar Station
Pourville
R. Scie
La Maison Blanche
Pourville
Quatre Vents Farm
N
Appeville
Bas de Hautot
0 500 1000 yards
0 500 1000 metres
to Arques

and out across the beach, where the 'sea wall' acted as a kind of dam. This ten-foot wall penned up the Scie and, with the riverbanks behind it broken, turned the shallow Scie Valley into a flooded marsh, ten feet in depth at the mouth and impassable to tanks.

This flooding was part of the work currently being undertaken to create the Atlantic Wall, Hitler's bastion against invasion. A 400-strong body of workers from the Todt Organisation was currently billeted in Pourville, working on these coastal defences. The only way out of the village was across a narrow bridge over the Scie, which leads up to the Dieppe road. This bridge was a solid stone structure, guarded on the eastern side of the river by a series of pillboxes.

Viewed from the sea, Pourville presents a wide, open aspect, with green slopes rising away to the east and west and a narrow, widening valley ahead, running inland to rising wooded ground. The beach is about a kilometre in length, a hundred metres wide at high tide and perhaps twice that or more at low tide. There was nothing menacing about this landing beach, no cliffs, no narrow exit gully and no apparent obstacles. There were, however, a number of German defensive positions, including some that formed part of the main Dieppe defences for the western headland but had spilled over the crest towards Pourville.

Like Puys, Pourville was an obvious landing area for anyone contemplating an assault on Dieppe, so it had already been endowed with a number of defensive positions consisting of pillboxes, trenches and dug-outs, some minefields and a quantity of wire. Some of these pillboxes, each equipped with machine-guns, covered the Scie bridge and access up the road towards Dieppe and the western headland. The Germans did not have many troops actually in Pourville – perhaps a strong platoon of some fifty men – but there were plenty more deployed in the defences above the village and, as at Puys, the German reaction to any landing was likely to be swift. If not extensive, the Pourville defences were deployed in depth – and depth is the essence of defence – and manned by resolute troops.

The assault would be led by the South Saskatchewans, 523 officers and men – another light battalion – commanded by Lieutenant-Colonel Cecil Merritt. The Saskatchewans were charged with going ashore at 0450hrs, just before dawn, and clearing the village to establish a firm base for the next unit to land, the Cameron Highlanders of Canada, another 500-strong battalion, commanded by Lieutenant-Colonel Alfred Gostling.

The plan required the South Saskatchewan Regiment to 'secure Green Beach with the minimum of delay to enable the Camerons of Canada to pass without opposition'. This was the first task but there were several others. The South Saskatchewans also had to move east from the beach to secure the western headland position overlooking Dieppe; there they would meet the Royal Hamilton Light Infantry, which had landed on the main beach in front of the port. This was the crucial task for the South Saskatchewans – taking the western headland was as vital as taking the eastern headland – and it is interesting to note that this task had been delegated to just one rifle company ('A' Company) in the battalion plan.

Lieutenant-Colonel Merritt had given each rifle company a specific job on landing. While 'A' Company were heading for the western headland and the batteries, 'B' Company would land to the west of the River Scie to clear Pourville and the slopes overlooking the Scie Valley. 'C' Company would meanwhile be moving up the right flank, onto the western slopes of the valley, and finally, 'D' Company would move inland and capture Quatre Vents Farm, so securing the route of the Cameron Highlanders towards St Aubin and Arques.

Quatre Vents Farm was the headquarters of the German 571st Regiment, and this position could pose a threat to the Camerons as they moved up the Scie Valley towards St Aubin; other enemy units here included an anti-aircraft (flak) battery and the staff of a radar station. All in all, if given the chance to occupy their positions in strength, the Germans could easily bar the road to Dieppe and the hinterland. If all went well, however, having secured Quatre Vents Farm, 'D' Company would then join 'A' in the attack on the western headland.

Given the size of Colonel Merritt's force and the varied tasks confronting it, there is nothing inherently wrong with this plan, except that it obliged Merritt to divide his battalion into four Company parts before the situation on the ground had revealed itself. That was a necessary and inevitable part of the plan – a rather hopeful one – but it posed a crucial question: if anything went wrong with any part of the plan was there sufficient force available anywhere to deal with it?

Still, all being well, while the Saskatchewans and the Hamiltons were taking the Western headland, the Calgary Tanks would have come ashore on the main Dieppe beach far below and be heading inland for St Aubin. The infantry units would ring Dieppe from Pourville round towards Puys, and form a perimeter from which the Tanks would surge inland to take the airfield at St Aubin and the castle at Arques-la-Bataille, which contained a German headquarters, and meet up there with the Camerons. If all went well the entire force would then withdraw to their boats through Dieppe. Anticipating that all would indeed go well, the South Saskatchewans and the Camerons embarked for Dieppe.

The South Saskatchewans embarked in two cross-Channel ferries, the *Princess Astrid* and the *Invicta.* After an eventful crossing, during which the careless handling of a grenade wounded seventeen men on *Invicta*, the men began to board their landing craft at 0300hrs. These consisted of two LCMs and ten LCAs which, arrayed in two columns and led by Lieutenant-Commander R. Prior RNVR in a motor gunboat, began to close the beach well before dawn. Finding the beach proved easy; H-Hour for the landing had been fixed for 0450hrs and the landing craft crunched onto the pebbles at 0452hrs, just two minutes late.

The landing at Pourville therefore enjoyed the benefit of surprise. It was still dark and the only noise that followed the thud of descending boat ramps was that of hundreds of nailed boots pounding across the shingle to the shelter of the sea wall. Only when the landing craft were reversing off the beach did the enemy come to life, putting up flares and sending a stream of tracer arcing over the landing area. Here the Saskatchewans were attempting to breach the wire on top of the sea wall and get into the village, a process aided by the discovery of some gaps the Germans had left in the wire for bathing parties.

Then matters started to go seriously wrong. It was discovered that the entire battalion had been put ashore on the western side of the River Scie instead of astride the river mouth; only one Company should have landed to the west of the river, all the others to the east of it. This fact took some time to emerge; only when the Saskatchewans were across the sea wall did they realise that the entire battalion had landed in the wrong place. This meant that 'A' and 'D' Companies must cross the bridge over the river before they could start clearing the eastern slopes of the headland or move on Quatre Vents Farm – and the Scie bridge was already under fire from machine-guns and mortars.

Before this gaffe was discovered a signal had been sent to Roberts on HMS *Calpe*: 'Cecil landed.' This was the last signal to come from Green Beach that day and the lack of subsequent communications left General Roberts completely confused; if the South Saskatchewans were ashore, where were the Cameron Highlanders – and what the hell were these battalions doing? The short answer is that they were fighting for their lives.

At Pourville, as elsewhere that morning, enemy reaction was swift. Merritt's Tactical HQ followed 'B' Company into Pourville village and established itself briefly in a house in the centre, where it was quickly subjected to enemy mortar fire and forced to move into the open; here a mortar bomb killed several signallers and wounded the battalion Regimental Sergeant-Major (RSM), Roger Strumm. This attack on the signals platoon had serious consequences: from then on communications within the battalion became extremely difficult, and with *Calpe* impossible.

'B' Company pressed on with clearing the village, house by house and against increasing opposition as the enemy woke up, recovered from his surprise and began to fight back hard and quickly. 'C' Company was also busily engaged clearing the western side of the village before moving up the far slope, rousting the Todt workers from their billets and attacking the German officers' mess outside the village, killing several officers and alarming a number of French prostitutes who had been entertaining the enemy overnight.

That done, 'C' Company slogged to the top of the western slope overlooking the village, where they were promptly held up by a machine-gun position on the edge of a wood. All of this was accomplished quickly; by just after 0600hrs the western slopes above Pourville had been cleared. During this time the Canadians made the interesting discovery that the Germans, while willing to fight hard from their trenches and pillboxes, were quick to surrender or flee as the Canadians closed in with the bayonets and grenades. Colonel Merritt could be satisfied with the situation west of the Scie but on the other side of the river, up the Scie Valley and on the hillside leading towards Dieppe, matters were not going so well.

The root of the problem was that unfortunate landing west of the river mouth. This meant that 'A' and 'D' had to cross the narrow bridge. This stone-built bridge was about 100ft in length and 10ft wide, defended across the river and on the far slopes by well-sited pillboxes, which engaged the Canadian companies with machine-gun fire as soon as they approached the bridge. Nor was it possible to outflank the bridge; the river was too deep and the approaches wired and mined.

The only way to get across to the east bank was by plucking up courage and sprinting across the bridge; this the Saskatchewans proceeded to do, but at considerable cost. Led by a very resolute officer, Captain Murray Osten, the men of 'A' Company charged the bridge or attempted to swim the river. Some of the first to try succeeded in surprising the enemy and got across to shelter behind a road block, but the pillbox machine-guns then came into play, piling up dead and wounded men on the bridge and its approaches, forcing others to take shelter in the village houses, firmly stuck and unable to advance. Or so it seemed.

'A' Company were held up at the bridge for almost half an hour taking casualties from snipers and mortar fire until Private Charles Sawden handed his rifle to a friend, took two grenades and knocked out the first pillbox, killing all inside. Private Sawden was killed later that day but his action freed up the forces pinned on the east bank of the Scie. 'A' Company then had to tackle the defences leading up the steep slope to the western headland, which were both well concealed and fully alert. Even so, the Company pressed on quickly, overrunning an artillery battery which was engaging the LCAs bringing the Cameron Highlanders of Canada into Green Beach.

The situation on Green Beach was becoming confused, with little coordination between the military and naval participants. Some support was being provided by the destroyer HMS *Albrighton*, which had been bombarding German positions on the eastern slopes while the Canadians were still stuck on the far side of the Scie bridge, but the Canadians were not able to take advantage of this shellfire at the time. By the time they were across the bridge, shore batteries had the range of *Albrighton* and had chased her back into the smokescreen. While the overall Saskatchewan plan was – just – being adhered to when the Camerons came ashore at around 0520hrs, it appears that 'D' Company were mostly over the bridge and anxious to get on to Quatre Vents Farm – an understandable ambition at this time with the Camerons coming ashore behind them.

The snag was that the road to Quatre Vents was under fire and 'A' Company, tasked to assault the defences on the eastern slope, had yet to move out of the way. Nor was 'D' Company complete; parts of this Company and all of 'B' Company, perhaps 100 men in all, were still west of the bridge and stuck on the edge of the village. Unless something was done, and done quickly, the South Saskatchewans' attack would stall. The battalion CO, Lieutenant-Colonel Merritt, solved this impasse in an action that was to win him Canada's first VC of the war.

The old adage 'Cometh the hour, cometh the man' has never been better illustrated than by the actions of Lieutenant-Colonel Merritt at Pourville that morning. Hearing that his battalion had been held up at the bridge, he left his HQ in the village centre and went forward to see for himself. Having seen, he acted. Crouched behind the houses, in ditches and behind the road block, his men were startled to see their colonel strolling down the road towards the bullet-swept bridge, his steel helmet dangling from one hand, his voice urging them to come forward out of cover and get across: 'Come on, boys, nothing to worry about, they can't hit a thing.'

Come forward they did, four men being killed among the first to do so. As they got up and rushed forward, Lieutenant-Colonel Merritt led them across the bridge, machine-gun bullets bouncing off the road and men falling on either side. The battalion colonel was displaying, in the words of his VC citation, 'matchless gallantry and inspiring leadership'. Nor did Merritt do this just once; having led the first group across the bridge he strolled back, collected another party and did it again . . . and again. How the Colonel managed to do this and survive simply beggars belief; one account records: 'The Colonel, when he saw we were being held up, crossed the bridge several times, urging the men forward and the men followed. The Canadian dead were piled up two deep for fifty yards or more along the bridge.'[1]

After bringing the last party across to the eastern bank, Merritt discovered that another pillbox was still in action on the far slope. Taking a few men with him, he ran up the road under cover of smoke and lobbed grenades through the pillbox's weapon slits. That done, and with the bridge now open, he returned to his HQ, telling his staff cheerfully that he had just 'bombed out a pillbox' and recommending this activity as something they should try before breakfast.

With more troops across the river the South Saskatchewans were now in a better position, but by now the enemy were fully alert and well able to stem the advance. Merritt had only two companies over the river, both somewhat reduced in strength, and this was not enough for the task of taking the eastern slope above Pourville and getting onto the western headland above Dieppe. In fact this task was probably beyond the capability of a single infantry battalion, and this battalion was totally without support.

As at Puys, the main support weapon available was the battalion's own 3in mortars, but these were virtually useless against pillboxes and trench positions and in any case the mortar crews rapidly ran out of ammunition. Merritt could also call on the 4in guns of the destroyer HMS *Albrighton*, but shore-to-ship communications were poor and in the general confusion little could be done to pick out targets and bring the destroyer's guns to bear. And so, in spite of great gallantry and tenacity, the South Saskatchewan advance on Dieppe came to a halt. They had secured Pourville and the western slopes and were hanging on grimly to the eastern slope leading to Dieppe. They had not, however, reached Quatre Vents Farm, or the German defences on the western headland.

In every essential the Pourville landing had failed before the Cameron Highlanders came ashore. The aim, as already described, was for the South Saskatchewans to secure the landing area and the surrounding slopes, the heights overlooking Dieppe and the route inland towards St Aubin airfield and Arques. None of this had been achieved. Largely because of the error on landing, the enemy had been given the chance to rally. Then, in crossing the Scie bridge, Merritt's battalion had lost perhaps a quarter of its strength and a considerable amount of time.

Time and the landing error apart – and some errors should have been anticipated – the basic flaw at Pourville would appear to lie in the initial plan. Merritt simply did not have the men, the support or the mobility to carry out these tasks if the enemy was given the chance to man his defences. Those defences were now manned and the Canadian landing at Pourville would make no further progress.

The Cameron Highlanders of Canada were coming ashore on Green Beach while Colonel Merritt's men were attempting to cross the bridge, battering their way towards Quatre Vents and fighting for the slopes around Pourville, and their efforts met with no more success. The Camerons, 503 officers and men, had been supposed to land at 0520hrs. This was the same time the assault went in on the Dieppe beaches; but, in the event, the Camerons went ashore half an hour after that, at 0550hrs, an hour after the Saskatchewans, in full daylight and on a beach already under fire. This was no unforeseen delay; the Camerons' CO, Lieutenant-Colonel Gostling, believed that the Saskatchewans would need at least an hour to clear the beach and had no wish to get involved in another battalion's firefight.

But the delay may have been a mistake. As the Camerons' LCAs closed the beach, a battalion piper playing in the bows of the leading craft, it quickly became apparent that the enemy gunners now had Green Beach ranged to the inch; shells and mortar bombs began to fall among the landing craft and a burst of machine-gun fire killed Colonel Gostling as he went ashore. Then, as with the Saskatchewans an hour before, many of the Camerons' landing craft landed on the west side of the Scie.

That there was yet another navigation error on Green Beach should not come as a great surprise. The Second World War LCA did not provide much of a viewing platform, being only a few feet above the water, and the LCA commander, the coxswain, usually a naval leading seaman or a Royal Marine corporal, would be too busy keeping station with the craft on either side to pay much attention to where he was actually going; any current or tidal drift could quickly carry the flat-bottomed landing craft off line. The important thing as far as the crew were concerned was to keep station and land in line with the others; an LCA on its own would rapidly be subjected to a barrage of fire to which it had no means of replying.

The error scattered the battalion and the death of the CO left it leaderless for a few vital minutes. The men on the western side of the beach faced no opposition since the Saskatchewans had wiped out the German positions on that side of the river; the snag was that the bulk of the Camerons landed on the west side, when they were needed to deal with the much greater opposition on the east. The battalion then split into companies and platoons as everyone tried to find out what was happening and get on with the job. A description of the situation is provided by one of the senior NCOs, Company Sergeant-Major George Gouk:

> On checking, I found that we only had a platoon from my company and one from 'D' Company. The Company commander had no means of communicating with anyone so we decided to swing left from the river to where we knew the enemy were. Snipers and mg's seemed to be in every house so we got busy on them and were doing a pretty good job when all of a sudden they opened up on us with their mortars. Then it was hell.
>
> Our casualties started mounting; every corner you turned you ran into mortar fire and they sure could place their shots. There was no stopping the boys then; they were seeing their friends being killed and wounded and the only thought in everyone's mind was to have revenge.[2]

This desire to close with the enemy led to another serious loss when Captain Young of the Camerons had his men fix bayonets and led them in a charge against an enemy position on the east bank of the Scie. The charge was pressed home with great resolution but Captain Young and many of his men were killed. Groups of men, Camerons and Saskatchewans, were milling all over Pourville, seeking out the enemy and engaging them where found, but this was not helping the battalions with their designated tasks.

The Camerons' second-in-command, Major Tony Law, then took charge of this scattered battalion, or those elements he could find, and reviewed the situation, first attempting to find out what was happening on Green Beach where all was clearly not going to plan. The Camerons' designated task, to advance along the Scie Valley to the airfield at St Aubin, now seemed less important than the need to assist the Saskatchewans in clearing the eastern slopes of the western headland and expanding the narrow bridgehead up the valley.

Even this took time. Those Camerons who had landed on the wrong side of the river mouth were held up crossing the wire-draped sea wall, which was now under constant fire. They were not able to do this until they chanced on the gaps cut previously by the Saskatchewans, and lost many good men in the process. Others then pressed forward into Pourville, where some Cameron officers sought out Colonel Merritt.

Major Law and Colonel Merritt duly conferred and agreed that Law should push up the valley along the west bank of the river and attempt to keep that rendezvous with the Calgary Tanks at Les Vertus Wood. No one at Pourville knew what was actually happening at Dieppe, but for the moment it seemed better to attempt the tank rendezvous and get at least part of the plan back on track. However, the Camerons had not gone far when they were engaged by enemy troops from Quatre Vents Farm and new enemy forces coming towards Pourville from Appeville.

The Germans had always been well aware of the importance of the Scie Valley to the defence of Dieppe, hence the work being done at Pourville by the Todt Organisation. All of this was designed to deny the route into the hinterland behind Dieppe to any landing force. Nor was it simply a matter of fixed defences – those pillboxes and that wire. As soon as the defenders realised that a landing had been made at Pourville, the reserve battalion of the 571st Regiment was ordered to the Scie Valley. This order was given at around 0530hrs and by 0630hrs the leading platoons of this battalion, having arrived on bicycles, were starting to take up blocking positions and reinforcing the troops at Quatre Vents Farm.

The problem confronting Law and his men was that lack of support and mobility. It will be recalled that in the original 'flanking plan', it had been suggested that tanks landing at Pourville might accompany the infantry. Tanks could have been landed there, though getting them off the beach might have proved difficult; even so, some work – perhaps a little blasting by assault engineers – could have got them over the wall and, in spite of fears to the contrary, the Scie bridge would have supported the weight of tanks.

However, tanks are slow and speed was now vital; a more useful asset at Pourville would have been some armoured cars or Bren-gun carriers. Bren-gun carriers were standard equipment in infantry battalions at this time, and with their aid it would have been possible to overcome the pillboxes and push up the road to confront the German infantry, which had no armoured assets of any kind. This is pure speculation; neither armoured cars nor tanks were factored into the Pourville plan – but it might have gone very much better if they had been.

As it was, the planners assumed that the Camerons would only need tank support when they linked up with the Calgary Tanks at St Aubin. In other words, tank support needed for the advance would only be provided in time for the withdrawal. So, without support, the Camerons did what they could, advancing up the valley from Pourville on foot, under observation from German troops mustering around Quatre Vents Farm. Quickly brought under sporadic fire, Law ordered his men to take what cover they could find in the woods and along the hedgerows but to keep pushing inland, ignoring the machine-gun and mortar fire.

This they did until they reached the end of the woods and came into the open right in front of a line of defended trenches; these were assaulted with the bayonet and the enemy swiftly evicted, but more machine-guns came into play and the Camerons were pushed to the left, down towards the Scie and the hamlet of Bas de Hautot, stopping eventually on a ridge above the river from where, had the tanks arrived, they should have been able to see the Calgary Regiment at Les Vertus. No tanks were in sight; the countryside inland from Quatre Vents Farm was firmly held by the enemy.

The Camerons could do no more. They had pushed up the Scie Valley against increasing opposition; now it was all too clear that there were no tanks ahead and no chance of further advances beyond Les Vertus Wood, where their advance was finally stemmed. There was nothing to do now but go back towards Pourville and hang on grimly for whatever relief was forthcoming.

This the Camerons were most reluctant to do. At around 0900hrs, undaunted by this new reverse, Law decided to cross the valley by the bridge at Bas de Hautot and mount an attack on the strong German position at Quatre Vents Farm, an act of considerable audacity for the farm was now crawling with enemy troops. Unfortunately for Major Law the Germans held the bridge at Hautot in sufficient strength to stop this move and so, stymied yet again, Law ordered the remnants of his battalion to pull back into Pourville. There, mustered with the remains of Merritt's force, they would hold until withdrawn.

So the Canadian advance from Pourville was brought to a halt and it never got going again. As the after-action report confirms:

> When it became apparent that the capture of objectives east of the village was impossible, the remains of the Saskatchewans and the Camerons took up positions on the ground they had gained and held them until it was time to withdraw. The enemy was content to limit himself to holding his positions . . . he had no desire to initiate

> counter-attacks which would bring him to closer quarters with the men who had come from the sea.[3]

Perhaps not, but it was not too long before the enemy realised that the Canadians had gone over from attack to defence and would shortly have to withdraw, not least because their hurriedly adopted positions in and around Pourville were coming under heavy fire and increasing pressure. The Pourville landing was over; the attack had stalled. Now the Germans would extract a heavy price during the withdrawal.

At this time the situation on Green Beach had improved somewhat with the arrival of some naval support to back up the battalion's mortars. These were now getting short of ammunition, and any slacking in their fire enabled the enemy to press forward. At irregular intervals throughout the morning the Canadians enjoyed a small measure of naval gunfire support, some from HMS *Albrighton*, some from MGB 317, which had supported the landing, and some from two LCMs equipped with Vickers medium machine-guns. These vessels concentrated their fire on the eastern slopes leading to Dieppe, but were unable to make it fully effective or silence the German guns.

The problem, yet again, was a lack of adequate communications. Supporting fire has to be directed and controlled. Under normal circumstances this task was delegated to a Forward Observation Officer (FOO; normally an artillery officer), who travelled with the infantry but was in constant radio contact with the ships and could move the naval gunfire about to where it was most needed. That at least was the theory; in the event, the FOO at Pourville, Captain Carswell, was never sure exactly where the South Saskatchewans were, other than somewhere on the eastern slopes, and his main asset, HMS *Albrighton*, was continually disappearing into the thick offshore smokescreen, pursued by enemy shells. According to the Captain of the *Albrighton*:

> Three shoots were started but the FOO was unable to spot the fall of shot. He also indicated targets on the cliff between Dieppe and Green Beach for direct bombardment and I think the ship did silence the fire of one gun position. The ship could not remain stationary for long as enemy fire was always accurate and always close.

Naval fire support would be needed to cover the withdrawal, but whether the Saskatchewans and Camerons got away at all would depend very largely on the actions of Roberts and Hughes-Hallett on *Calpe*. They alone could authorise the withdrawal – using the codeword 'Vanquish' – and send in the boats to get the men off.

This could prove difficult for neither Roberts or Hughes-Hallett had much idea of the situation on Green Beach and the information they did have tended, for some reason, to be optimistic. Indeed, it is one of the great mysteries of the entire Dieppe Raid that the bulk of the information reaching the Force Commanders on *Calpe* implied that all was going reasonably well when the exact opposite was usually the case.

As related, Roberts had been informed that 'Cecil had landed' and then that the Camerons had got ashore. Silence then fell apart from a message claiming that the radar station near Pourville had fallen and the South Saskatchewans were on the western headland. Then silence fell again, until 0846hrs when a doom-laden signal arrived from Pourville, asking for the evacuation of casualties from the sea wall on Green Beach. This was a reasonable and not unexpected request – the wounded should be extracted as soon as possible – but it seems to have sown some alarm on *Calpe*, where Roberts issued an order for the total evacuation of Green Beach at 1030hrs – a timing later put back, with dire effect, to 1100hrs.

The withdrawal from Pourville needs to be seen in the context of all the other withdrawals at the end of that fatal day and is described in Chapter 13, but it should come as no surprise that the German Army's follow-up to it was characteristically swift. As Peter Young was to remark, 'I have fought a lot of people but if you have not fought the Germans you don't know what fighting is. Whatever the situation, they will always find something to throw at you – and their junior officers and NCOs always show great initiative.'[4]

This account has concentrated on the actions of the two Canadian battalions but it is worthwhile pausing to consider the reactions of the enemy troops, who came back fighting within a matter of minutes and held their positions with courage and considerable skill. These were supposed to be 'second-grade' troops, but they fought with great tenacity and brought the Canadian advance to a standstill. Then they came swarming after them when the Canadians pulled back to the beach.

The root of the Pourville problem seems to rest on the fact that the landing simply lacked weight. It was not just the lack of support from warships and aircraft, though there was precious little of that, but the landing was not made in sufficient strength for it to succeed. Once the enemy was on the alert two or three battalions were not enough to carry the attack forward. Granted, the South Saskatchewans had enjoyed the advantage of surprise, but too much cannot be left to surprise. Three years into this hard war was a little late in the day to assume that the Germans would be caught totally unprepared or not react quickly to any threat.

The effect of these mistakes and the strong, swift German reaction contributed in no small measure to the casualty figures on Green Beach. From the 523 officers and men of the South Saskatchewan Regiment who landed on Green Beach, 353 got back to England; 167 of these survivors were wounded. Eighty-four men were killed and another 89 made prisoner. Only 6 of 25 officers survived the raid unscathed and uncaptured.

From the Cameron Highlanders of Canada, of 503 officers and men who went ashore, 268 returned to England, 103 of them wounded. Sixty men were killed and 167 were captured. Only 8 of 32 officers got back unwounded. The losses for both battalions on Green Beach come to a joint total of 39 per cent. As we shall see later, much of this loss occurred during the withdrawal phase.

RED AND WHITE BEACHES

DIEPPE

It is vital to the success of the operation as a whole that White and Red beaches be in our hands with the minimum delay.

Operation Order, JUBILEE

READING ANY ACCOUNT of the Dieppe operation, personal or official, gradually fills the reader with a growing sense of doom. Everything seems to hinge on what happened elsewhere. Everywhere the same basic problems – inadequate intelligence, a poor plan, a lack of adequate support, communications failures, no alternative to the pre-planned assault, a lack of surprise, the rapid enemy response – become ever more obvious, yet nothing is done, the slaughter continues and the casualties mount.

And so the assaults go in, culminating in the most desperate one of all, the frontal attack by two battalions, one each from the Essex Scottish and the Royal Hamilton Light Infantry, plus a regiment of the Calgary Tanks, on the one-mile-long stretch of shingle beach directly before the port of Dieppe.

This frontal assault, a bloody climax to the events on the other beaches, had always been the most controversial part of the operation. Even to the amateurs planning the Dieppe operation, there was something uniquely hazardous about making a frontal assault on the beach at Dieppe. It smacked of another Light Brigade at Balaclava, or a Pickett's Charge at Gettysburg – in boats.

Four months after the Raid, in December 1942, Churchill himself queried the entire frontal assault concept employed at Dieppe:

> At first sight it would appear to a layman very much out of accord with the accepted principles of war, to attack the strongly-fortified town front without first securing the cliffs on either side and to use our tanks in frontal assault off the beaches by the Casino etc., instead of landing them a few miles up the coast and entering the town from the back.[1]

Quite so. A lot of opinion, informed or otherwise, would agree with these comments, but that basic point had not escaped the RUTTER planners. As already described, there were two plans for the Dieppe assault. One, calling for a frontal attack on the town, was favoured by General Montgomery, while Mountbatten favoured putting the weight into flanking attacks and avoiding a direct assault completely. The reasons for these differences and the rejection of the 'flanking attack only' option have already been explained and the decision to carry out both flanking attacks and a frontal assault was taken by the CCS as early as 18 April, four months before the attack; sanity did not return in the intervening weeks.

However, it was also clear that if the planners wanted a frontal assault on Dieppe and wanted it launched within half an hour of the flanking attacks at Puys and Pourville, then a good deal of support was going to be necessary in the form of heavy naval gunfire and aerial bombing. In effect, this shelling and bombing was the Plan 'B', an alternative for any failure at Puys and Pourville. If the flanking forces failed to clear the headlands, this shelling and bombing would – or at least might – make up the difference. When the heavy shelling and bombing was cancelled, the entire operation became extremely hazardous; when the flanking assaults failed, a tragedy became certain.

It is important to grasp this point firmly and hang onto it. The demands of the situation were quite clear and the priorities stark. If the Canadians landed on the main beach while the enemy were in full possession of the headlands, their destruction was inevitable. Therefore, the headlands must be cleared and there were only two ways to do this. One was the plan adopted, sending in troops from the flanks to take physical possession of the headland defences. The second option was to so shatter these defences by shelling and bombing that they would be untenable and out of action when the troops came ashore on the beach below. The reader and the historian enjoy the benefits of hindsight, but the issue is clear and always was clear: no possession of the headlands, no beach landing.

There was nothing scientific about the central assault at Dieppe. It simply required two infantry battalions to land on the shingle under the sea wall and advance directly into the town, clearing the way for the tanks and opening a route the armour could follow due south to link up with the Camerons at St Aubin and Arques. Various tasks would then be performed and the force would withdraw via Dieppe.

To achieve this end the battalions were to land on two parts of the main beach, each part with a designated codeword. The eastern landing area, Red Beach, close to the harbour entrance, was to be assaulted by the Essex Scottish. The western area – White Beach – and the Casino that occupied the promenade between the houses and the sea wall were handed to the Hamilton Light Infantry. Both units would be followed by thirty Churchills from the Calgary Tanks equipped with machine-guns and 6-pdr guns, landing in three waves directly onto the shingle but not tasked to support the assault infantry; sappers would clear a path off the promenade and the tanks were to speed through the town further inland and join the Camerons at St Aubin.

Having got ashore, the Essex Scottish were to clear the eastern end of the port and the harbour – where the Royal Marine 'A' Commando would be busy seizing the German landing craft – before linking up with the Royal Regiment coming over the headland from Puys. Meanwhile the Hamiltons, having cleared the beach and the Casino, were to turn west and meet the South Saskatchewans coming over the western headland from Pourville. It all sounded perfectly straightforward but two major drawbacks inhibited this simple plan, both the fault of the planners.

Firstly, the planners either relied on poor intelligence or failed to correctly interpret the intelligence they did have – probably the latter. The German defences in the town and on either headland were much stronger than the Allied planners supposed, and the German troops were well led and far from 'second-rate'. Secondly, the support made available to the assaulting battalions at Dieppe was *completely inadequate.*

The Germans had taken a considerable amount of trouble with the

Dieppe defences, constructing pillboxes and trenches on both headlands and along the promenade, equipping these positions with machine-guns and mortars, and hiding more of these weapons in the narrow caves carved out of the chalk cliffs overlooking the esplanade. Cannon – 30mm and 20mm – and the turret of a French tank cemented into the esplanade defended the street exits leading into the town, which were also blocked by concrete anti-tank barriers.

One curious omission in the German armoury was anti-tank guns. By 1942 the Wehrmacht possessed a wide range of anti-tank artillery, including the formidable 88mm, which was making life a misery for British tank crews in the Western Desert of North Africa, but there are no accounts of anti-tank guns at Dieppe. Indeed, the hulls and turrets of the Churchills are frequently mentioned in accounts of this operation as being invulnerable to shellfire, so the enemy resorted to shelling their tracks, with very beneficial results: most of the Calgary Tanks knocked out that day were halted by the loss of their tracks.

Another feature of the defences was the Casino building, which ran across the promenade and overlooked White Beach. The Germans had been in the process of destroying this building, but on the day it was turned into a strongpoint, with weapons firing down on the Canadians from every door and window. All these positions, on the headlands or in the town, were strongly manned, and the troops manning them, if not of first-class quality, were perfectly capable of putting up a stout resistance from their fixed defences.

These defences were also in depth, which is the essence of defence. If the Canadians got off the beach they would then have to cross the open bullet-swept promenade and fight their way into the town, raked by fire from the headlands every step of the way. Granted, their Isle of Wight training had laid great stress on street-fighting skills, but street-fighting is notoriously hard on infantry – and, curiously, there were no plans for the infantry to be supported in this fight by the Calgary Tanks. The infantry were to secure the headlands, the town and the port while the tanks were to pass through Dieppe and get to St Aubin and Arques.

All this is academic. The tanks and infantry never got more than a few hundred yards from the beach, and it is not hard to see why. The prime problem with attacking this central position is a basic one: unless the two headlands, western and eastern, were in friendly hands before the main assault went in, the landing craft and their passengers would be faced with an overwhelming amount of plunging fire from artillery, mortars and machine-guns. As we have seen from the events described in the previous chapters, neither headland was in any danger of capture when the Hamiltons and Essex Scottish went ashore, half an hour after the battles began at Puys and Pourville. In the event and as a result, the central landings were shattered by German fire before the troops even reached the beaches. The only remedy would have been to support the landing forces with a great volume of naval gunfire or aerial bombing, shattering the defences and dismaying the garrison; as we know, neither of these assets was in place.

The idca of bombing Dieppe had been shelved, partly for fear of killing French civilians and partly because General Roberts believed, or had been persuaded to believe, that the main effect of heavy bombing would be to fill the streets of the town with rubble and inhibit the passage of his tanks. As for the naval gunfire, the Admiralty, who had no intention of exposing one of their scarce capital ships to attack by the Luftwaffe, rejected out of hand a request by Combined Operations HQ for a battleship or monitor capable of pounding the headlands with 15in or 16in shells.

Here was a major error and another failure of command responsibility. When the request for such support was denied, the entire operation should have been called off and the powers that be at Home Forces and Combined Operations left in no doubt of the reason; no aerial bombardment, no heavy gun support, no assault landing. Granted, the Navy offered some support in the shape of the 4in guns of several Hunt-class destroyers but no one could seriously maintain that this was adequate compensation for the firepower of a capital ship.

Instead of the 15in guns of HMS *Warspite* or the monitor HMS *Terror*, the Navy offered the 4in guns of eight small destroyers, HMSs *Calpe*, *Fernie*, *Albrighton*, *Berkeley*, *Brocklesby*, *Bleasdale* and *Garth*, plus the Polish destroyer *Slazak*. Not all these ships were on bombardment duties; HMSs *Calpe* and *Fernie* were command ships and *Slazak* was guarding the eastern end of the invasion convoy. In the event, just four destroyers (*Albrighton*, *Berkeley*, *Bleasdale* and *Garth*) bombarded the headlands during the Red and White Beaches assault. Two of these destroyers, *Albrighton* and *Garth*, had also been tasked to support the landings at Berneval, Puys and Pourville, but even if every Hunt-class destroyer had been pounding the headlands with her main armament, the volume of fire would still have been inadequate.

To compare the effect of a 4in projectile with that of a 15in or 16in shell is ridiculous. It is like comparing a gentle tap on the front door with the sudden arrival of a speeding train; the difference in sheer weight of fire is profound. Had the defenders of the two headlands been on the receiving end of a few 15in shells, the survivors, crawling from their shattered casemates, would have been in no condition to offer any resistance to the landings taking place below. Much the same applies to the proposed bombing. Though naval gunfire was heavier and more accurate, a heavy bombing raid on the town and headlands just before the landing would have been some compensation for the absence of a capital ship and given the defenders something else to think about other than engaging the troops below. A brief strafing of the defences by fighters just before the landing was simply not sufficient.

The RAF was anxious to help the landing force but the help they had in mind was quite inadequate. In lieu of a smashing attack by the heavy bombers of RAF Bomber Command, JUBILEE was offered a brief strafing attack with cannon on the headlands at or about H-Hour by six squadrons of RAF fighters. In addition, three RAF squadrons would lay a smokescreen across the beach area as the landing craft closed the shore. This smokescreen proved a mixed blessing; apart from blinding the coastal gunners, it obscured the shore from the naval observers on the bombardment ships, and so reduced the accuracy of naval gunfire. There were no easy options at Dieppe. The sum total of these failures was that the troops went in to find the headlands and the town defences alert, undamaged and active; what followed was no less tragic for being quite inevitable.

The Canadians crossed to Dieppe in three assault landing ships – the *Glengyle*, the *Prince Charles* and the *Prince Leopold* – and were in their LCAs by 0320hrs. They experienced no problems of any kind as they approached the Dieppe beach, on time and directly in line with their landing area. There was no enemy reaction until the beach was in plain sight but, following reports of the landings at Pourville and Puys, the enemy were fully on the alert. At 0445hrs the approaching armada of landing craft was detected by a flotilla of German ships waiting off the harbour and by observers on the headlands. Starshells were fired, the landing craft stood out starkly in the glaring white light of flares, the Germans rushed to their positions and the battle for the Dieppe beaches was on.

It was now around 0450hrs and the Canadian LCAs, now in line abreast, were heading for the shore. H-Hour was 0520hrs and at around 0510hrs, with sufficient daylight available, the four destroyers opened fire on the beach and the houses and hotels across the promenade, producing a bombardment that was instantly seen as inadequate. Then, when the LCAs were about a mile from the shore, RAF fighters swept overhead, blasting the buildings at the rear of the promenade and the headlands above the port with cannon fire . . . and that was that. Within a few minutes all the support the Canadians were to get had already been expended. It was, said the US Brigadier-General Lucian Truscott, observing this prior bombardment from HMS *Fernie*, 'not nearly so heavy or impressive as I should have liked'.

By now, with the men in the landing craft easing their cramped limbs for the dash up the beach, the headlands had been smoked out by more RAF aircraft but the guns on the headlands had been set to fire on fixed lines and could engage the beach without needing to see it. Then the dawn breeze shredded the smoke and the German gunners were able to pour fire directly onto the incoming craft. What followed is best described by recounting briefly what happened to the LCAs and LCTs of the first wave.

Thanks in part to the strafing of the headlands, the first wave of LCAs managed to land their troops with light casualties, the men dashing down the ramps and sprinting up the steeply shelving beach towards the sea wall. Not everyone made it for the machine-guns were now in action, raking the beach with fire, cutting down anyone who hesitated.

The Royal Hamilton Light Infantry, landing at the western end of the beach close to the Casino, seemed to have suffered most. Their commanding officer, Lieutenant-Colonel R.R. Labatt, scion of a Canadian brewing family, lost most of his headquarters, including the vital signals section, to machine-gun fire before he reached the sea wall, and as he flung himself down and looked about him, he saw his battalion being shot to pieces. The rifle companies on his right had been hit by mortar fire while still in their landing craft and had then landed directly in front of a pillbox, which poured fire into the bow doors as soon as they opened. Those to his left were in no better case, their path to the sea wall littered with dead and wounded men. Some of the survivors were now crouching in hollows on the open beach, others were huddled against the sea wall, hundreds of anxious faces turned in his direction, mutely asking what to do next.

Further up the beach to the east, the commander of the Essex Scottish, Lieutenant-Colonel Fred Jasperson, was in similar trouble. He had seen men falling on either hand as he ran up the beach towards the sea wall where the survivors were gathered. Those who had crossed the wall were now held up by another belt of wire, between the wall and the esplanade. Bangalore torpedoes were brought up but failed to make much impression on these tangled thickets, and when men crawled across the wall and attempted to cut the wire by hand, the machine-gunners and snipers had an easy target. The Essex Scottish were pinned on Red Beach and looked likely to stay there.

There was no easy way forward on White Beach, either. Behind the wall lay the wire, and overhanging the beach and the wall stood the Casino from where snipers and machine-gunners were picking off anyone who moved. Within minutes of their craft crunching on the cobbles, both infantry battalions had been stopped and were taking casualties. Come what might and at whatever cost, they had to get off the beach.

What was needed now was some support to beat down the enemy fire. The Calgary Tanks, which should have landed with the infantry, could have provided this but they were only now coming in, some fifteen minutes behind the first infantry wave. The first tank wave landing on Red Beach consisted of three LCTs, each craft containing three Churchill tanks. These tanks had been equipped with a rolled-up bundle of wooden palings, a primitive form of carpet, which, it was hoped, would provide some grip for the tank tracks on the rolling shingle of the beach. As it transpired, losing a track was the least of the tank crews' problems.

The first LCT managed to unload its three tanks under fire but while these armoured vehicles – named 'Calgary', 'Company' and 'Chief' – got off unscathed to grind about the beach, the LCT was so damaged and holed by shellfire that it sank as it pulled back off the shore. The second craft grounded and was then delayed, well aground and under a storm of fire, because the tank crews had failed to warm up their engines before the landing and the cold engines refused to start – a small error that had a grievous effect. Frantic minutes passed while the three tanks remained stuck on the launching ramp, tanks and LCT under heavy fire.

When the second three tanks – 'Cat', 'Cougar' and 'Cheetah' – finally got off their riddled craft, they quickly found a place where the shingle had piled up against the sea wall, crossed the wire without difficulty and were last seen heading across the promenade towards the town centre. The LCT had by now lost its bow door, and most of the crew were killed or injured before it could reverse off the beach and pull out to deeper water; those on board were taken off by the destroyer *Slazak* before this LCT sank, but it had landed its tanks.

One of the minor myths of the Dieppe operation is that the tanks remained stuck on the shingle and never got off the beach, a belief encouraged by a number of subsequent German photographs showing tanks, minus their tracks, stopped and burning on the beach. A number of tanks did suffer such a fate but there is no general truth in the story. In fact, the Calgary Tanks put twenty-nine tanks ashore at Dieppe, and of these fifteen got off the beach and onto the promenade. Disembarking into deep water drowned two and the rest were knocked out on the beach, either by shellfire or from slipping their tracks on the shingle.

A considerable number of tanks got over the wall and onto the promenade, and it was there that their problems really began. The various exits from the promenade had been blocked with anti-tank obstacles which the tank crews had no means of removing; that task had been delegated to the Canadian engineers, the sappers, and most of them had been killed. Most of the tanks therefore stayed on the promenade, the crews engaging the enemy positions with their 6pdr guns until they ran out of ammunition and then staying inside their tanks – quite the safest place to be in Dieppe that day – until obliged to surrender.

Those tanks that got onto the promenade could have made a difference, not least in cutting down some of the fire from the buildings behind the promenade and from the Casino, but that was not their prime task. Besides, there was no way of elevating the turret guns to hit targets on the headlands, and the direct fire of the Churchill 6pdrs could not have engaged the defences further back; what was needed there was naval gunfire or howitzers, which deliver a plunging fire, or heavy mortars, but there was nowhere to deploy artillery on the Dieppe seafront, even had artillery been factored into the plan. Confined to the promenade, their commander already dead, the Calgary Tanks were a wasted asset.

The engineers who might have cleared the obstacles barring exit from the promenade were still either on their landing craft or already dead on the beach. Parties from the Royal Canadian Engineers had been put ashore with no other task in mind – to blast any obstacle barring the exits and get the tanks moving inland – and their losses in attempting to do so were very high. Of the 169 sappers who went ashore, no fewer than 152 were killed or wounded or captured; of the 17 who got back to the UK 10 were wounded. This represents a loss rate among the sappers of some 90 per cent, but in spite of this sacrifice the tanks remained on the promenade.

The problem this caused should not be underrated. General Roberts had agreed to the cancellation of the heavy bombing at least partially because he had been told that intensive bombing would fill the streets with rubble, making the passage of the tanks impossible. Rubble was not the only obstacle: there were also those anti-tanks walls and concrete pillars. They also had to be removed, and the only people who could do that were the sappers. When the engineers were cut down on the beach, the tanks were destined to stay on the esplanade.

One Canadian tanker describes the tanks' main activity that day as 'going round and round in bloody circles, using up our gas and ammo, being shelled, rolling over people'. Unable to get forward, the tanks rumbled about the open promenade, engaging any enemy they saw but contributing very little to the vital task of opening a way off the beach for the infantry.

Lacking any such support, the struggle on the beach continued, with the same story repeating itself in both Red and White sectors. The craft in the second wave, LCTs 4, 5 and 6, suffered, if anything, more than the three LCTs of the first wave. LCT 4 carried three tanks and 'B' Company of the Essex Scottish. The craft was hit by shellfire as it closed the beach; the tanks got off but were then struck by shellfire themselves. This knocked them off their tracks, leaving tanks and crews stranded on the beach. 'B' Company stayed in the elusive shelter of the LCT hold until the tanks were clear, then went down the ramp in a wild rush for the sea wall, leaping through gaps in the wire and finding shelter against the sea wall without more than a few casualties, while LCT 4, empty and abandoned, burst into flames, drifted out to sea and sank.

Fire was now sweeping LCT 5. Hit by mortar bombs, which landed on the bridge, killing her captain and crew, the LCT got to the beach and unloaded her tanks. The first of these got up the beach, found a place where shingle had piled up and crossed the sea wall to the promenade; the other two threw their tracks on the shingle and remained on the beach under fire.

The last vessel of the second wave, LCT 6, made three attempts to beach before landing and unloading her three tanks, all of which made it to the promenade and were last seen heading across the open ground for the rear of the Casino. Other troops on board also landed, but at least one platoon of thirty men declined to go ashore in spite of a direct order from the captain, who wanted to kedge his vessel off and get back out to sea. These exhortations seem to have taken some time for, in his report, the captain of LCT 6 records: 'All the infantry except thirty were landed and after waiting fifteen minutes for them to go ashore, I withdrew from the beach.'

It is hard to blame these men for their reluctance to land – the noise, the confusion, the sights glimpsed through the open ramp and bow doors would have daunted anyone – and it is a fact that most of the thousand or so Canadians who returned to the UK after the Raid owed their survival to the fact that they never went ashore.

The third wave of LCTs, consisting of LCTs 7, 8, 9 and 10, closed the beach at around 0605hrs. This final wave brought in another squadron of Churchills – twelve tanks – and the command element of the assault force, the two Brigadiers, Sherwood Letts of the 4th Brigade and William Southam of the 6th Brigade, as well as Lieutenant-Colonel Johnny Andrews, CO of the Calgary Tanks. Brigadier Southam also carried, unwisely and in defiance of orders, a copy of the JUBILEE operational plan. This later fell into the hands of the enemy, affording them great interest and, one suspects, considerable amusement.

The Brigadiers were to set up their HQs in churches near the sea front and get a grip on the battle, but neither man had the chance to do so. It may have been assumed that by the time these senior officers got ashore, the situation on the beach would have been stabilised; but that was not the way it was at Dieppe that morning.

Brigadier Southam, coming in on LCT 7, got a rapid introduction to the problems ashore when a mortar bomb hit his craft, blowing him off the upper deck and down into the hold. Shaken but otherwise unhurt, rallying his headquarters team about him, Southam followed the tanks off the craft and was promptly blown into the water by the explosion of an artillery shell, which killed a number of men in the Brigade Signals section and put most of the brigade radios out of action. The LCT then reversed off the shore only to sink later; the Brigadier, now without his Signals link, joined his men on the beach.

Another range of difficulties attended the landing of Brigadier Letts from LCT 8. The first tank to disembark broke down on the ramp, barring the way to the other tanks and causing chaos on board, where the CO and Headquarters Section of the Calgary Tanks were also anxious to get off. The LCT's commander then decided to go out to sea, reorganise and come in again. This second landing, made closer to the western headland, attracted a great amount of enemy fire which caused a number of casualties. These included Brigadier Letts, hit by a shell splinter. When

LCT 8 finally got to the beach, Lieutenant-Colonel Andrews drove his tank off into deep water and was killed when he abandoned it to seek shelter ashore. The last tank on LCT 8 remained on board as the craft was, according to one account, 'quite literally blasted off the beach by shell fire'.

The last LCT in the third wave carried three experimental flame-throwing tanks and a variety of other stores and vehicles, including one of those scout cars that might have proved so useful at Pourville. The bulk of the cargo was engineering stores, including a bulldozer and several tons of explosive for clearing road blocks, as well as infantry and sappers. Greeted with heavy fire, this craft grounded in the centre of the beach and immediately received a salvo of mortar bombs, which landed in the cargo hold, killing a number of men but miraculously not detonating the explosives.

In these circumstances it is hardly surprising that the unloading of this LCT was a shambles. The first tank started out before the ramp was in position and tumbled into deep water. The second got to the beach, where its flame container was set alight by tracer bullets. The third rolled backwards in the hold, crushing to death some wounded soldiers lying on the deck, and lost a track to shellfire as soon as it hit the beach.

By now all the LCT officers and many of the crew had been hit. The craft broached to across the waves, while those aboard who were still alive attempted to take shelter from the mortar bombs and machine-gun fire that continued to lash the craft. Further down the beach other craft – LCAs and LCTs – were also ablaze, while the beach itself was littered with dead and wounded men and a few grounded tanks. The Canadians still came in to land, but the landing on Red and White Beaches had clearly stalled. The gallantry of the LCT crews in this part of the operation should not be forgotten. Ten LCTs had gone in; five of them were promptly sunk by shellfire and another three were badly damaged; 50 per cent of the LCT crews were either killed or wounded.

What was needed now – what had always been needed – was some way of suppressing the enemy fire so that the troops could move forward off the beach. The support coming from the bombardment destroyers and the landing craft was clearly inadequate, which left the task to the ground-strafing fighter aircraft of the RAF. So far that support had been confined to the brief strafing of the guns at Varengeville and the headlands above Dieppe. That was all the planners envisaged, partly because that was considered sufficient, partly because of the difficulty of spotting exactly where the landing forces were. It would not have helped if the RAF had added their attacks to the other travails of the assault troops. Nevertheless, there were now hundreds of RAF aircraft either over Dieppe or heading in that direction; why was not some of this force directed to help the assault?

The short answer is that ground support was not built into the plan. An examination of the operational orders reveals that the RAF were tasked to engage the enemy and bomb gun batteries, but there is no mention of any other support for the ground troops in the form of ground strafing of enemy defences or regular attacks on the headlands. This was largely due to the current state of ground-to-air communications, which were non-existent; the 'cab-rank' of ground-attack fighters, tasked to support the troops below, which was such a feature of the 1944 Normandy campaign, had not yet been thought of.

Indeed, as far as Leigh-Mallory was concerned, the ground forces were a form of bait. In the RAF vision of things the Raid would lure the Luftwaffe to Dieppe, where the RAF would fall upon them in vast numbers, inflicting massive losses and so establishing British air superiority over the Channel. The RAF certainly put a lot of effort into the Dieppe operation. The air element included sixty-seven squadrons of fighters – all but fifteen of them Spitfire squadrons – seven bomber squadrons (five of Bostons and two of Blenheims), a Beaufighter squadron and, from the US Eighth Army Air Force, the 91st Bomber Group of four B-17 Flying

Fortress squadrons. With such a force available Leigh-Mallory anticipated knocking the Luftwaffe out of the sky.

It was not to work out like that; when the RAF and Luftwaffe losses were finally compared it was discovered that the RAF had lost 106 aircraft and the Luftwaffe 48. RAF losses were made up of 88 fighters and 18 smoke-laying aircraft or bombers; 67 RAF pilots were killed. These figures alone illustrate that the balance of advantage in the air battle went to the Germans, largely because the British fighter mainly employed at Dieppe, the Spitfire V, was totally outclassed by the Focke-Wulf 190. Dieppe, seventy miles from the south coast of England, was also at the extreme end of the Spitfire V's range; RAF fighters, other than the few Mustangs available, could not stay over the beaches for more than ten minutes, and their pilots fought the FW 190s with one eye on the petrol gauge.

German fighters, FW 190s and Messerschmitt 109s, appeared over the beaches at around 0700hrs and German bombers, Dorniers and Heinkels, appeared at around 0930hrs, attacking the fleet offshore and attempting to bomb the beaches; by the end of the day most of the Allied shipping had sustained some bomb damage.

On the British side light bombers were available, but not for ground support. RAF Bostons bombed the heavy coastal batteries around Dieppe but to little avail; the bombs were too light and the battery casemates too strong for the bombs to have much effect, and the offshore fleet came under increasingly effective fire. Where the RAF was useful was in laying and maintaining the smokescreen that shielded the fleet from observed fire. On the other hand, this smokescreen concealed much of what was happening ashore from the commanders offshore.

RAF efforts, while gallant and persistent, cannot therefore be counted among the few successes of that dreadful day. Losses were heavy, ground support was limited or non-existent, the bombing ineffective and the smokescreen a mixed blessing. And not a few RAF losses were due to the fire put up by the ships.

It would be possible to go on recounting the events on the Dieppe beach but the picture is surely clear. Within half an hour of the assault going in, the landing here had failed. All order had been lost, there were tanks on the promenade and tanks – mostly knocked out – on the beach. There were men on the beach, huddled under the sea wall and crouching in the ditch between the sea wall and the promenade. Many of these men were wounded and most of those out on the beach were either dead or pretending to be dead; any sign of life attracted a sniper's bullet or a burst of fire.

Worst of all, there was no one in command. Lieutenant-Colonel Johnny Andrews of the Calgary Tanks was dead. The commanding officers, Lieutenant-Colonel Jasperson of the Essex Scottish and Lieutenant-Colonel Labatt of the Royal Hamilton Light Infantry, were ashore but in no better case than their men, pinned down and unable to influence events, with no communication with the Force Commanders on *Calpe* who seem to have had no clear idea of the situation. The only communication link between shore and *Calpe* came from a scout car, stranded on the beach and manned by a signals corporal and a wounded officer. The problem was that nobody else knew that this link existed, and getting across the fire-swept beach to the scout car in order to send a signal was an exploit fraught with hazard.

There was, however, one possible way off the beach – through the corridors and gaming rooms of the three-storey Casino, which loomed above that part of the beach now carpeted with the dead and wounded of the Royal Hamilton Light Infantry. These wounded were being cared for under fire by one of the heroes of the Dieppe operation, the regimental padre of the Hamiltons, Captain Reverend John Foote, who won Canada's second Victoria Cross in this war for his courage on the beach that morning.

In the days before the Raid the Germans had been busy destroying the Casino, seeing it as a means whereby a landing force could get under cover from the beach to the town. With a raid now actually in progress, they had sent men into the building and were engaging the troops on the beach from the windows. The Canadians were returning this fire with rifles and Brens, and from time to time small parties of men were dashing across the few yards between the beach and the Casino and vanishing inside. Once inside, they began to fight their way from room to room, blasting a way forward with grenades and bursts of Sten-gun fire, a certain amount of help from the tanks cruising about outside and the assistance of some sappers with explosives.

The fight for the Casino was a 'soldiers' battle', fought by junior officers, NCOs and private soldiers, largely on their own initiative, often meeting the enemy in hand-to-hand combat in the dark rooms and corridors. It took over an hour, but the Casino was finally in the hands of the Hamiltons by shortly after 0700hrs. A message was then sent from Lieutenant-Colonel Labatt, announcing that the Casino had fallen; it reached Roberts on *Calpe* at 0712hrs and had the direst effect.

Roberts had been receiving a number of reports from the beach since the landings began. Many of these were garbled and some were plain wrong, but the sum total had created the impression that the landings on Red and White Beaches, if costly, were still going well. The news that the Casino had fallen only seemed to confirm the impression that, given another push, the German defences at Dieppe would crumble and success attend the rest of the operation. This being so, Roberts decided to commit his floating reserve, the French Canadian Fusiliers Mont-Royal, to the fight taking place at Dieppe.

12

THE FLOATING RESERVE GOES IN

With a courage terrible to see, the Marines went in to land . . .

REPORT ON OPERATION JUBILEE, 1942

THE HANDBOOK USED by the military world is full of good advice on the basic principles a commander should employ for the successful conduct of war. These begin with the need 'to select and maintain the aim', move onto the need for a 'concentration of force', then list many more essentials including the need to avoid 'reinforcing failure'.

'Reinforcing failure' is considered a bad move for a military commander because it resembles throwing good money after bad, an action which all sensible people would wish to avoid. The snag for the military commander is that he first has to discover whether the battle he is conducting has indeed become a failure, and if so what he should do about it. His ability to make that decision depends very largely on the information he is able to obtain.

The 'fog of war' can be a very real thing. Before 0700hrs it was clear to the Military Force Commander on HMS *Calpe*, Major-General Roberts, that all was not going well on the beaches at and around Dieppe. The snag was that actual details were very hard to come by, not least because the beaches were obscured by the heavy smokescreen laid to shield the offshore fleet from the coastal batteries, so it was difficult for those afloat to see what was happening on the beaches. For that Roberts had to rely on radio messages received from the battalions ashore, and that method was proving both inadequate and contradictory.

Communication problems were to plague military operations throughout the Second World War. It may therefore be helpful if the basics of military communications are explained here, taking as an example the signals set-up of a battalion and a brigade.

A battalion commander would be in radio contact with the four Rifle Company commanders and the Rifle Company commanders would be in contact with their subordinate platoon commanders, perhaps using the same radio, but on a different wavelength (or 'net') from that used by the CO and the Company commanders. These would be referred to as the 'battalion net' and the 'company net'. This set-up enabled the battalion commander to get a message forward even when one Company was failing to respond; since they were all on the same 'net', a message from the battalion CO to 'B' Company could be relayed via the commander of 'A' Company. In addition, since all the Company commanders had their ears glued to the radio sets on that net, everyone knew what was going on. This was no reason for idle chatter, for the enemy too would be listening to these transmissions. Those using the radios were supposed to follow strict radio procedures and use the appropriate or previously agreed codewords.

The battalion commander would not be listening in on the brigade net, the radio contact between the battalion and all the other battalions in the Brigade and with his direct superior at Brigade Headquarters, but the brigade net signaller would be close by, ready to call the CO over if the Brigadier came on the air and wanted to talk to him. Since the Brigade might be deployed over a much wider area, this net would use a more powerful radio set than that used by the battalion and be manned by the men of the Battalion Signals section. And so the process of communications would proceed, to Division and Corps and Army, with links up and down and everyone fully in the picture.

This, however, would be perfection; radio communications were usually a nightmare. Often unreliable and spasmodic, radio signals could be interrupted by buildings and woods, by hills and valleys, by malfunctions in the equipment and by enemy jamming. These difficulties could make command virtually impossible for a commander, and accounts abound on the problems caused by communications failures.

If his radio communications failed the commander was deaf and blind and dumb. Unable to ascertain the situation, he was incapable of making a decision based on accurate information, but he probably had to make one anyway, based on whatever information was to hand. It follows from this that by 1942 any experienced commander had become almost paranoid about his communications, and strained every effort and the nerves of his staff to ensure their reliability.

In this respect at least it is difficult to fault the JUBILEE commanders. All the evidence suggests that they were fully aware of the importance of good communications on JUBILEE and had made every effort to provide a sound communications net and back it up in case any part of it broke down. The two headquarters ships, HMSs *Calpe* and *Fernie*, were so festooned with wireless aerials that they could hardly traverse their guns, and indeed had been forbidden to take part in the shore bombardment for fear that the concussion from the gunfire would damage the aerials.

The planners had arranged a sound signals set-up, making every allowance for breakdowns. What they were not able to do was to prevent the breakdown of communications on the beach caused by enemy action. Indeed it is one of the tragic ironies of the Dieppe operation that after so much care and attention, this vital function failed as a result of factors completely beyond the planners' control – not at the command end but at the sharp end, where shells and gunfire ruled events.

As we have seen, the result was a complete signals breakdown in every sector. The Berneval signals set-up failed completely when SGB 5 ran into that German coastal convoy. The Royal Regiment lost all its communications on Blue Beach when a salvo from HMS *Garth* brought a section of the cliff top down on the signallers below. At Pourville, Colonel Merritt had his radio shot from his hand and the German mortars followed the signals section around the village with such persistence that the signallers believed they were being tracked by radar. Everywhere signallers, marked out by the tall aerials of their sets, found themselves a target for snipers.

On Red and White Beaches there are reports of a shell landing on LCT 7 'which decimated the brigade signals section', and Brigadier Southam's signals set was destroyed when a tank ran over it. Even Lord Lovat found it best to close *Calpe* in his landing craft to report the success at Varengeville – and during the attack he had used flares rather than radio to order the assault on the guns. Other signal sections suffered heavy casualties when mortar shells struck their landing craft.

The destruction of the JUBILEE signals set-up was so complete and from such varied causes that it might be laughable had the outcome not been so serious. Nor was the destruction of so many sets the only problem. The only means the men ashore on Red and White Beaches had of communicating with the *Calpe* was via a radio set in a scout car manned by the Hamilton's Signals officer, Major Guy Rolfe. The problem was that no one knew Rolfe had contact with *Calpe*, and anyway getting messages to him across that fire-swept beach was virtually impossible. The failure of communications at Dieppe was almost total, but this is one failure for which no one can be blamed.

However, as we have seen, a certain number of radio signals were reaching Roberts and Hughes-Hallett on *Calpe* and, or so we must hope, they were also in receipt of reports from the landing craft unloading the wounded onto *Calpe*, from the wounded themselves, who would be most anxious to report what had happened, and from the captains of the bombardment destroyers which were manoeuvring off the beach. For some reason, the sum total of this information – and that message from Red Beach that 'The Essex Scottish were across the beach and in the houses' – induced General Roberts to believe that the time was right to commit his reserve.

This information was wrong. It seems to have arisen from the action taken by a small group of Essex Scottish soldiers who had indeed managed to get off the beach, over the promenade and into the houses along the Boulevard de Verdun, on the far side of the promenade. Over the next half-hour other groups, a few men at a time, managed to join them and when about thirty or so had been assembled, this party, amounting now to a platoon, made its way towards the harbour where they were quickly spotted, brought under fire by German troops on the eastern headland and forced back into cover. This group made the deepest incursion into Dieppe that day and – probably – it was the news of this exploit, signalled back to *Calpe*, that convinced Roberts that all was not yet lost.

The actual situation on Red and Green Beaches at this time, around 0730hrs, was extremely grave. The bulk of the two infantry battalions had been pinned on the beach for well over an hour and taken heavy casualties. The Essex Scottish, lying on the open Red Beach, were under heavy fire from the eastern headland and unable to move. The Hamiltons had taken the Casino but at some cost, and a heavy gun built into the seaward side of the Casino was still in action, firing into any incoming craft at point-blank range.

The command set-up ashore had also collapsed. Colonel Labatt of the Hamiltons was unwounded and had been ordered by Brigadier Letts to take command of the 4th Brigade, or what was left of it. Labatt wrote later:

> It was a grim feeling to be placed in command of this fine brigade only to take over when there was no tactical solution. The Royal Regiment at Puys could not be reached, and the Royal Hamilton Light Infantry had been practically wiped out and any movement on the part of the Essex Scottish meant its destruction and the end of any organized resistance.[1]

This was no more than the simple truth; by the time Labatt took over, the Essex Scottish had suffered some 75 per cent casualties and very few of them had got off the beach. Further up the beach, small parties of Canadians had passed through the Casino and got into the town, but all order had been lost and these men were on their own. And German troops from the country around Dieppe were now starting to arrive.

In spite of the rapid reaction of the German troops in and around Dieppe, the landings had clearly come as a complete surprise to the German High Command. The initial landings were reported to von

Rundstedt's Headquarters at 0525hrs but the scale of the landings was not clear. Later reports of landings at various points along the coast from Puys to Pourville then created the impression that this was a major incursion. Troops inland were put on full alert or, as in the case of the 10th Panzer Division, fifty miles away at Amiens, put on stand-by for a move to the coast. Other units, including an SS Division, were also ordered forward; had this indeed been a major incursion, the Germans had more than enough forces on hand to deal with it.

As it was, the landings had been effectively defeated in the first half-hour. The only question confronting the Force Commanders now was how to get the surviving troops off the beaches without further loss. Or at least, that should have been the question. The withdrawal would present its own complications but for the moment General Roberts was not thinking of withdrawal. Encouraged by Hughes-Hallett, he was willing to throw his last cards onto the table.

General Roberts later became the scapegoat for the entire JUBILEE operation – most unjustly in this author's opinion – but his decision to add another two units to the holocaust on the beach is very hard to defend. Granted, some of the messages gave ground for optimism, but there is more to command than simply listening to information that tells you what you wanted to hear. There is, for example, the evidence of one's own eyes. Had General Roberts emerged from his headquarters cabin on *Calpe* he would have seen plenty of evidence to contradict any radio report. The complement, the crew, of HMS *Calpe* numbered fewer than one hundred men. By 0700hrs the decks of this little destroyer were crammed with some two hundred wounded and dying Canadian soldiers, brought off every landing beach and delivered to *Calpe* in the hope of finding doctors.

Nor was this all: off *Calpe* other landing craft were bobbing about, their upper works riddled by shell and machine-gun fire, their decks running with blood, and they too had wounded men in urgent need of assistance. The physical evidence that the Dieppe operation was a shambles was there for anyone with the wit to see it, yet Roberts decided to commit his reserve, an action which the report on the Raid describes as 'one of the most unfortunate errors of the whole operation'.

The only way to analyse this decision is through the signals logs and the messages coming from the beaches. At 0610hrs, Roberts received a message from Red Beach, relayed from *Fernie*, that 'the Essex Scottish were across the beaches and in the houses'. A few minutes later, at 0615hrs, another message arrived from Labatt, stating that the Hamiltons were in the Casino.

The reports reaching Roberts seemed to indicate that the Raid still had a chance of success. He knew that the Casino had been taken and now believed that his tanks, supported by the Essex Scottish, had penetrated the town. It also appeared to him – heaven knows how – that the Pourville landing was proceeding according to plan. He still had the Fusiliers Mont-Royal and the Royal Marine 'A' Commando at his disposal and the decision was taken to use them in support of the troops ashore, the Fusiliers to back up the Essex Scottish on Red Beach, the Royal Marines to push in behind the Royal Hamilton Light Infantry on White Beach.

The Fusiliers Mont-Royal were a 584-strong battalion, commanded by Lieutenant-Colonel Dollard Ménard, and the Royal Marines 'A' Commando, just 369 officers and men, was commanded by Lieutenant-Colonel J. Picton-Phillips. The Fusiliers Mont-Royal had been waiting all morning in the boat pool, and they greeted their commitment to the battle with an outburst of cheers.

As for the Royal Marines, they had spent much of the day in a state of confusion. In the original plan they had been tasked with sailing into the harbour at Dieppe aboard the gunboat HMS *Locust*, capturing a fleet of forty German landing craft tied up there and sailing them back to England. This is another of those quixotic JUBILEE objectives with no basis in reality, as a little forethought by the planners would surely have revealed.

Had the Marines even reached the German landing craft they would probably have found that half of them were under repair or maintenance, with their engine parts spread about on the quayside or on the upper decks. Very few of these landing craft would have been fully fuelled, certainly not for a seventy-mile voyage back across the Channel to Newhaven. It is not hard to imagine the chaos that would have followed as the Marines hunted about the dockyard for diesel or attempted to fit the German engines back together. It would have been far simpler to equip each Marine section with a pickaxe and have them sink these craft at their moorings. Fortunately this venture into the harbour never came off.

An early-morning conference between Major-General Roberts, Captain Hughes-Hallett and Commander R.E.D. Ryder, VC, decided that since Puys had not been taken and the German positions on the eastern headland were still in action, any attempt to enter the port by HMS *Locust* and the Royal Marines Commando should be abandoned. The Marines on HMS *Locust* were already attempting to close the port and under fire from a shore battery when this decision was reached.

'Things were pretty confused what with the smoke and shelling,' recalls one Marine on HMS *Locust*. 'Someone near me on the bridge said, "Where's the entrance? – I can't see the Mole." I took hold of him and said, "The harbour Mole's over there; it's the one with the bloody great gun on it – the one that's firing straight at us."'[2]

HMS *Locust* contained the Commando HQ, 'A' Company and a demolition team and had arrived off the harbour entrance at 0520hrs. There she was promptly hit twice by the big gun on the mole, losing two men killed and six wounded. After being ordered to withdraw, she joined the destroyers bombarding the shore batteries, where she was eventually joined by French Chasseurs – fast armoured motor launches – bringing the rest of the Commando, and the Marines on *Locust* transferred to these craft. The 'A' Commando then joined the Fusiliers Mont-Royal as Force Reserve to await further orders.

On being ordered to land on Red Beach and support the Essex Scottish, the Fusiliers Mont-Royal embarked in twenty-six LCAs assembled from the boat pool for the run-in to the beach. This run-in was not prolonged; it began on the seaward side of the smokescreen that aircraft and the destroyers were still maintaining a few hundred yards offshore. As the LCAs emerged on the landward side, perhaps 200 yards from the beach, the Fusiliers were immediately struck by a blizzard of fire.

Within minutes, two craft had been hit by mortar fire and sunk; most of the rest were taking hits from machine-gun fire and men on board were already being killed or wounded. Nor was this all: those officers who dared to put their heads over the bulwarks saw that their craft were being carried to the west and looked likely to land on White Beach, behind the Hamiltons, rather than in support of the Essex Scottish by the harbour mouth. Nothing could be done about this; the only thought in every man's mind was to get ashore and away from this hellish fire.

The bulk of the Fusiliers landed on White Beach, a number of them, several companies, perhaps three hundred men, at the extreme western end, right under the headland, where grenades hurled down by Germans up above added to their problems. Everywhere the landing was chaos, with losses soaring among the troops. The battalion second-in-command, Major René Painchaud, recalls seeing what appeared to be a company of men under the western cliff, 'all of them dead, or wounded'.

Some soldiers were so traumatised by what they encountered beyond the smokescreen, the noise, the dead, the sheer unexpectedness of all this, that they were incapable of movement; they simply lay on the beach until they were killed. Another Fusiliers officer, Major Guy Vandelac, records: 'We realised it was pretty hopeless the minute we hit the beach and knew that everything was *kaput.* We could not believe it could go so wrong. We were never told about the sea wall and thought it was just an open beach we would be landing on.'[3]

The Fusiliers went in at around 0700hrs. Their commanding officer, Lieutenant-Colonel Ménard, was hit on landing and then hit again and again, the last bullet injuring his spine. Of thirty-one Fusiliers officers who went ashore that day, all but four were killed, wounded or captured – only four returned to England. Colonel Ménard was evacuated off the beach and made it back to England with just 120 of the 584 men he had led ashore. More than one hundred were killed on White Beach and the rest, many of them wounded, went into captivity.

The Fusiliers Mont-Royal never stood a chance. Within minutes of landing, a fine battalion was reduced to scattered groups clinging to holes in the shingle, sheltering behind wrecked tanks or huddled against the sea wall. Many of them were already wounded, all order had been lost and the survivors were being picked off without mercy by snipers. It was now the turn of the Royal Marines, and Marine 'Knocker' White of the 'A' Commando takes their story forward:

> At dawn we still hadn't gone ashore and palls of smoke and murderous gunfire were coming from the beach and cliffs. We tried to force our way in on HMS *Locust* but it was hopeless so we went back out to sea and hung about. Then we heard that a second plan was to be put into operation to land us further along the beach and get into the dock from the rear. We transferred from *Locust* into LCAs and LCMs.[4]

The orders given to Picton-Phillips were 'to land on White Beach, skirt the town to the west and south and attack the batteries on the East cliff'. Jacques Mordal, a French writer, later commented that this 'over-optimistic plan needed an advance of two-and-a-half miles over ground where no one had yet advanced so much as twenty yards'.[5]

Major Robert Houghton, then the second-in-command of the 'A' Commando, recalls:

> We had been on the French Chasseurs and transferred into LCAs for the assault. While we were waiting on the far side of the smoke-screen there were plenty of shells flying about. Once we went through the smoke, like the Fusiliers we were carried to the west and I went ashore almost in front of the Casino. My LCA contained the unit's Rear-HQ and a demolition team, which meant that it also contained a horrifying quantity of explosives. The fire which met us from the shore was very heavy and very accurate, but we just went on.[6]

The Marines were embarked in two LCMs (landing craft mechanised) and five LCAs, with Colonel Picton-Phillips leading the way in an LCM. 'With a courage terrible to see,' says the official history, 'the Marines went into land determined, if fortune so willed, to repeat at Dieppe what their fathers had accomplished at Zeebrugge.'

Lieutenant Buist, in charge of the Chasseurs, saw the Royal Marines go in:

> It was not long before I realized that this landing was the sea version of the Charge of the Light Brigade. A barrage of fire from the cliffs showed that the beach was under heavy fire and shells soon started to fall around the small group of landing craft, which we tried to screen with smoke. I shouted across to ask Colonel Phillips, asking if he wanted to continue but I doubt if he heard me. Anyway, he grinned and waved to show that he meant to land at all costs.

According to 'Knocker' White:

> Our craft got hit and stopped but we boarded another one . . . someone shouted that the Colonel was waving us back but then another shell came in and hit our engine compartment. I saw a poor stoker leap overboard with his clothes on fire then our Troop OC, Captain 'Pops' Manners, said very calmly, 'I think we had better abandon ship, lads', which we promptly did as the fuel tanks were hissing and threatening to blow up. Luckily we drifted into the smoke which saved us from the murderous machine-gun fire – we were only 200 yards or so from the shore.[7]

Captain Peter Hellings takes up the story:

> When the fire became intense, the Colonel stood up on the landing craft to direct the remainder of the party and lead his Commando onto the beach under the most intense mortar and machine-gun fire. As the range shortened the fire increased until there was no doubt that any attempt to reach the town over that beach would mean certain death. The Colonel refused to turn back until he had proved it was useless to continue.[8]

'We were in the Colonel's LCM and were hit repeatedly on our way to the beach,' writes Marine J. Farmer, '. . . and then I saw the bravest act I have ever seen. Colonel Phillips saw that it was hopeless and stood up in full view of us and pulled on a pair of white gloves and semaphored to the other assault boats to turn back. He was shot and killed in a matter of seconds.'

Major – now Major-General – Houghton recalls:

> I did not see that [the Colonel's death] because my LCA had been carried to the west and actually ran aground some way offshore, the tide now being out. The LCA cox'n was not keen to go in again but

he did and we came ashore under fire on White Beach. I have no idea where the CO got those white gloves from but he certainly saved the rest of the unit from certain destruction.[9]

Sergeant Knuthoffer in Colonel Picton-Phillips's boat:

For 10 Platoon, the moment of truth came when the LCM surged in all on its own towards touch-down on a fire-swept beach occupied by prostrate bodies and a few desperate groups clinging to cover. A look in any direction showed only too clearly that along the whole stretch of beach the landing of Canadian tanks and infantry had been smashed to a standstill.

For those of us who could see over the side the feeling at that moment was not of panic or unreasonable fear – but sheer amazement and disbelief. Not a logical reaction but a short space of a few seconds when the brain tries to reject what has been fed in. 'Get out fast, spread out, and run like hell for cover.'

Our LCM ground to a stop some way off the beach, an isolated target for everything in range. Within seconds it was down by the stern, broached to and the front ramp jammed shut. Even if the mind had fully registered and retained the detail, it would still be impossible to present a realistic impression of events from then on; it can be attempted only by listing some parts of the jigsaw clearly remembered.

A group at the front of the craft, trying to kick the ramp down. The CO, the crewmen and others hit and falling about. A scrum at the back end, men trying to dodge small arms fire coming down amongst them. Those looking over the shore side or trying to climb out, getting it in the head or chest and crashing back on to those behind them. Some Bren-gunners at work, one immortal bawling for full magazines. Another enthusiast, firing from a sitting position, threatening to shoot the head off anyone moving sideways. The theory was that at this point you pass through the fear barrier; it was just a matter of curiosity to see who got you first.

Steady mortar fire added to the pandemonium, but as the stern settled down even more, the deck was half awash, and it was not realized that this water included either petrol or diesel. Whatever it was, it ignited promptly when a burning smoke canister was dropped into it. The bright one who dropped the canister probably saved several lives by forcing everyone to bale out – and it at least shifted the menace of the sitting Bren-gunner who, with his legs afire, was over the side like a flash of light, taking his weapon with him. Being unable to disembark either through the front ramp or over the shore side, the start of a raging fire became a deciding factor even for those who had been slow in realizing that their number was coming up.

An effective smoke screen and very rapid movement meant that evacuation was carried out without many extra casualties. A quick check that those lying in the fire were dead – and then with anti-tank bombs and 36-grenades cooking and going off – instinct took over and saved the problems of planning the next move. Nobody made it ashore except as POWs later, and the half-platoon which came back were those who were able to get out in one piece and had the confidence to swim out towards home in the hope of being picked up.[10]

Sergeant Knuthoffer swam two and a half miles out to sea before he got onto a ship and returned to England.

In spite of Lieutenant-Colonel Phillips's brave efforts to warn them off, the 'A' Commando continued to land. Sergeant Jim Hefferson takes up the story:

We knew we were going in to reinforce the Canadians and even

> after the Colonel was killed, we still went on. His craft was on fire but no one on my LCA saw any signal to turn back. We got out over the side onto the beach but as we lowered the ramp, our right section and part of the centre section were wiped out by machine-gun fire. The rest got away, though some got clipped on the way up the beach. There were bodies everywhere with a yard-wide river of blood on the edge of the sea. Craft and tanks were burning, planes diving over and the mortar fire was throwing large stones everywhere off the shingle.
>
> After what seemed a long time, we got behind a Churchill tank which was bogged down and I got a bullet along my ribs, and after that a bloody grenade went off. I saw it rolling and the lever coming off. Then it stopped and I got a lot of shrapnel and worst of all, after being blind for a year in the POW camp, they took out my right eye. My platoon commander was Lieutenant Smale.[11]

Lieutenant Ken Smale recalls the events on White Beach. 'A scene of horror and carnage where people had, quite literally, been blown to pieces. We charged up the beach and took shelter behind a Churchill tank; I never realized I would be so keen to press my nose against a lump of steel.'[12]

Lieutenant Smale also got off the beach and swam out to sea, only to be picked up some miles offshore by a German E-Boat and taken prisoner. Ken Richardson's LCA was hit close to the beach:

> We slithered over the side into the water and got ashore, still under fire, with more men being hit. The fire was very heavy and with my heavy pack and Bren-gun it was difficult to get up the beach, which was very steep shingle. It was a frightening sight; I saw the beach strewn with dead Canadians, abandoned tanks beached and burning, LCTs perched at crazy angles. I managed to get behind a

> tank, completely exhausted, with a fraction of the section and our troop commander. We could not see the enemy but there was plenty of sniping and heavy mortar and machine gun fire from the cliffs . . . this was not what was intended.
>
> When we were told to go, I inflated my life-jacket and got into the water – it was very cold. I swam out towards the craft but I didn't think I could make it. The shellfire, hitting the water, seemed to numb me like an electric shock. I don't know how far I swam but it was like attempting to swim the bloody Channel. I was eventually picked up by an LCT, which was full of wounded, men lying all over the deck. When we got back, we were mustered into units and told to inform our next of kin. We lost a lot of good people.

Like all the units committed to JUBILEE, the 'A' Commando suffered severely; of the 17 officers and 352 other ranks of the 'A' Commando who sailed to Dieppe, 66 were killed or captured on the beach and many others were injured or killed in the landing craft. The Royal Hamilton Light Infantry lost 372 men killed or captured; many of those captured were wounded, as were half of the 217 men who made it back to England. Only one Royal Hamilton officer returned unwounded.

Of the Essex Scottish on Red Beach, of the 555 men who sailed for France, only 52 came back; 121 were killed on the beach and 382, again many of them wounded, were taken prisoner. The tank crews, protected by armour plate, had fewer men killed but most of them were taken prisoner. Only one of the five commanding officers and one of the two brigadiers who landed on the Red and White Beaches made it back to England. A disaster has rarely been more complete.

The events on these two beaches add up to a two-part tragedy. Some of this – the pinning of the two assault battalions on the beach – should have been anticipated once the demand for support had been denied. But the commitment of the Fusiliers Mont-Royal and the Royal Marines was an avoidable and unnecessary catastrophe, which has to be laid at the door of Major-General Roberts. Although he was undoubtedly under great pressure, greater than anyone can imagine, the decision to send the Floating Reserve in was a clear mistake and an obvious one even when the benefits of hindsight are set aside.

It was not simply a matter of not 'reinforcing failure'; commanders are supposed to commit their reserves in order to exploit success, and there was precious little evidence that success was attending any of the landings that morning. The decision simply added more men to the casualty list and resulted in more men being pinned down ashore – now the Force Commanders had to get them off.

THE WITHDRAWAL
1100–1300HRS

It remains our task to batter and wipe out the enemy at Dieppe with all our means and in the shortest possible time.

ORDER FROM VON RUNDSTEDT, TO THE DIEPPE GARRISON, 0700HRS, 19 AUGUST 1942

A WITHDRAWAL IN THE face of the enemy is one of the most difficult of military manoeuvres. It usually involves pulling back from an existing position while still maintaining a front against the enemy, thereby dividing one's force, with some pulling back and some staying put to cover the withdrawal. This alone can be difficult; no one wants to be left behind and unless the troops are highly disciplined and kept well in hand by their officers, any withdrawal can all too easily degenerate into a rout.

These inherent problems are compounded when the withdrawal is out to sea. This part of the action will involve close liaison with both the landing craft, which will lift the troops off the beaches, and the offshore fleet which will, with any luck, cover the last stages of the withdrawal across the beach with gunfire. The problems and solutions of the withdrawal must therefore be factored into the initial plan.

In order to appreciate the difficulties confronting the troops at Dieppe it would be as well to explain how a well-conducted amphibious withdrawal is managed. The first requirement is that the troops are thoroughly briefed beforehand and know *exactly* what is going to happen and where their part will be played. Any failure here can result in confusion and panic.

A withdrawal will usually be made in phases and the first phase is to evacuate the wounded and any prisoners. Then go any men who can be spared, the Headquarters staff, drivers and signallers, and all but a few medics. At this stage someone has to decide whether some of the wounded cannot be moved; if not, they must be left to the mercy of the enemy, a hard decision that can cause a certain amount of angst among the troops, though the Germans were noted for taking good care of wounded prisoners.

The decks having been cleared, the main withdrawal begins, again in phases. It will be necessary for some troops to go back from the front line and establish a line of resistance, probably some way short of the beach, in the hope of freeing the re-embarkation area from observed fire. When this fall-back position has been established, the troops engaged with the enemy break off the action and pull back – fast.

These troops would normally pass through those holding the line of resistance and establish another one even further back. This leapfrog process continues until the troops are on or close to the beach where the landing craft, summoned in from somewhere offshore, should now be waiting. Now comes the really difficult part, especially if the enemy are pressing hard on the heels of the retreating troops. It is now necessary for a number of troops to cross the beach and board the landing craft while others maintain a front against enemy pressure.

This is a real test of discipline, training and leadership. Nobody wants to be left behind and those boarding the craft must do so in an orderly fashion or the boats will be swamped. Assuming this stage of the embarkation goes well, there will then come a final moment when those remaining ashore will have to abandon their positions and sprint for the last of the landing craft. This moment will be eased if some of these craft have guns and can spray the beach with gunfire, so deterring the enemy from interfering while the last boats are loaded and pull away.

The above description is one of perfection; only in the most ideal circumstances would a withdrawal go so smoothly. Ideal circumstances were not generally available on the beaches of Dieppe that day, but something close to it can be found in the withdrawal of No. 4 Commando from Orange Beach 1. Although the Germans were active and engaged the retreating Commandos with rifle fire, the Commando withdrew to the beach at Vasterival in good order while their 3in mortars, previously established on the beach, engaged the enemy machine-guns and denied the enemy any chance of close pursuit. Most of the wounded were evacuated, German prisoners being pressed into service to carry the stretchers, but some wounded had to be left behind on Orange Beach 2. The landing craft were waiting, just offshore but afloat, not grounded, in places where the men could wade out to them. The Colonel, Lord Lovat, wading out knee-deep, was one of the last to board. Once the men were embarked, the craft withdrew under a smokescreen without further loss.

This success was not accidental. In their pre-Raid planning, Lovat and his men had practised this phase of the operation repeatedly, taking into account many possible situations: withdrawing under fire, withdrawing with wounded and withdrawing when closely pursued. One result of this training was that everyone knew what action he should take during this phase of the operation and simply got on with the job. On the other beaches, with less well-prepared troops, it was different.

The decision to pull the troops out was made by General Roberts, in consultation with Hughes-Hallett, at around 0900hrs. 'By nine o'clock,' said Hughes-Hallett, 'it was obvious that the military situation was serious and it was becoming steadily more difficult for ships and craft to close the beaches.' General Roberts was initially reluctant to order a withdrawal; at one point he even attempted to go ashore himself but on being dissuaded from this action he accepted the inevitable and said, 'Bring them home.'[1]

The signal to withdraw, the codeword 'Vanquish', went out at 0950hrs when the withdrawal was set for forty minutes later, at 1030hrs. This was swiftly amended to 1100hrs, partly in order to let the word reach the troops and partly to allow time for the RAF bombers to thicken up the smokescreen, but this alteration in timing added to the later confusion.

Hughes-Hallett then had to send word to Commander H.V. McClintock, the officer in charge of the boat pool, ordering the landing craft into the beaches for the evacuation. Orders also went out to the bombardment destroyers, urging them to shell the German positions on the headlands and reduce their ability to hamper the evacuation. HMS *Brocklesby* duly shelled the slopes around Pourville, and HMS *Garth*, though low on 4in ammunition, engaged the guns on the eastern headland.

There were, however, two mistakes, one caused by a misinterpretation of the revised order to start the evacuation at 1100hrs and another by a signals failure. The commander of one of the landing craft flak, LCF 1, Lieutenant F.M. Foggitt, thought that the signal to withdraw referred only to his craft and the LCAs he was escorting, and duly led them back to England without lifting any soldiers off the beach; an LCF and those landing craft would have been very useful on the beaches later that morning.

Having received his orders from Hughes-Hallett, McClintock had to get them to the coxswains of the craft in the boat pool. Since these were without radios the only way to do this was by closing the craft and passing on the order by loudhailer. To speed this task McClintock elected to inform the craft waiting to the west while his assistant, Lieutenant-Commander Durham, took the word to the landing craft waiting to the east.

McClintock had carried out part of this task when he was forced to withdraw out to sea. He had now reached the conclusion that it would be impossible to pull the troops off the Blue, Red or White Beaches and, having ordered the craft he had collected to set course for home, he attempted to make his way to *Calpe* to report to the Force Commanders. Unable to find the command ship, McClintock then sent a radio message to *Calpe*, recounting what he had done and stating that, in his opinion, any further withdrawal of troops was impossible. Then the second error arose. On receiving McClintock's message, Hughes-Hallett replied, 'If no further evacuation possible, withdraw to four miles offshore.' Only part of this message was picked up by McClintock who read it as 'No further evacuation possible, withdraw.'

Taking this as confirmation of his own conviction, McClintock set sail for England, taking with him a considerable number of LCP (L)s. Nor was this all: on the way out, he ran into another group of landing craft led by Lieutenant Jack Koyle from the transport *Duke of Wellington*, and ordered this group to return to England as well. The fleet of landing craft duly crossed the Channel and were back in Newhaven that evening, without a single soldier on board.

The effects of that missing 'If' were to be far-reaching. It reduced the number of craft available for the evacuation and thereby deprived many of the troops ashore of the means of getting off the beach in one lift. A considerable number of craft had already been lost in the landing phase; now three groups of landing craft, those led by Foggitt, McClintock and Koyle, had been ordered back to England. It remained to be seen whether those that remained were sufficient to lift the wreckage of the 2nd Canadian Division off the beaches – and it would now take more 'lifts' to do it.

Here too there was an unexpected problem. In the original plan, the entire JUBILEE force, having carried out its various tasks, would withdraw across the beaches at Dieppe. However, since the Green Beach forces had never been able to link up with the Calgary Tanks and were still fighting in the Scie Valley, the Cameron Highlanders and the South Saskatchewans would have to be withdrawn through Pourville – where they were currently under close attack from an aggressive enemy pressing down the valley.

The withdrawal of the Camerons and the South Saskatchewans down the Scie Valley to Pourville was well handled. Colonel Merritt was well aware of the dangers of a precipitate withdrawal and to prevent any panic even ordered his men to fall back slowly, as on parade, with their rifles at the slope. Meanwhile the Beachmaster on Green Beach, Lieutenant-Commander Redvers Prior, was attempting to contact the boat pool by radio. No reply being received, he clambered on top of a pillbox and attempted to contact some craft offshore by flag signal. This action quickly attracted the attention of the enemy machine-gunners; by the time the morning was over, Lieutenant-Commander Prior had been wounded four times.

His action did attract the attention of at least one LCA, which closed the beach at 0930hrs only to be driven off by shelling and machine-gun fire. Undaunted, Prior tried again; half an hour later another craft came in, only to be chased off by enemy fire. There was no further sign of relief until just after 1100hrs when, probably following the general evacuation order, four landing craft were seen approaching the beach, emerging from the smokescreen to be greeted with a storm of fire. In the past hour, after the Canadians had withdrawn into Pourville, the Germans had come forward and reoccupied their positions on the surrounding slopes; they now had the beach in plain sight and well within range.

Even so, the four craft managed to beach, but because the tide was now out they grounded some 200 yards from the sea wall behind which the wounded and the first troops to evacuate were waiting. To get to the boats the Canadians – including the stretcher-bearers – had to run a gauntlet of fire. Heavy losses were sustained while dashing across the beach, and further confusion arose when the men reached the landing craft. These four LCAs could have taken off about 120 men; more than 200 attempted to get on board and the space available was not nearly sufficient, even before the stretcher cases were manhandled on board.

Chaos then intensified when it was discovered that one LCA had been so badly holed by fire that it was unable to get off the beach. The men who had rushed on board promptly abandoned that craft and tried to board another one, but that craft was already overcrowded and sank a few hundred yards offshore, tipping the men into the water. Only two of the four craft, each crammed with men, made it out to the waiting destroyers; both these craft had been so badly damaged by fire that they could not be used again.

No one should be blamed for this chaos. The rule for boarding a landing craft during an evacuation is 'one man, any boat'; this is not the time to worry about staying with your unit or finding the craft that brought you ashore. It usually means that some craft are overloaded and some craft half empty. But two things are essential: first, that the craft should remain in water deep enough to avoid grounding when the men surge on board; and, secondly, that the craft should not be so crowded that it is in danger of capsizing. In the circumstances then prevailing on Green Beach, neither rule was, nor could be, observed.

The situation there has been well described by one of the landing-craft officers:

> Going in through the smoke I found men swimming out to get away from the machine-gun fire. There were corpses in the water and those alive had little strength left. I picked up about twenty men out of the water, and ignoring their protests, headed for the beach. By this time one engine was not working and our steering was defective.
>
> I stopped the boat before a group of men who had waded out, four of them carrying a stretcher. We were now bow-on to a machine-gun position and it was impossible to manoeuvre the craft owing to the steering defect and the weight of men now clambering over the bow and stern – many were shot in the back as we pulled them over the bow. When every man in the vicinity was on board we had great difficulty dragging wounded men away from the lowered ramp. I gave the order to pull back and we went astern on one engine which was slow progress but the steering was working again and we were able to get out to sea.

The crux of the problem facing the landing-craft crews was that so many men were now trying to get on board that the crews became fully involved simply preventing capsize. They were also busy keeping these men away from the ramp and the propellers, and trying to persuade frantic soldiers, many of them wounded, that they simply could not take any more on board. This proved an impossible task; heavily overloaded as they hauled back off the beach, many of the LCAs turned over, and all this, be it remembered, while a pitiless fire from the shore was flaying both men and boats.

In spite of the best efforts of the officers and NCOs, order was rapidly being lost ashore; every boat that came into the beach was rushed by the troops. As the chaos increased, more and more men gave up the attempt to get on one of the landing craft and elected to swim out to sea, hoping to be picked up beyond the smokescreen; some of these men made it, some of them were hit by snipers and some of them simply drowned. The landing craft kept coming in but their numbers were steadily shrinking as more craft were swamped by troops and capsized or were hit by enemy fire and sank. Eventually it became clear that the evacuation from Green Beach could achieve no more and had to be abandoned.

Colonel Merritt and his company commanders had elected to stay until the end and were taken prisoner. Sometime before noon the last boat got away, leaving some 160 officers and men from the South Saskatchewans and the Camerons still on the beach and still fighting. The Battalion Adjutant of the South Saskatchewans, Lieutenant Buchanan, sums up: 'No words of mine can describe the sheer courage of that last half hour of hell but as the last craft left the shore we saw the fellows that had to remain behind waving us on, and still keeping the Jerries away from the sea wall.'

Matters were going no better on the main beach before Dieppe. The first task was to get the withdrawal order to the beach, where only two signal sets were in operation, that of Major Rolfe on White Beach and that of Brian McCool, the Principal Landing Officer; neither was in touch with the troops and they had difficulty getting the 'Vanquish' message to the two battalion COs, Labatt and Jasperson. Fortunately the news eventually filtered out to most of the men, but further confusion arose when the execution of this order went back from 1030hrs to 1100hrs and not everyone got the message.

On White Beach, the men in the Casino did get the message. About 150 of them gathered at the seaward end of the building, ready to sprint across the sea wall and the beach when the landing craft appeared. Matters were not going so well just to the west, where the men of the Fusiliers Mont-Royal who had drifted into the White sector were stuck at the bottom of the western headland, enduring machine-gun fire from the eastern headland and a steady rain of hand-grenades from German forces on the cliff top overhead. This party, some two hundred strong, was captured at around 1030hrs by a German patrol which came down a cliff path and took them by surprise.

On Red Beach, Colonel Jasperson received news of the evacuation at 1100hrs via a runner from Colonel Labatt who was now in command of the Brigade. At 1020hrs Hughes-Hallett ordered the landing craft to start closing the beach and at first the evacuation from Red and White Beaches appears to have been well ordered.

The landing craft were organised in two groups, one for each beach, and they were provided with another smokescreen – which, though generally beneficial, prevented the men ashore seeing them come in. In addition there were clearly not enough craft; each cox'n was ordered to land, fill his boat with men and take them out to the waiting destroyers before returning for another load, an order that was not received with much enthusiasm.

At 1100hrs another flight of Boston bombers swooped over the beach and the headlands to thicken up the smokescreen and, as if waiting for such a signal, the German batteries on the headlands commenced a heavy fire on the beach and the offshore waters. Nor were the landing craft on time; a full twenty minutes were to elapse before the first came nosing through the smoke and into a great blast of shells, mortar bombs and machine-gun bullets. This fire was reported back to *Calpe* by Major Rolfe: 'Boats coming in under intense fire. Want lots of support. They cannot get in. Much smoke and air support wanted.'[2]

Once again, alas, the signals net had gone on the blink, and Rolfe was no longer in direct touch with Roberts on *Calpe*. Roberts could, however, hear a relay on the link with *Fernie* and fifteen minutes later he heard another report from Rolfe: 'You had better hurry. It is getting a bit hot hereabouts. Boats are being hit and sinking. "Bill" [Brigadier Southam] does not think it possible to evacuate unless you get everything possible in here.'[3]

The premature departure of those landing craft to the UK was now taking effect. There were no more boats to send in and those reaching the beach were in trouble, as the following messages make clear: 'Request lots of support. Enemy engaging craft. Need smoke and all support possible for assault craft. Bill.' And from Brian McCool: 'Situation here no damn good. Need LCAs, LCSs, LCTs. Lots of smoke and Leigh-Mallory [i.e. air cover].'[4]

The problem with providing gunfire support was, ironically, the smoke-screen. This was now drifting over the beaches and the immediate offshore area, blinding the destroyers and cutting off the view of the headlands from the Hurricanes that were trying to strafe the enemy gun-pits. The evacuation was getting under way but it took a great deal of time.

At 1211hrs, more than an hour after the evacuation should have started, McCool reported to *Fernie*: 'Very few personnel have been evacuated. 1000 is maximum.' McCool was being optimistic; the evacuation of 1000 men in an hour would have been a miracle. Major Rolfe was providing a more accurate assessment from his wrecked scout car on White Beach:

1243hrs. White Beach not good. Red not so bad . . .

1305hrs. Give us quick support. Enemy closing in on beach. Hurry it up please.

1307hrs. We are evacuating. [Rolfe meant that he was abandoning his scout car, but in fact he stayed to send one more message.]

The scenes on Red and White Beaches during this time were quite terrible, each a larger replica of those taking place at Pourville. Of the four LCAs that made up the first wave into White Beach, all were immediately rushed by troops, one was promptly overturned and then hit by artillery fire, all on board being killed. The other three craft managed to limp out to the destroyers, each carrying some seventy men, about twice the safe number.

Another eight LCAs, supposed to land on White Beach, actually arrived on Red, where six were quickly hit by shellfire and destroyed. These were the last craft even to attempt a landing on Red Beach. The two surviving craft got away – one carrying no fewer than eighty men – but were so badly damaged that they sank shortly after delivering their passengers to the destroyers.

In these desperate circumstances it is hardly surprising, and an indication of that desperation, that a large number of men decided to give up the landing-craft option and swim for it. Royal Marine Richard McConkey of the 'A' Commando was one of the early swimmers, following the abortive landing of the Floating Reserve:

> I was in a landing craft directly behind Colonel Phillips's boat. We saw him stand up in murderous fire and wave us to retreat but then we also got hit. I swam away but I saw someone still hanging on, so a Marine called Jock Cowan and I swam back and hauled him off. He said, 'I canna' swim, Mac', and I said, 'You canna' sink either, you've got a Mae West lifejacket on.' That was Willy McKnight. Then a scaling ladder floated past so we put him on that and towed him out to sea, heading for home.
>
> We were picked up by HMS *Brocklesby*, and they gave us dry gear and put us below, but then their Skipper came down and said, 'Can any of you Marines use an Oerlikon anti-aircraft gun?' So my mate Knocker White went up and soon had it blazing away. We got

> hit six times on the *Brocklesby* and went aground once, but they stayed to pick up survivors – what guts that Skipper had! We came back to Pompey doing four knots under air attack most of the way![5]

Knocker White had helped tow Willy McKnight out to sea:

> Our QMS, Wiggy Bennet, was in the water shouting, 'Save your weapons, boys' – when we cleared the smoke I noticed the sea was full of jellyfish – then the ship came up, manoeuvred between us and the shore and picked us up. When the officer asked if anyone could handle the Oerlikon 20mm, as the crew had been killed or wounded, I went up. I had done a gunnery course at Scapa Flow, and couldn't say no, mostly firing at Stuka dive-bombers – and they gave us plenty of stick and sank another ship, the destroyer *Berkeley*, with a direct hit amidships. The withdrawal had been fixed for 1100hrs and our brave skipper made for the shore and turned stern on, to pick up any survivors. The screws were hurling up stones, we were in shallow water.
>
> The scenes on that beach at Dieppe I shall never forget. There seemed to be hundreds of wrecked landing craft of all descriptions, tanks hardly a few yards up the beach and dead bodies, mostly Canadians, all over the shingle. Every gun was going on the ship, as the gunners were letting fly with everything we had at the Spandaus in caves on the cliffs; when the skipper finally decided to shove off I thought we had had it. We were well aground, masses of shingle were thrown into the air by the ship's screws but we eventually made it and steamed for Blighty, as fast as we could though their bombers continued to bomb us until dark. We made it to Portsmouth about midnight I guess.

As this account confirms, the Royal Navy were doing all they could to support the troops ashore while under air attack from dive-bombers and being shelled from the cliffs. HMS *Brocklesby* went within 500 yards of the shore off the main Dieppe beach to bombard the headlands and ran briefly aground. HMS *Berkeley*, also sailing close to the beach, was hit amidships by a bomb which killed a number of the crew and broke the ship's back. Since she could not be towed back to Britain her crew and a host of Canadian soldiers, many of them wounded, were taken off by HMS *Albrighton*, which then sank the *Berkeley* with a torpedo.

Efforts to get the men off continued, as did the mad dash for every boat that approached the beach. Four LCAs touched down on Red Beach and were promptly mobbed by a mixed bag of soldiers from every battalion, who broke cover behind abandoned tanks and the sea wall in an attempt to get away, only to be cut down by machine-guns as they massed in a great group around the boats. One account of this event from a medical officer describes what happened:

> The men were literally running en-masse for the boats. I yelled and yelled but I might as well have spared my breath. No one was going to help me move my wounded. Machine-guns on the cliffs did frightful execution. Some of the boats pushed off, all hopelessly overloaded. It was murder . . . the sea was full of men and bodies.

Brigadier Southam's report confirms that order had been lost:

> The approach of the landing craft was the signal for a headlong rush by several hundred men who waded into the water, shoulder deep, in an attempt to board them. Some boats were hit, others swamped. It was my thought that none would get away. I walked to that area where many men, some wounded, were sheltering behind a beached LCT. I ordered that the men should prepare for the arrival of more landing craft and made it clear that priority should go to the

> wounded, adding that I would settle any disobedience with my pistol. About this time I met Colonel Labatt, who had just swum ashore after being on the way out to a boat. He was wearing only a duffle coat and was, in his own words, 'pooped'.[6]

Labatt had been organising the withdrawal from the Casino, which the Hamiltons had evacuated in good order, assembling on the beach to await the landing craft while a number of men stayed in the Casino to hold back the enemy. When the landing craft arrived, however, the usual scenes occurred. All the boats were promptly overloaded and all were immediately raked with fire by the Germans.

All this took place sometime after noon. Scores of men were now swimming out through the smoke, but on the beaches the evacuation continued and the chaos increased. Those tanks which had not been knocked out, about ten in all, had returned to the beach where they were abandoned. The crews tended to stay in the safety of their armour until captured; only one tank soldier got away from Dieppe, again by swimming out to the ships offshore.

Another man who got away was Lieutenant-Colonel Ménard of the Fusiliers Mont-Royal, the only commanding officer to return to the UK from Dieppe. Colonel Ménard had been badly wounded and was carried aboard an LCT by his men. He was taken off the damaged and now sinking LCT two miles offshore, along with eighty other soldiers. Lieutenant-Colonel Labatt had tried to swim out to an LCT only to find it under fire and in the process of being sunk; he swam back to the beach where he found the Hamiltons' padre, John Foote, calmly moving about, doing all he could to help the wounded and the dying.

This could not go on; with all order lost, many boats sunk and men now obliged to swim out to sea in hope of rescue, attempts to get more men off Red and White Beaches were clearly unsustainable and everyone knew it. At 1308hrs, Major Rolfe, about to abandon his scout car, sent one last message to Roberts on *Calpe*: 'There seems to be a mass surrender of our troops to the Germans on the beach. Our people here have surrendered.'

The evacuation had already been called off. At around 1300hrs *Calpe* had sailed close to the beach where the enemy fire was beginning to slacken. All resistance had ceased, no boats were approaching the beach and the only movement observed was of German troops and vehicles coming out of their positions and moving down towards the shore.

Calpe was at once engaged by shore artillery and pulled back into the smokescreen. As she disappeared, a message to General Konrad Haase, the 302nd Divisional Commander, informed him: 'The British Navy has gone. Remnants of the landing force are still holding out. Request permission to clear up the battlefield.' This permission having been granted, the 571st Infantry Regiment began to move forward into Pourville and onto the Dieppe beaches. There was no further resistance and the surrender of the remaining troops went ahead without further bloodshed.

Major Houghton of the 'A' Commando reports:

> We had gone on as long as we could and got as far inland as we were able. We could do no more as we were completely out of ammunition – I had no cartridges left, even for my revolver. The Germans were perfectly correct – no complaints there. We were herded together and I spent that night in a brick factory with hundreds of other prisoners, sleeping with my head on a sack of cement.[7]

What happened then was strictly routine. The prisoners were rounded up, searched and marched through the town to captivity, many being held overnight in the brickworks. The Canadian wounded were taken care of, some locally, some in hospitals as far away as Rouen. In about an hour the beaches of Dieppe, Puys and Pourville had been cleared of prisoners and wounded – only the dead remained, and they too would be cleared away over the next few days, more bodies being collected off the beaches for a week or more as they came ashore with every tide. The Dieppe Raid was over – the time for recriminations had begun.

14

A VERDICT ON DIEPPE

The waters have since been muddied so successfully that hardly anything about the Raid is undisputed.

ANDREW ROBERTS,
EMINENT CHURCHILLIANS

With the Raid over, the boats gone and their ammunition exhausted, the thousands of Canadian troops left on the beaches were faced with the unpalatable option of surrender. Lieutenant-Colonel Labatt refers to this action as:

> The most unpleasant decision of my life . . . but there was nothing further we could do and we were already losing men, wounded chaps drowned by the incoming tide. We had some German airmen whom we had taken prisoner and I sent one of them into the open with a white towel. He waved to his pals and thirty or forty of them leapt onto the sea wall and covered us with sub-machine guns or rifles. Everybody stood up, and that was that.

The Dieppe beach was an abattoir – dead bodies floating in the sea or rolling about in the waves, supported by their life-jackets. Other bodies and body parts washed to and fro on the edge of the shingle. The beach, wreathed in smoke from burning landing craft, was littered with bodies, and loud with the moans of wounded men who lay out on the shingle or huddled in piles against the sea wall. It was, says one German account, 'a picture of horror', and now, trailing wearily off the beach, their hands raised in surrender, came scores then hundreds of men.

All along Red and White Beaches and further along the coast at Pourville, the Canadians surrendered, adding their numbers to those already taken at Puys. In all of these places the Germans made no objection to the Canadians collecting and taking care of their wounded, and in many cases came forward to offer a helping hand. Less helpful were some Allied aircraft, mostly Spitfires, who returned to strafe the Dieppe beaches soon after the surrender, sending the prisoners and their guards scrambling for cover.

After the men from Red and White Beaches had been assembled on the promenade, the officers and men were separated, the men being marched off to the brickworks, the officers taken away for interrogation. This questioning provided the Germans with very little useful information, since the Canadians restricted their replies to the official 'name, rank and number', declining to say where they had come from, or what the raid had been for. Indeed, when he was asked that question, Brian McCool, the Beachmaster, replied, 'If you could tell me the answer to that question, I would be very grateful.'

More than sixty years after the Dieppe Raid, that remains the big question. There is nothing in the RUTTER outline plan to justify the post-Raid claims that the operation was mounted to explore the likelihood of the Allies seizing a port at the start of an invasion, to provide lessons for a later landing or the invasion of Continental Europe, or as a 'reconnaissance in force'. The only logical answer is that the Dieppe Raid, Operation RUTTER/JUBILEE, should be taken for what it was – a raid, the largest so far, but still a raid, with a range of objectives, which would again remind the Führer that the British were still in the war and fighting back.

The Raid can also be seen as a development of what had already happened at Vaagsø and Lofoten and therefore as a logical extension of previous experience, notably by an increase in scale, in terms of numbers and in the use of tanks. The two previous operations in Norway had also had a range of objectives – to destroy fish-oil factories and sink shipping, and to take prisoners and bring back volunteers for the Norwegian forces in the UK – but no one has suggested that either operation, both of them far less costly and far better run than Dieppe, was also designed to test arrangements for the invasion of a Nazi-dominated Continent.

Besides, as has already been mentioned, most of the strategic reasons quoted for the Dieppe Raid were thought up after the operation was over and seen to be a costly failure; this being so, some solid gains from the operation had to be found, if only to divert public and political wrath away from the commanders. The truth, the real cause of failure, lies in the fact that, unlike Vaagsø and Lofoten, Dieppe was planned by people with little knowledge of amphibious operations. Even worse, a cursory inspection reveals that Mountbatten and Hughes-Hallett had little experience of even land-based military operations; both men were destroyer captains, not Army officers.

Ex post facto claims are not uncommon in military history. To give an example of a later claim being introduced to give weight to an argument or justify a campaign: advocates for the Allied bomber offensive claim, quite correctly, that the bombing forced the Germans to deploy over two million men in the homeland to man the anti-aircraft defences and clear up the rubble. They also cite the Luftwafffe's need to concentrate on the production of fighter aircraft for the defence of the Reich as the factor that prevented the enemy developing a long-range bomber, and the fact that some 15,000 88mm dual-purpose guns were deployed for anti-aircraft use, guns that might have been used to fend off Russian tanks in the East. These are perfectly valid claims, but they formed no part of the original stated objective of the Allied bomber offensive, which was the dislocation and destruction of the German military-industrial machine.

The claim that Dieppe provided some useful lessons for D-Day is supported by a number of people, including those who took part in the Raid. Major-General Robert ('Titch') Houghton, who landed at Dieppe as second-in-command of the Royal Marine 'A' Commando, says:

> Although the Raid did me, a professional Royal Marine, absolutely no good at all, I remain firmly of the opinion that an operation of that nature was vital as a prelude to the D-Day planning. And that whatever may be said of him, Mountbatten was correct in saying that casualties were saved on D-Day as a result of the Dieppe raid – which in isolation was a shambles.[1]

This view is endorsed by the CIGS, General Sir Alan Brooke – later Field Marshal Lord Alanbrooke. At a meeting with Churchill on 30 June 1942, when the Prime Minister requested an assurance that things would go well at Dieppe, Brooke allegedly jumped in to state that the request was unreasonable: if one knew how the Raid would turn out there would be no reason to launch it. He then added that the object was to find out whether or not a cross-Channel operation could be successfully mounted and, finally, that 'no leader would be willing to plan a major invasion unless this operation [RUTTER] was attempted'.[2] This might seem conclusive but, again, if the aim was to test whether a cross-Channel operation could be mounted, why was that aim not mentioned in the RUTTER plan?

The final and most vocal advocate for the usefulness of the Raid is Lord Louis Mountbatten, who claimed that 'the battle of D-Day was won on the beaches of Dieppe' and that thousands of D-Day casualties were saved by the application of the lessons learned at Dieppe. 'Dieppe was one of the most vital operations of the Second World War. It gave to the Allies the priceless secret of victory . . . if I had the same decision to make again, I would do as I did before.' Few people would go that far and the claim that this shambles was a 'vital operation' seems a little far-fetched, but the last sentence does indicate that Mountbatten accepted the responsibility for launching the JUBILEE operation.

The core claim therefore is that the Dieppe Raid, either intentionally or subsequently, provided many useful lessons for the D-Day landing of 1944. Some of the innovations employed by some commanders on the D-Day beaches – the use of specialised armour, close support for the troops during the landing phase, and landing the infantry in the third or fourth wave when the armour was ashore and active – certainly made a major contribution to getting the troops ashore and off the beaches quickly and with acceptable losses. It could be that the shambles at Dieppe pointed out the need for these innovations. But one of the objects of this book is to point out that these assets were equally necessary at Dieppe, two years before D-Day, and that that fact should have been obvious to the JUBILEE planners.

It is noticeable that where these innovations were not employed on D-Day, as the Americans neglected to employ them on OMAHA beach, the troops were pinned down on the beach and took terrible losses as at Dieppe; just under half of the 10,000 D-Day casualties were taken by the two US divisions and the assault engineer support teams that landed on OMAHA on 6 June 1944. The casualty figures certainly indicate that something went very wrong here; if Dieppe provided a number of lessons to the Allies, the US Army – or General Omar Bradley – declined to learn from them.

On OMAHA beach the Americans lost 4700 men;[3] on the Anglo-Canadian beaches along the Calvados coast – SWORD, JUNO and GOLD – the losses were about 1000 men killed, wounded and missing per beach – say 3000 in all. This startling difference in the casualty rate between OMAHA and the other three beaches on this strip of coast is mainly due to the use by the British and Canadians of improved means of getting the troops *off the beach* – better assault tactics and specialised armour. But whether these benefits can be directly and solely attributed to the lessons learned at Dieppe is at least debatable.

As we have seen, the Canadian infantry were stuck on the beach and massacred while the Calgary Tanks, rather than being tasked to support the infantry on the beaches or in Dieppe town, were supposed to rush through the town and link up at Arques with the Camerons coming from Pourville. In the event, many of the tanks did get off the beach but they then got held up on the promenade, and the engineers who might have blasted a path through the obstacles had already been cut down on the beach. To the credit of their commanders, many tanks then tried to help the infantry by engaging German positions. But individual initiative and bravery are no substitute for a sound plan, or even an alternative plan –

the plan for tank and infantry cooperation at Dieppe was virtually non-existent.

It has been alleged that the inability of the Calgary Tanks to get off the beach led to the development by Major-General Sir Percy Hobart of the specialised armour of the 79th Armoured Division, 'Hobart's Funnies': those mine-clearing, bridge-building, flame-throwing tanks, the Crocodiles, Crabs, Petards and Bobbin tanks, collectively known as AVREs (Armoured Vehicles, Royal Engineers), that punched great holes in the Atlantic Wall on D-Day and so enabled the landing forces to get off the beaches quickly.

Here again, though, the later argument on the benefits of JUBILEE is flawed by an examination of the facts. The claim that those bridging, petard- and fascine-laying tanks helped the D-Day tanks off the Normandy beaches, as opposed to getting stuck on the beach as at Dieppe, is undermined by the fact that half of the Calgary Tanks *did* get off the beach; their problems came later.

However, although the tanks got off the beach, the infantry did not. Dieppe made it abundantly clear that unsupported infantry would probably never get off the beach and that naval gunfire support and tactical bombing had a part to play in helping them. So too did the use of tanks; the infantry must have armour on hand from the moment they stepped ashore, and tank tactics must be merged with those of the assault infantry.

The problem of assaulting a defended coast and the creation of the 'Funnies' led to a radical change in the British Army's assault techniques. The greatest asset possessed by the D-Day troops was the Duplex-Drive or DD tank, an amphibious floating version of the Sherman tank, which was able to come ashore with the LCAs – if not before – and provide tank support to the infantry as they crossed the beach. So it was that on D-Day 1944, the first wave to land on the British and Canadian beaches – GOLD, JUNO and SWORD – consisted of 'swimming tanks' – DD tanks – that would engage the coastal guns and strongpoints on the beach. Then came a wave of AVREs to clear the beach obstacles and open up paths through the minefields for the fighting tanks and infantry. Only then, and sometimes after another wave of DDs had landed, did the infantry come ashore, in the third or fourth wave of the assault.

This change in tactics saved countless lives on D-Day, 1944. It *may* have been brought to the surface by the tragic events at Dieppe; it is equally likely that it was the result of an accumulation of experience from other, later operations – and some common sense among the planners. Landings, in North Africa, Sicily and Italy, in 1943 and 1944, also provided lessons for the D-Day planners. Not all of these operations were successful, either; Salerno was very costly and the lethargic start to the Anzio operation led to a stalemate, but all of these later landings, being actual invasions, were on a much larger scale than JUBILEE and closer to the events of D-Day.

The second major claim for lessons learned at Dieppe is that the failure to seize the port made it necessary for the Allies to develop the artificial Mulberry harbours used to supply the D-Day troops. But this is also a claim too far; seizing Dieppe port was not among the listed objectives of the raid. Had that been the objective, another plan would have been laid to seal off the town. While the design and development of the Mulberry harbours certainly took place after the Raid, the need for artificial harbours had been discussed between Churchill and Mountbatten as early as May 1942, months before the Dieppe Raid and more than a year before the outline plan for D-Day, the so-called COSSAC plan, was drawn up by General Morgan.

It therefore appears that while the Dieppe Raid provided lessons that at least the British and Canadian planners and commanders employed for D-Day, not all the claims made for the Raid are borne out by the facts. Many were reached *ex post facto,* created after the Raid to account for or justify the horrific losses. The above account of some useful lessons learned at Dieppe – not least how not to do it – merely serves in some measure to balance an otherwise dreadful account laid at the planners' door.

One of the most interesting facts about the aftermath of the Dieppe Raid is the absence of recriminations, at least for a while and especially in Canada. The greater part of the losses were sustained by the 2nd Canadian Division; what happened to those men was little short of criminal, not least because they were steadily deprived of adequate support and never provided with any alternative plan should the venture go wrong. So it is surprising that no attempts were made to pass the blame for this catastrophe to their, usually British, planners and commanders. This may be partly due to the fact that, as we saw on p. 122, a large part of the plan was prepared by a Canadian officer, Lieutenant-Colonel Churchill Mann, who was the 'planning adviser' to General Roberts.[4] Moreover the Canadians had no use for scapegoating; to quote the words of Canadian Lieutenant-Colonel Cecil Merritt who won the Victoria Cross at Dieppe, 'We were very glad to go, we were delighted. We were against a very difficult situation and we didn't win but to hell with this business of saying the generals did us dirt.'[5]

In the decades since the raid, accusations of incompetence have arisen in Canada and the search for someone to blame has, if anything, intensified. The traditional scapegoat has been Major-General Roberts, largely because at the pre-Raid briefing he allegedly remarked that JUBILEE would be 'a piece of cake'. Evidence to support this allegation is scanty, but for years after the Raid a piece of cake was sent anonymously to Roberts on 19 August, a bitter reminder of what had actually transpired. The Dieppe Raid destroyed his career. In the spring of 1943 he was removed from command of the 2nd Division and sent to command a recruiting depot. After the war he retired to Jersey in the Channel Islands and died there in 1962.

General Roberts was no more or less to blame than any of the other senior participants, and to single him out for special condemnation is quite unfair. The two charges that can be specifically laid at his door are, firstly, that he was wrong in not resisting the cancellation of bombing support and that he had deluded himself that bombing would only result in streets filled with rubble blocking the passage of tanks. This might have been true, but without such support the assault troops would probably not get off the beach. Roberts should have insisted on the promised bombing or naval gunfire support, even to the point of recommending a cancellation of the raid to the COS or the Canadian Government. His second failure lay in ordering the Floating Reserve to land when it should have been clear that the operation was by now a disaster; by 'reinforcing failure' he was simply adding to the casualties.

Apart from those two errors, Roberts is no more to blame than many other people. As Lord Lovat said later, 'Roberts was obviously not the right fellow but I don't know of anybody who could have done it right that day.'

Lovat has put his finger on the problem: given the situation, nobody could have made the Dieppe operation work. The Raid went awry for a large number of avoidable reasons and no amount of subsequent justification about lessons learned can gloss over that fact. The errors were often fundamental and in many cases inexcusable – errors that should not have occurred and probably would not have occurred had the planners and commanders known their job.

The selection of Dieppe for the raid was the first mistake. Dieppe was simply not the right place for an amphibious assault, for the terrain was against it. As we have seen, the choice lay between a direct assault on a well-defended position and flanking attacks which, in the event, were easily held on or just off the beaches. Dieppe was a target that soldiers wise in amphibious warfare would have left well alone. From that basic error, many others flowed.

This fact and many other snags might have been revealed had the planners made or obtained a proper 'appreciation of the situation'. This would have pointed out the possibilities, the opportunities and the problems, and enabled the planners to estimate the chances of success before committing themselves to the operation at all. The failure to carry out such a basic procedure is further evidence of incompetence.

This leads us to the command structure and the fact that no one person was solely responsible for the success or failure of the Raid. Instead there were three commanders – a Triumvirate – none of them experienced in amphibious warfare and all with their own agenda. This system was not unusual in 1942, as Major-General Houghton confirms:

> That was the way it was done at the start of the war. Every Service supplied a chief and they drew up a plan and decided collectively what should be done. It did not work and in the end, by 1943, we had gone over to the American system, in which there clearly was a single commander who had advisers but was solely responsible for the operation. That did not happen at Dieppe.[6]

We have seen how Baillie-Grohman accepted, albeit reluctantly, the substitution of eight small destroyers for the heavy guns of a capital ship and how Leigh-Mallory abandoned the idea of a heavy bombing raid in favour of a few minutes of ground strafing and a lot of smoke; in both cases, their Service loyalty pressed them to accept and defend a decision that fatally undermined the possibilities of success at Dieppe.

This error was not corrected because, when JUBILEE was mounted, other factors prevailed. Hughes-Hallett was in favour of the Raid and accepted the RUTTER plan, with some minor variations, because he was a Combined Operations man who wanted this raid to proceed. Leigh-Mallory was for the operation as he hoped it would cause a major air battle in which the Luftwaffe could be greatly written down. Roberts wanted the operation to go ahead because his Canadians were thirsting for action. Their various motivations blinded them all to the fact that the plan for RUTTER/JUBILEE was fundamentally flawed.

These flaws have been extensively discussed, and can be summarised as follows. The first thing a commander planning an attack should consider is the ground – and Dieppe was not geographically suitable for an amphibious landing. The beach exits – especially at Puys – were too narrow and impossible to breach if the enemy chose to defend them. This also indicates a general failure to gather or evaluate the necessary intelligence.

Secondly, the Raid suffered from an inflexible plan and a failure to weigh up the difficulties of getting the troops off the beaches. The German commander, General Konrad Haase of the 302nd Division, makes this point in his post-action report to von Rundstedt at the German General Headquarters: 'The British Operational Order fixed every detail of the action for each unit. This method of planning made the failure of the raid inevitable in the event of unexpected difficulties.'

Third is the gradual erosion of naval and RAF support, without which the frontal assault on the Red and White beaches was suicidal. Finally, a whole series of snags, mistakes and errors – including the unexpectedly rapid German response, numerous communications failures and the withdrawal of landing craft during the retreat – all pushed up the casualty figures.

One other question remains: could the Raid have succeeded if a different plan had been devised? At this point historians should be careful: hindsight is a wonderful gift, but the Dieppe plan has to be evaluated from the perspective available at the time, when many of the errors that seem so obvious after the event were not so clear-cut. However, if we accept that a seaborne assault at Dieppe was always a high-risk proposition, what alternatives were there?

One way to evaluate the raid is to relate the prior need to the subsequent plan or actions. The major failure at Dieppe was an inability to get the troops off the beaches. The attack promptly stalled and casualties quickly mounted. We have argued here that a beach assault on Dieppe was fundamentally impossible in the event of opposition. This being so, could a beach assault have been avoided? The short answer to that is – probably not. Could it have been better managed? The answer to that question is – probably yes, if the problem had been appreciated and thought through.

The main task was to get the troops off the beaches. If that could not be done from the seaward side without great loss, it had to be done from the land. In other words, the two landward exits, certainly at Puys and Pourville, and possibly the two headlands, should first have been attacked from behind. This would have required the use of parachute or glider forces to seize the landward exits. This was not impossible: the RUTTER plan had involved the use of paratroops to knock out the coastal batteries; this being so, it is hard to see why paratroopers could not have been used to seize the exit from Blue Beach or attack Quatre Vents Farm.

The use of paratroops had been abandoned for JUBILEE because it was considered that their weather requirements, low winds and good visibility, were an unwanted additional element. In the event, the weather was not a factor in the JUBILEE operation; evidence for this is provided by the fact that a large part of the JUBILEE force, as planned, crossed the Channel in small assault boats. Assault boats are designed for shipping troops between the transports and the nearby shore, not for seventy-mile voyages across the open sea; if the weather was good enough for small boats it was calm enough for the employment of paratroopers.

As to how these paratroop soldiers might have been used, General Haase makes some interesting comments only slightly tinged with hindsight:[7]

> The British did not employ parachutists. If they had attacked the Puits [Puys] position simultaneously with airborne troops and from the sea, the initial position of the defenders would probably have been critical. Since fire control observation on the big ships was

> poor because of the smokescreen, the landing force had no artillery support whatsoever.

These paratroopers, from James Hill's 1st Parachute Battalion, could have landed before dawn, either close to the beaches or on flat ground on or close to the airfield at St Aubin. Colonel Hill's men had already been tasked to attack the coastal batteries for RUTTER, a task passed to Nos. 3 and 4 Commandos for JUBILEE, so the Parachute Brigade staff were already familiar with the ground and the main details of the operation.

Once on the ground, well behind the enemy coastal defences, the effect of this parachute force could have been decisive. The distance back to the coast is short, night-time navigation difficulties were negligible (there was the River Arques and a railway line to provide direction) and the arrival of troops, at the landward end of the Puys gully or in Dieppe town just prior to the seaborne assault, would, at the very least, have alarmed and distracted the garrison.

General Haase makes a similar point regarding the use of tanks at Pourville. The attack there stalled because the Germans were quickly able to man fixed defences, pillboxes and strongpoints which the unsupported Canadian battalions had no means of overcoming. Haase comments:

> The British completely miscalculated the strength of the German defences and tried to overcome them by landing the main body of their forces, particularly the tanks, right in front of Dieppe. They persisted with this plan even though they knew the strength of the defences, concrete constructions, anti-tank walls, machine gun positions, etc.
>
> This we know from their maps. It is also inconceivable why they did not support the battalions which landed at Pourville with tanks. An attack with tanks against the hill west of Dieppe and the Ferme Quatre Vents might have been successful.[8]

As we have seen, the reason given for not employing tanks at Pourville was a fear that the Scie River bridge would not support their weight. This factor had to be considered, for the Churchill tank weighed 38 tons. On the other hand, the Scie bridge was made of stone and an evaluation after the Raid stated that it would have been up to taking the weight – a factor that could probably have been calculated prior to the operation by a competent engineer using air photographs.

General Haase had obtained the copy of the JUBILEE orders that Brigadier Southam had unwisely taken ashore. With that and a set of maps Haase was fully conversant with what the landing force knew and had attempted to do, and clearly was unimpressed with the plans laid to bring those two parts together. By any objective standard he was right; at almost every level the Dieppe Raid was an unimpressive piece of work.

That said, some praise is due, and the gallantry of the Canadian soldiers is beyond all praise. Their willingness to press on during the Raid was quite outstanding and their lack of self-pity after it was both remarkable and a great credit to them as soldiers. Canada is rightly proud of them.

The Commandos can also reap a harvest of praise, not least for their sheer professionalism and for their willingness to press on in the face of adversity. The first was demonstrated by Lovat's No. 4 Commando at Varengeville, the second by Peter Young and the men of No. 3 Commando at Berneval. Credit must also go to the destroyer officers and men and the gallant crews of the landing craft; the Dieppe Raid was a field for valour.

Praise to the brave and all credit to them, but what were the real lessons of the Dieppe Raid? Not those so often advanced, surely? All the subsequent claims for this operation in terms of 'lessons learned' and 'techniques tested' were biased by the need to justify the losses and, perhaps, to divert attention from the main lesson, a very comprehensive one – on how not to do it.

This area of command – the need to admit failure – also requires investigation; one grows tired of reading those stirring tales where the gallantry and sacrifice of the men – the common soldiers – are used to conceal the glaring incompetence of the commanders. In 1794, after the failure of the Duke of York's campaign in Flanders, Arthur Wellesley, then an infantry colonel but later Duke of Wellington and a very competent commander, ruefully remarked, 'Well, at least I have learned what one ought not to do and that is always something.' The same comment might hold true for those who took the trouble to study the lessons of the Dieppe Raid, but many of the lessons of Dieppe were quite fundamental – there was no need to learn them again at such a terrible cost.

The first requirement of any military commander is simple: he must know his job. It is painfully evident that many of the commanders and planners involved in the Dieppe Raid did not know their jobs and failed to appreciate the problems and requirements of amphibious operations – or even, as with Mountbatten and Hughes-Hallett, of military operations of any kind. Ignorance of amphibious operations was very common in 1942 but that is no excuse for senior officers 'learning on the job' at the expense of the soldiers. If common sense had ruled the day rather than hubris, the Raid would either have been cancelled or the plans drastically revised. It was not one of those many operations that begin well and then deteriorate. It failed from the very first moment the troops stepped ashore and got worse thereafter.

Moral courage was also lacking: the courage needed to admit doubts, to refuse to be talked out of legitimate objections or to decline to go along with a flawed plan. The Dieppe commanders failed to remember that loyalty should flow down as well as up; their loyalty was due to the nameless soldiers in the landing craft as much as to their peers and superiors and the dictates of the Service. There were *people* here, dying on those stony beaches; they deserved better of their commanders.

A VERDICT ON DIEPPE

The Dieppe Raid provides many examples of why matters go wrong in war, and that is its only lasting value. As in most arcas of human affairs, when things go wrong, the process of failure begins at the start, with the basic concept; once that has gone awry, matters rarely recover. So it was at Dieppe; those who go there today and know enough about that day of violence in 1942 will not find it hard to visualise what took place and will wonder at it all, at the madness that led men to die here in such numbers.

It is customary to end these accounts on a positive note, recalling all the brave deeds and the contribution this event made to the eventual victory. There are few such consolations in the story of Operation JUBILEE. The Dieppe Raid was an avoidable disaster. Those who seek for glory in war will not find it on the beaches of Dieppe. Those who seek tales of valour need look no further.

ENDNOTES

Chapter 1: The Road to JUBILEE, 1939–42

[1] Conversation with the author, 2004.

Chapter 2: After Dunkirk, 1940–41

[1] Bernard Fergusson, *The Watery Maze*, p. 43.

[2] Ibid., p. 42.

Chapter 3: The Commander, the Commandos and the Canadians, 1940–42

[1] Conversation with the author, 1988.

[2] Ibid.

[3] Ibid.

[4] Robin H. Neillands Archive.

[5] Ibid.

[6] Ibid.

[7] Ibid.

[8] Ibid.

[9] Ibid.

[10] C.P. Stacey, *The Canadian Army 1939–45*, p. 44.

Chapter 4: Political Pressures, 1942

[1] Winston Churchill, *The Second World War*, Vol. IV, p. 305.

[2] Field-Marshal Lord Alanbrooke, *War Diaries 1939–45*, A. Danchev and D. Todman (eds), London: Weidenfeld & Nicolson, 2001, p. 242.

[3] Ibid, p. 248.

Chapter 5: Planning RUTTER, April–July 1942

[1] Fergusson, *The Watery Maze*, pp. 87–8.

[2] Alanbrooke, *War Diaries*, p. 236.

[3] Hughes-Hallett Papers, Imperial War Museum.

[4] Villa, *Unauthorised Action*, p. 3.

[5] Hughes-Hallett Papers, Imperial War Museum.

[6] Stacey, *The Canadian Army 1939–45*, p. 57.

[7] Robertson, *The Shame and the Glory*, pp. 69–71.

[8] Conversation with the author, 1988.

Chapter 6: Remounting Jubilee, 22 July–18 August 1942

[1] *A Reappraisal of the Dieppe Raid: Planning and Intelligence* (IWM K93/1476), *The Dieppe Raid Combined Report: COHQ, 1st October 1942* (BR1887 IWM).

[2] Ismay Papers (2/3/242–62).

[3] Ibid.

[4] Villa, *Unauthorised Action*, p. 35.

[5] Department of Documents, Imperial War Museum.

[6] Alanbrooke, *War Diaries*, p. 284.

[7] Atkin, *Dieppe 1942*, p. 47.

[8] Hughes-Hallett Papers, Imperial War Museum.

[9] Ibid.

Chapter 7: Yellow Beach 1 and 2, Berneval

[1] RHN Archive.

[2] Conversation with the author, 1987.

[3] Ibid.

[4] RHN Archive.

[5] Ibid.

Chapter 8: Orange Beach 1 and 2, Varengeville

[1] Lord Lovat, *March Past*, p. 239.

[2] Ibid., p. 242.

[3] Conversation with the author, 2005.

[4] Lovat, *March Past*, p. 242.

[5] Ibid., p. 254.

Chapter 9: Blue Beach, Puys

[1] Terence Robertson, *The Shame and the Glory*, p. 240.

[2] After-action report, Imperial War Museum.

[3] Ibid.

Chapter 10: Green Beach, Pourville

[1] Robertson, *The Shame and the Glory*, p. 280.

[2] Ibid., p. 288.

[3] Department of Documents, Imperial War Museum.

[4] Conversation with the author, 1987.

Chapter 11: Red and White Beaches, Dieppe

[1] Liddell Hart Archive.

Chapter 12: The Floating Reserve Goes In

[1] Atkin, *Dieppe 1942*, pp. 193–4.

[2] RHN archive.

[3] Atkin, *Dieppe 1942*, p. 186.

[4] RHN archive.

[5] Atkin, *Dieppe 1942*, p. 190.

[6] Conversation with the author, 2004.

[7] RHN archive.

[8] Ibid.

[9] Conversation with the author, 2004.

[10] RHN archive.

[11] Ibid.

[12] Ibid.

NOTES

Chapter 13: The Withdrawal, 1100–1300hrs

[1] Hughes-Hallett Papers, Imperial War Museum.

[2] After-action report, Imperial War Museum.

[3] Ibid.

[4] Ibid.

[5] RHN Archive.

[6] Atkin, *Dieppe 1942*, p. 229.

[7] Conversation with the author, 2004.

Chapter 14: A Verdict on Dieppe

[1] Conversation with the author, 2004.

[2] The diary entry for 30 June (Alanbrooke, *War Diaries 1939–45*) makes no mention of this conversation. It does, however, refer to a 'meeting with the PM and Mountbatten to discuss the large raid which is to be carried out next Saturday morning on Dieppe'. This would appear to confirm that Churchill knew about JUBILEE before he left for the Middle East.

[3] Joseph Balkoski, *Omaha Beach*, Pennsylvania: Stackpole Books, 2004 pp. 350–2.

[4] Villa, *Unauthorised Action*, p. 10.

[5] Ibid., p. 247.

[6] Conversation with the author, 2004.

[7] Report to OKW by von Runstedt.

[8] Ibid.

BIBLIOGRAPHY

Sources for the Dieppe Raid are widespread in the official archives of Britain and Canada but the main sources used are listed below. Much credit must be given to my Canadian aide, Paul McNicholls of Victoria BC, for his research among Canadian veterans. Main UK sources can be found in the Department of Documents at the Imperial War Museum, notably the Hughes-Hallett Papers and various reports, other official reports and correspondence on RUTTER/JUBILEE; in the Liddell Hart Archive at King's College; and in the National Archives at Kew. Details and references are given in the footnotes.

Atkin, Ronald, *Dieppe 1942*, London: Macmillan, 1980

Buckley, Christopher, *Norway, The Commandos, Dieppe*, London, 1951

Bull, Peter, *To Sea in a Sieve*, London: Peter Davies, 1956

Churchill, Winston, *The Second World War vol. IV: The Hinge of Fate*, London: Cassell, 1951

Dunning, James, *The Fighting Fourth*, Stroud: Sutton, 2003

Durnford-Slater, John, *Commando*, London: Kimber, 1953

Fergusson, Bernard, *The Watery Maze: The Story of Combined Operations*, London: Collins, 1961

Ford, Ken, *Dieppe 1942: Prelude to D-Day*, Oxford: Osprey, 2003

Hough, Richard, *Mountbatten: A Hero of Our Time*, London: Weidenfeld & Nicolson, 1980

Leasor, James, *Green Beach*, London: Heinemann, 1975

Lovat, Lord, *March Past*, London: Weidenfeld & Nicolson, 1968

Maguire, Eric, *Dieppe*, London: Jonathan Cape, 1963

Mellor, John, *Forgotten Heroes: The Canadians at Dieppe*, London: Methuen, 1975

Mills-Roberts, Brigadier Derek, *Clash by Night*, London: Kimber, 1956

Neillands, Robin, *By Sea and Land: The Royal Marines Commandos 1942–1982*, London: Weidenfeld & Nicolson, 1984

Neillands, Robin, *The Raiders: The Army Commandos, 1940–1945*, London: Weidenfeld & Nicolson, 1985

Roberts, Andrew, *Eminent Churchillians*, London: Weidenfeld & Nicolson, 1994

Robertson, Terence, *The Shame and the Glory: Dieppe*, Toronto, 1962

Stacey, C. P., *The Canadian Army, 1939–45*, Ottawa: Department of National Defence, 1948

Terraine, John, *The Life and Times of Lord Mountbatten*, London: Hutchinson, 1968

Thompson, R.W., *Dieppe at Dawn*, London: Hutchinson, 1956

Villa, Brian Loring, *Unauthorised Action; Mountbatten and the Dieppe Raid, 1942*, Oxford: OUP, 1989

Whitaker, Brigadier W. Denis, *Dieppe: Tragedy to Triumph*, Toronto, 1992

Young, Peter, S*torm from the Sea*, London: Kimber, 1958

Ziegler, Philip, *Mountbatten: The Official Biography*, London: Collins, 1985

INDEX

INDEX

INDEX

INDEX